The

INVESTOPEDIA®

Guide to Wall Speak

The terms you
need to know to
talk like **Cramer**,
think like **Soros**,
and buy like **Buffet**

Edited by Jack Guinan

The

INVESTOPEDIA®
Guide to Wall Speak

The terms you
need to know to
talk like **Cramer**,
think like **Soros**,
and buy like **Buffet**

Edited by Jack Guinan

New York Chicago San Francisco Lisbon London Madrid Mexico City
Milan New Delhi San Juan Seoul Singapore Sydney Toronto

The *McGraw·Hill* Companies

1 2 3 4 5 6 7 8 9 0   DOC/DOC   0 1 5 4 3 2 1 0 9

ISBN   978-0-07-162498-5
MHID   0-07-162498-8

McGraw-Hill books are available at special quantity discounts to use as premiums and sales promotions, or for use in corporate training programs. To contact a representative please e-mail us at bulksales@mcgraw-hill.com.

This book is printed on acid-free paper.

To my family, especially my parents, and to three very special little investors–Lana, Bridgette, and Shaun

Acknowledgments

We would like to extend a huge thank you to our families, including our wives, Nicole and Heidi, children, parents, grandparents, and siblings. Thanks also to the hardworking editors, financial analysts, and contributors who have made Investopedia the incredible success it is today. Some of these individuals are Tom Hendrickson, Shauna Carther, Tara Struyk, Chad Langager, Casey Murphy, Rachel Humenny, Albert Phung, Edmund Chua, and the often unappreciated tech team led by Chris Dailey.

Special thanks goes out to Jack Guinan, whose witty financial cartoons have been a mainstay on Investopedia's home page for many years; his countless hours of work helped this book become a reality.

Finally, thank you to the Forbes Family and Forbes.com. In April 2007, Investopedia was acquired by Forbes Media LLC. We are honored to be a part of the Forbes Digital family and appreciate their role in helping Investopedia continue to grow. The Forbes mantra of being the "Capitalist Tool" is a perfect fit for our vision for Investopedia as we strive to give individual investors the power to take control of their financial futures through education.

—The Investing Guys
Cory Janssen and Cory Wagner
April 2009

Introduction

"Okay everyone, I believe this is the sell signal that we've been looking for."

nvestopedia was started in the summer of 1999. If you remember your stock market history, our timing couldn't have been worse. By the time we had formally incorporated the business in February 2000, we were at the peak of the dot-com bubble—not exactly the best time to start a dot-com in the financial industry.

Nevertheless, we pushed on. We had grand plans to create the biggest and best financial site on the Internet. It was going to be a bigger and better version of the top sites that millions of investors and would-be investors were visiting every day.

It didn't take us long to figure out that our ambition far exceeded the resources we had at the time. (At that point, Investopedia had only two employees: us.) That being the case, we decided to focus on something we could tackle. It turned out to be something that, as university students, we were learning every day and had a passion for. As we soon realized, it was also an area that almost every Web site and publication to this day ignores or puts on the back page: financial education.

At the time, we believed that if we started building our financial dictionary, our company would develop the momentum it needed to move on to bigger and better things. However, although we originally intended to use financial education as a platform to launch us toward the creation of more traditional financial content, the site continued to evolve as a source of educational content and tools for individual investors.

We didn't know it at the time, but we had stumbled upon a niche that nobody else was filling. Today we have an enormous database of content devoted to helping individuals improve their financial IQ, including a dictionary of more than 9,300 terms. It is, in our humble opinion, the most comprehensive dictionary of its kind.

In addition to the dictionary, Investopedia boasts one of the Web's most popular stock simulation games and thousands of pages of free educational content produced by more than 200 subject-matter experts worldwide and supported by a team of analysts and editors at our head office in Edmonton, Alberta.

As you read *The Investopedia Guide to Wall Speak* there are a few things you should know about Investopedia and our philosophy:

1. **We're unbiased.** One of our biggest pet peeves with the financial industry is that so many of the "experts" out there are trying to sell you something and so many of the talking heads in the financial media offer a biased perspective. How are we different? We have no financial products to sell, and so we can stay true to what is important: explaining financial concepts so that you can make your own decisions about what's best for you.

2. **Plain English and common sense reign supreme.** We've yet to meet anybody who has a need for the complex explanations in financial textbooks. Investopedia provides simple definitions of

financial terms and concepts. Then we take it a step further by cutting through the jargon and providing real-world examples and interpretations. In the end, finance and investing are much easier to understand when explained in plain English. Why do it any other way?

3. **No one cares about your money more than you do.** It sounds obvious, but how many people actually take control of their financial futures? This isn't to say that seeking advice from a financial professional is a bad idea; in fact, many people can benefit from having an advisor. But even with professional help on your side, you still need to be equipped with financial knowledge that lets you understand where your money is being invested. Only then will you have the confidence to sit down with your financial professional and ask the tough questions that will ensure that your money (and your advisor) is working for you.

Why Finance Rules

Part of the reason Investopedia has become so popular is that in terms of financial education for young people, there tends to be a huge void. We'd rank finance and money as being as important as history, health, math, and science. We all learn arithmetic, but how many of us are taught to budget properly and manage a checking account? How many high school graduates do you know who can explain the benefits of compounding? In our opinion, understanding how much you'll make by investing at 10% for 10 years and knowing how much interest you'll pay by holding a balance on your credit card are some of the most important lessons out there.

This country (if not the world) is guilty of some major financial mistakes. This isn't just Main Street we're talking about; Wall Street has made plenty of mistakes too. Therefore, we believe that the need for financial education among young people applies not only to those who might fall prey to adjustable-rate mortgages or credit card debt but also to the Wall Street set who staked their futures on collateralized debt obligations (CDOs), mortgage-backed securities (MBSs), and other creations of financial engineering that have emerged over the last few decades.

Similarly, there has been no shortage of talk about the world's "credit binge," but this discussion rarely addresses what we view as the root cause: lack of education. Just look at the credit crisis: A general lack of knowledge extended all the way down the line, from the homeowner who didn't read the details of his or her mortgage document, to the investment bank that sold it, to the institutional investor who bought it, to the credit rating agency that rated it, and to the politician who failed to regulate it. The common theme is that nobody really understood these esoteric and exotic securities.

Much as the dot-com bust was a wake-up call for investors, we hope that the silver lining of the current crisis is that we learned a collective lesson: Wealth is not created by mountains of debt. It is the result of hard work, smart investments, and the creation of goods and services that make life better. That's true for both individuals and nations. We hope that Investopedia can play a role, albeit a small one, in preventing future financial crises, whether personal or economic.

"Dad when I grow up, I'm gonna jump up-n-down, yell at my computer and call everyone on Wall Street a moron, just like you."

copyright JackGuinan

10-K

What Does *10-K* Mean?

A comprehensive report summarizing a company's performance; it must be submitted annually to the Securities and Exchange Commission. Typically, the 10-K is more detailed than the annual report and includes information such as company history, organizational structure, equity, holdings, earnings per share, and subsidiaries.

Investopedia explains *10-K*

The 10-K must be filed within 60 days (it used to be 90 days) after the end of the fiscal year.

10-K = yearly; 10-Q = quarterly

RELATED TERMS:

- *Balance Sheet*
- *Earnings per Share—EPS*
- *Securities and Exchange Commission—SEC*
- *Shareholders' Equity*
- *Capital Structure*

401(K) PLAN

What Does *401(k) Plan* Mean?

A qualified plan established by employers by which eligible employees can make salary deferral (salary reduction) contributions on a posttax and/or pretax basis. Employers may make matching or nonelective contributions to the plan on behalf of eligible employees and also may add a profit-sharing feature to the plan. Earnings accrue on a tax-deferred basis.

Investopedia explains *401(k) Plan*

Contributions in 401(k) plans usually are capped by the plan and/or IRS regulations limiting the percentage of salary deferral contributions by employees. There are also restrictions set on employee withdrawals; penalties may apply if an employee makes a withdrawal before reaching retirement age as defined by the plan. Plans that allow participants to manage their own investments often provide a group of investments from which employees can choose. Otherwise, investment professionals hired by the employer direct and manage the employees' investments.

RELATED TERMS:
- *403(b) Plan*
- *Roth IRA*
- *Traditional IRA*
- *Qualified Retirement Plan*
- *Tax Deferred*

403(B) PLAN

What Does *403(b) Plan* Mean?

A 403(b) plan, also known as a tax-sheltered annuity (TSA) plan, is a retirement plan for employees of public schools, certain tax-exempt organizations, and certain ministers. 403(b) plan accounts can be any of the following types: (1) an annuity contract, which is provided through an insurance company; (2) a custodial account, which is invested in mutual funds; or (3) a retirement income account set up for church employees. Generally, retirement income accounts can invest in either annuities or mutual funds.

Investopedia explains *403(b) Plan*

The features of the 403(b) plan are very similar to those of the 401(k) plan. Employees may make salary deferral contributions that usually are limited by regulatory caps.

RELATED TERMS:
- *401(k) Plan*
- *Individual Retirement Account*
- *Tax Deferred*
- *Qualified Retirement Plan*
- *Traditional IRA*

"Son, baseball's like investing.
You do better if you're not always
trying to hit a homerun."

ABSOLUTE RETURN

What Does *Absolute Return* Mean?

The return that an asset achieves over a certain period of time; it considers appreciation or depreciation (expressed as a percentage) of the asset, which is usually a stock or a mutual fund. Absolute return differs from relative return because it looks only at an asset's return; it does not compare returns to any other measure or benchmark.

Investopedia explains *Absolute Return*

Generally, mutual funds seek returns that are better than those of their peers, their fund category, and/or the market as a whole. This type of fund management is referred to as a relative return approach to fund investing. Absolute return funds seek positive returns by employing investment strategies that often are not permitted in traditional mutual funds, such as short selling, futures, options, derivatives, arbitrage, leverage, and unconventional assets. Alfred Winslow Jones is credited with forming the first absolute return fund in New York in 1949. Today, the absolute return approach to fund investing has become one of the fastest growing investment products in the world; it's called a hedge fund.

RELATED TERMS:
- Mutual Fund
- Return on Investment
- Yield
- Return on Assets
- Total Return

ACCOUNTS PAYABLE (AP)

What Does *Accounts Payable (AP)* Mean?

An accounting entry that represents an entity's obligation to pay off a short-term debt to its creditors; it is found on the balance sheet under current liabilities. Accounts payable often are referred to as "payables." AP also may refer to a business department or division that is responsible for making payments owed by the company to suppliers and other creditors.

Investopedia explains *Accounts Payable (AP)*

Accounts payable debts must be paid off within a specific period to avoid default. For example, at the corporate level, AP refers to short-term debt payments to suppliers and banks. However, APs are not limited to corporations. People also have APs owed to creditors. For example, the phone company, the gas company, and the cable company are types of creditors. Each creditor provides a service and then bills the customer after the fact. The payable is essentially a short-term IOU obligation of the customer. If people or companies do not pay their bills, they are considered to be in default.

RELATED TERMS:
- Accounts Receivable
- Current Liabilities
- Receivables Turnover Ratio
- Balance Sheet
- Liability

ACCOUNTS PAYABLE TURNOVER RATIO

What Does *Accounts Payable Turnover Ratio* Mean?

A short-term liquidity measure used to quantify the rate at which a company pays off its accounts payable to suppliers. The accounts payable turnover ratio is calculated by taking the total purchases made from suppliers and dividing it by the average accounts payable amount during the same period.

$$\text{Accounts Payable Turnover} = \frac{\text{Total Supplier Purchases}}{\text{Average Accounts Payable}}$$

Investopedia explains *Accounts Payable Turnover Ratio*
The measure reveals how many times per period a company pays its average payable amount. For example, if the company makes $100 million in purchases from suppliers in a year and at any specific point holds an average accounts payable of $20 million, the accounts payable turnover ratio for the period is 5 ($100 million/$20 million). A falling turnover ratio is a sign that the company is taking longer to pay off its suppliers, which could be a bad sign. A rising turnover ratio means that the company is paying off suppliers at a faster rate, which is good.

RELATED TERMS:
- *Accounts Payable—AP*
- *Current Ratio*
- *Receivables Turnover Ratio*
- *Accounts Receivable—AR*
- *Liquidity*

ACCOUNTS RECEIVABLE (AR)

 What Does *Accounts Receivable (AR)* Mean?
Money owed by customers (individuals or corporations) to vendors in exchange for goods or services rendered. Receivables usually come in the form of operating lines of credit and are usually due within a relatively short period, ranging from a few days to a year. On a balance sheet, AR often is recorded as an asset because it represents cash legally owed by a customer.

 Investopedia explains *Accounts Receivable (AR)*
When a company has receivables, that means that it has made a sale but has not collected the money from the purchaser yet. Most companies operate this way. This allows frequent customers to avoid the hassle of making cash payments for each transaction. In other words, the company receives an IOU for goods or services rendered. People have ARs as well in the form of a monthly or biweekly paycheck. It's the company's IOU for services (work) rendered. ARs are the opposite of APs (accounts payables).

RELATED TERMS:
- *Accounts Payable—AP*
- *Asset*
- *Receivables Turnover Ratio*
- *Accrual Accounting*
- *Balance Sheet*

ACCRUAL ACCOUNTING

What Does *Accrual Accounting* Mean?

An accounting method that measures the performance and status of a company regardless of when cash transactions occur; financial transactions and events are recognized by matching revenues to expenses (the matching principle) at the time when the transaction occurs rather than when payment actually is made (or received). This allows current cash inflows and outflows to be combined with expected future cash inflows and outflows to provide a more accurate picture of a company's current financial condition. Accrual accounting is the standard accounting practice for most big companies; however, its relative complexity makes it more expensive to implement for small companies. This is the opposite of cash accounting, which recognizes transactions only when there is an exchange of cash.

Investopedia explains *Accrual Accounting*

The need for this method arose because of the complexity of business transactions and the need for more accurate financial information. Selling on credit and projects that provide future revenue streams affect a company's financial condition when they occur. Therefore, it makes sense to reflect those events during the same reporting period in which the transactions occur. For example, when a company sells a television to a customer on credit, the cash and accrual methods view this transaction differently. The cash method does not recognize the sale until actual cash is received, which could be a month or longer. Accrual accounting, in contrast, recognizes that the company will receive the cash at some point in the future. Therefore, even though the cash has not been collected yet, the sale is booked to "accounts receivable" and thus sales revenue.

RELATED TERMS:
- Accounts Receivable
- Accrued Interest
- Income Statement
- Accrued Expense
- Cost of Goods Sold—COGS

ACCRUED EXPENSE

What Does *Accrued Expense* Mean?

An accounting expense (current liability) recognized on the company's books before it actually is paid for. Such expenses are typically periodic and are recorded on a company's balance sheet because of the high probability that they ultimately will be collected.

Investopedia explains *Accrued Expense*
Accrued expenses are the opposite of prepaid expenses. Typical company accrued expenses include wages, interest, and taxes. Even though they will be paid on a future date, they are recorded on the balance sheet until the moment they are paid. An example would be interest that accrues on a simple bank loan.

RELATED TERMS:
- *Accrual Accounting*
- *Balance Sheet*
- *Liability*
- *Accrued Interest*
- *Gross Income*

ACCRUED INTEREST

What Does *Accrued Interest* **Mean?**
(1) A term used to describe an accrual accounting method when interest from a payable or a receivable has been recognized but not yet paid or received. Accrued interest occurs as a result of the difference in the timing of cash flows and the measurement of those cash flows. (2) The interest that has accumulated on a bond since the last interest payment up to but not including the settlement date.

Investopedia explains *Accrued Interest*
(1) An accrued interest receivable occurs when interest on an outstanding receivable has been earned by the company but has not been received yet. A loan to a customer for goods sold would result in interest being charged on the loan. If the loan is extended on October 1 and the lending company's year ends on December 31, there will be two months of accrued interest receivable recorded as interest revenue in the company's financial statements for the year. (2) Accrued interest is added to the contract price of a bond transaction, reflecting interest earned since the last coupon payment. Because the bond has not matured or the next payment is not yet due, the owner of the bond has not received the money officially. Therefore, when the bond is sold, the accrued interest is added to the sale price.

RELATED TERMS:
- Accrual Accounting
- Coupon
- Settlement Date
- Accrued Expense
- Interest Rate

ACID-TEST RATIO

What Does *Acid-Test Ratio* Mean?

A stringent test to determine whether a firm has enough short-term assets to cover its immediate liabilities without selling inventory; the acid-test ratio is far more strenuous than the working capital ratio because the working capital ratio allows for the inclusion of inventory assets. The acid-test ratio is calculated as follows:

$$= \frac{(\text{Cash} + \text{Accounts Receivable} + \text{Short-term Investments})}{\text{Current Liabilities}}$$

Investopedia explains *Acid-Test Ratio*

Companies with ratios <1 cannot pay their current liabilities and therefore should be viewed with extreme caution. If the acid-test ratio is much lower than the working capital ratio, this means current assets are highly dependent on inventory. Retail stores are examples of this type of business. The term is said to have come from the method gold miners used to verify that a gold nugget was real. Unlike other metals, gold does not corrode in acid; if a nugget did not dissolve when submerged in acid, it was the real thing and was said to have passed the acid test. Today, if a company's financial statements pass the figurative acid test, this indicates the company's financial integrity.

RELATED TERMS:
- Current Assets
- Current Ratio
- Working Capital
- Current Liabilities
- Liability

ALPHA

What Does *Alpha* Mean?

(1) A measure of performance on a risk-adjusted basis. Alpha takes the volatility (price risk) of a mutual fund and compares its risk-adjusted performance with a benchmark index. The excess return

of the fund relative to the return of the benchmark index is a fund's alpha. (2) The abnormal rate of return on a security or portfolio in excess of what would be predicted by an equilibrium model such as the capital asset pricing model (CAPM).

Investopedia explains *Alpha*

(1) Alpha is one of five technical risk measures that are used in modern portfolio theory (MPT); the others are beta, standard deviation, R-squared, and the Sharpe ratio. These indicators help investors determine the risk-reward profile of a mutual fund. Simply stated, alpha often is considered to represent the value that a portfolio manager adds to or subtracts from a fund's return. A positive alpha of 1.0 means the fund has outperformed its benchmark index by 1%. Conversely, a similar negative alpha would indicate an underperformance of 1%. (2) If a CAPM analysis estimates that a portfolio should earn 10% on the basis of the risk of that portfolio yet the portfolio actually earns 15%, the portfolio's alpha would be 5%. The 5% is the excess return above the predicted CAPM return.

RELATED TERMS:
- *Beta*
- *Capital Asset Pricing Model—CAPM*
- *R-Squared*
- *Sharpe Ratio*
- *Standard Deviation*

AMERICAN DEPOSITARY RECEIPT (ADR)

What Does *American Depositary Receipt (ADR)* Mean?

A negotiable certificate issued by a U.S. bank representing a specified number of shares in a foreign stock that is traded on a U.S. exchange. ADRs are denominated in U.S. dollars, with the underlying security held by a U.S. financial institution overseas. ADRs help reduce administrative and duty costs that otherwise would be levied on each transaction.

Investopedia explains *American Depositary Receipt (ADR)*

ADRs are an excellent way to buy shares in a foreign company and realize any dividends and capital gains in U.S. dollars. However, ADRs do not eliminate the currency and economic risks for the underlying shares in another country. For example, dividend payments in a foreign currency would be converted to U.S. dollars, net of any conversion expenses and foreign taxes. ADRs are listed on the NYSE, AMEX, or Nasdaq.

RELATED TERMS:
- Derivative
- Global Depositary Receipt—GDR
- MSCI—Emerging Markets Index
- Security
- Spiders—SPDRs

AMERICAN STOCK EXCHANGE (AMEX)

What Does *American Stock Exchange (AMEX)* Mean?
The third-largest stock exchange by trading volume in the United States. The AMEX is located in New York City and handles about 10% of all securities traded in the United States.

Investopedia explains *American Stock Exchange (AMEX)*
The AMEX has merged with the Nasdaq. It was known as the "curb exchange" until 1921. It used to be a strong competitor of the New York Stock Exchange, but that role has been filled by the Nasdaq. Today, almost all trading on the AMEX is in small-cap stocks, exchange-traded funds, and derivatives.

RELATED TERMS:
- Dow Jones Industrial Average
- Index
- Nasdaq
- New York Stock Exchange—NYSE
- Stock Market

AMORTIZATION

What Does *Amortization* Mean?
(1) The paying off of debt in regular installments over a period of time. (2)The deduction of capital expenses over a specific period (usually over the asset's life). More specifically, a method measuring the consumption of the value of intangible assets, such as a patent or a copyright.

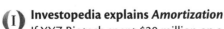

Investopedia explains *Amortization*
If XYZ Biotech spent $30 million on a piece of medical equipment with a patent lasting 15 years, the company would record $2 million each year in amortization expense. Although amortization and depreciation often are used interchangeably, technically this is

incorrect because amortization refers to intangible assets, whereas depreciation refers to tangible assets.

RELATED TERMS:
- Asset
- Earnings before Interest, Taxes, Depreciation, and Amortization—EBITDA
- Intangible Asset
- Depreciation
- Tangible Asset

ANNUAL PERCENTAGE YIELD (APY)

What Does *Annual Percentage Yield* (APY) Mean?
The effective annual rate of return after considering the effect of compounding interest; APY assumes that funds will remain in the investment vehicle for a full 365 days and is calculated as follows:

$$= (1+\text{periodic rate})^{\#\text{ Periods}} - 1$$

Investopedia explains *Annual Percentage Yield* (APY)
APY is similar to the annual percentage rate insofar as it standardizes varying interest rate agreements into an annualized percentage number. For example, suppose you are considering whether to invest in a one-year zero-coupon bond that pays 6% at maturity or a high-yield money market account that pays 0.5% per month with monthly compounding. At first glance, the yields appear identical— 12 months multiplied by 0.5% equals 6%—but when the effects of compounding are included, it can be seen that the second investment actually yields more: 6.17% (1.005^(12 − 1) = 0.0617).

RELATED TERMS:
- Certificate of Deposit—CD
- Compound Annual Growth Rate—CAGR
- Compounding
- Yield
- Money Market Account

ANNUITY

What Does *Annuity* Mean?
A financial product designed to pay out a stream of payments to the holder at a later point in time. Annuities are used primarily as a means of securing a steady cash flow for an individual during his or her retirement years.

Investopedia explains *Annuity*

Annuities can be structured in many ways, such as by the duration of the time in which payments from the annuity can be guaranteed or can be created so that upon annuitization, payments continue as long as the annuitant or spouse is alive. In addition, they can be structured to pay out funds for a fixed amount of time, say, 20 years, regardless of how long the annuitant lives. Annuities also can provide fixed periodic payments or variable payments. Variable annuities allow the annuitant to receive greater payments if the investments of the annuity do well but smaller payments if the investments do poorly. Although it is riskier than a fixed annuity, this allows the annuitant to benefit from strong returns from the annuity fund's investments. Annuities are flexible and therefore are suitable for many types of investors.

RELATED TERMS:
- *Bond*
- *Interest Rate*
- *Tax Deferred*
- *Defined-Benefit Plan*
- *Mutual Fund*

ARBITRAGE

 What Does *Arbitrage* Mean?

The simultaneous purchase and sale of an asset to profit from a difference in the price; a trade that creates profit by exploiting price differences in identical or similar financial instruments in different markets. Arbitrage is the result of market inefficiencies; it is a mechanism that helps ensure that prices do not deviate substantially from fair value for long periods.

 Investopedia explains *Arbitrage*

Arbitrage is not a long-term investment strategy but a short-term trading strategy to exploit short-term pricing inefficiencies. Arbitrage helps ensure that prices do not deviate too far from an asset's fair value for long periods.

RELATED TERMS:
- *Ask*
- *Currency Swap*
- *Volume*
- *Bid*
- *Spread*

ASK

What Does *Ask* Mean?

The price a seller is willing to accept for a security; also known as the offer price. The ask price quote also stipulates the number of shares offered at that price. Sometimes called "the ask."

Investopedia explains *Ask*

This is the opposite of bid, which is the price a buyer is willing to pay for a security. The terms "bid" and "ask" are used in nearly every financial market in the world in regard to stocks, bonds, currency, and derivatives. An example of an ask in the stock market would be $5.24 × 1,000, which means that someone is offering to sell 1,000 shares at $5.24.

RELATED TERMS:
- Bid
- New York Stock Exchange
- Stock Market
- Bid-Ask Spread
- Spread

ASSET

What Does *Asset* Mean?

(1) A resource with economic value that an individual, corporation, or country owns or controls with the expectation that it will provide future benefit. (2) A balance sheet item that reflects what a firm owns.

Investopedia explains *Asset*

(1) Assets are purchased to increase the value of a firm. One should think of an asset as something that can generate cash flow. It could be a company's plant and equipment or an individual's rental property. (2) In the context of accounting, assets are either current or fixed (noncurrent). Current means within one year: cash, accounts receivable, and inventory. Fixed assets are expected to provide benefits beyond one year: manufacturing equipment, buildings, and real estate.

RELATED TERMS:
- Balance Sheet
- Depreciation
- Tangible Asset
- Current Assets
- Intangible Asset

ASSET ALLOCATION

What Does *Asset Allocation* Mean?

An investment strategy that aims to balance risk and reward by spreading investments across three main asset classes—equities, bonds, and cash—in accordance with an individual's goals, risk tolerance, and investment horizon. Historically, different asset classes have varying degrees of risk and return and therefore behave differently over time.

Investopedia explains *Asset Allocation*

There is no simple formula to determine the proper asset allocation for every individual. However, the consensus among financial professionals is that asset allocation is one of the most important investment components. In other words, individual securities selection is secondary to the way an investor allocates investments across stocks, bonds, and cash. Some mutual funds, called life-cycle, or target-date funds, use asset allocation to provide investors with portfolios that align with an investor's age, appetite for risk, and investment objectives. However, some critics argue that these kinds of standardized funds are problematic because individual investors require individual solutions, not a one-size-fits-all approach.

RELATED TERMS:
- Correlation
- Modern Portfolio Theory—MPT
- Risk
- Diversification
- Portfolio

ASSET TURNOVER

What Does *Asset Turnover* Mean?

The amount of sales generated for every dollar's worth of assets; it is calculated by dividing sales in dollars by assets in dollars:

$$\text{Asset Turnover} = \frac{\text{Revenue}}{\text{Assets}}$$

Investopedia explains *Asset Turnover*

Asset turnover measures a firm's efficiency at using its assets in generating sales or revenue; the higher the number, the better. It also reflects pricing strategy; companies with low profit margins tend to have high asset turnover, whereas those with high profit margins have low asset turnover.

RELATED TERMS:
- *Fundamental Analysis*
- *Inventory Turnover*
- *Net Sales*
- *Revenue*
- *Turnover*

ASSET-BACKED SECURITY (ABS)

What Does *Asset-Backed Security (ABS)* Mean?
A financial security backed by a loan, a lease, or receivables other than real estate and mortgage-backed securities. Asset-backed securities are an alternative to investing in corporate debt.

Investopedia explains *Asset-Backed Security (ABS)*
An ABS is essentially the same thing as a mortgage-backed security except that the securities backing it are assets such as loans, leases, credit card debt, a company's receivables, or royalties but not mortgage-based securities.

RELATED TERMS:
- *Asset*
- *Corporate Bond*
- *Derivative*
- *Mortgage-Backed Securities—MBS*
- *Securitization*

AVERAGE DIRECTIONAL INDEX (ADX)

What Does *Average Directional Index (ADX)* Mean?
The Average Directional Movement Index is used in technical analysis as an objective value for the strength of trend; it is nondirectional so that it will quantify trend strength whether it is up or down. ADX usually is plotted in a chart window along with two lines to create one indicator; it is derived from the relationship of the lines.

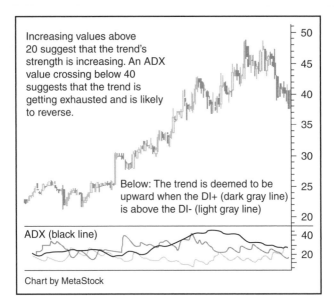

Increasing values above 20 suggest that the trend's strength is increasing. An ADX value crossing below 40 suggests that the trend is getting exhausted and is likely to reverse.

Below: The trend is deemed to be upward when the DI+ (dark gray line) is above the DI- (light gray line)

ADX (black line)

Chart by MetaStock

Investopedia explains *Average Directional Index* (ADX)
This analysis is a method of evaluating trend and can help traders identify the strongest trends and show them how to let profits run when the trend is strong.

RELATED TERMS:
- Benchmark
- Index
- Uptrend
- Downtrend
- Trend Analysis

O.K, here we are pal, Wall Street. That'll be 250 basis points!

copyright JackGuinan

BALANCE SHEET

What Does *Balance Sheet* Mean?

A financial statement that summarizes a company's assets, liabilities, and shareholders' equity at a specific point in time. The balance sheet gives investors an idea of what the company owns and owes as well as the amount invested by the shareholders. The balance sheet follows the formula *assets = liabilities + shareholders' equity*. Each of the three segments of the balance sheet has many accounts within it, documenting the value of each one. Accounts such as cash, inventory, and property are on the asset side of the balance sheet, and accounts such as accounts payable and long-term debt fall on the liability side. Accounts on a balance sheet differ by company and by industry, as there is no set template that accurately accommodates the differences between different types of businesses.

Investopedia explains *Balance Sheet*

It is called a balance sheet because the two sides of the sheet balance out. This makes sense: A company has to pay for all the things it has (assets) by borrowing money (liabilities) or getting it from shareholders (shareholders' equity). The balance sheet is one of the most important pieces of financial information issued by a company. It is a snapshot of what a company owns and owes at that point in time. The income statement, in contrast, shows the company's revenues and profits over a certain period. One statement is not

17

better than the other; together they present a complete picture of a company's finances.

RELATED TERMS:
- Asset
- Liability
- Shareholders' Equity
- Income Statement
- Retained Earnings

BANK GUARANTEE

What Does *Bank Guarantee* Mean?

A guarantee issued by a lending institution ensuring that the liabilities of a debtor will be met. In other words, if the debtor fails to settle a debt, the bank will cover it.

Investopedia explains *Bank Guarantee*

A bank guarantee enables the customer (debtor) to acquire goods, buy equipment, or draw down loans and thus expand business activity.

RELATED TERMS:
- Cash and Cash Equivalents
- Letter of Credit
- Risk
- Debt
- Liability

BANKER'S ACCEPTANCE (BA)

What Does *Banker's Acceptance (BA)* Mean?

A short-term credit investment created by a nonfinancial firm and guaranteed by a bank.

Investopedia explains *Banker's Acceptance (BA)*

Acceptances are traded at a discount from face value on the secondary market. Banker's acceptances are very similar to T-bills and often are used in money market funds.

RELATED TERMS:
- Bond
- Commercial Paper
- Treasury Bill—T-Bill
- Certificate of Deposit—CD
- Money Market

BANKRUPTCY

What Does *Bankruptcy* Mean?

A legal proceeding initiated by a person or business that is unable to pay its outstanding debts; the bankruptcy process begins with a petition filed by the debtor (most common) or on behalf of creditors (less common). All the debtor's assets are measured and evaluated, after which the assets are used to repay a portion of the outstanding debt. Upon the successful completion of bankruptcy proceedings, the debtor is relieved of the debt obligations incurred before filing for bankruptcy.

Investopedia explains *Bankruptcy*

Bankruptcy offers an individual or business a chance to start fresh by forgiving debts that simply cannot be paid while offering creditors a chance to obtain some measure of repayment that is based on what assets are available. In theory, bankruptcy benefits an overall economy by giving persons and businesses a second chance and providing creditors with a measure of debt repayment. Bankruptcy filings in the United States can fall under one of several chapters of the Bankruptcy Code: Chapter 7 (which involves liquidation of assets), Chapter 11 (company or individual "reorganizations"), and Chapter 13 (debt repayment with lowered debt covenants or payment plans). Bankruptcy filings vary widely from country to country, leading to higher or lower filing rates, depending on how easily a person or company can complete the process.

RELATED TERMS:
- Bear Market
- Credit Crunch
- Subprime Loan
- Chapter 11
- Debt

BASIS POINT (BPS)

What Does *Basis Point (BPS)* Mean?

A unit equal to 1/100 of 1%; it is used to denote a change in a financial instrument (usually a fixed-income security). The basis point is used commonly for calculating changes in interest rates, equity indexes, and the yield of a fixed-income security.

Investopedia explains *Basis Point (BPS)*

Converting percentage changes in basis points is done as follows: 1% change = 100 basis points, and 0.01% = 1 basis point. Thus, a bond whose yield increases from 5% to 5.5% is said to increase by 50 basis points; when interest rates rise 1%, they have increased by 100 basis points.

RELATED TERMS:
- Bond
- Interest Rate
- Yield
- Corporate Bond
- Pip

BEAR MARKET

What Does *Bear Market* Mean?

A market condition characterized by falling stock prices, widespread pessimism, and snowballing negative sentiment that causes investors to sell stocks; this leads to further pessimism. Although figures vary, a downturn of 20% or more across broad market indexes such as the Dow Jones Industrial Average (DJIA) or the Standard & Poor's 500 Index (S&P 500) over a two-month period is considered a bear market.

Investopedia explains *Bear Market*

A bear market should not be confused with a correction, which is a short-term trend that lasts less than two months. Although corrections are often a great time for a value investor to jump into the market, bear markets are quite risky to time because one never knows when a market has hit bottom. It is difficult for investors to make money in a bear market unless they are short sellers.

RELATED TERMS:
- Bull Market
- Market Economy
- Stock Market
- Downtrend
- Short Sale

BEHAVIORAL FINANCE

What Does *Behavioral Finance* Mean?

A field of finance that proposes psychology-based theories to explain stock market anomalies. Within behavioral finance, it is assumed that the information structure and the characteristics of market participants systematically influence individuals' investment decisions as well as market outcomes.

 Investopedia explains *Behavioral Finance*
Many studies have documented long-term historical phenomena in securities markets that contradict the efficient market hypothesis and cannot be captured plausibly in models that are based on perfect investor rationality. Behavioral finance attempts to fill the void.

RELATED TERMS:
- *Efficient Market Hypothesis—EMH*   • *Fundamental Analysis*
- *Market Economy*
- *New York Stock Exchange—NYSE*   • *Quantitative Analysis*

BENCHMARK

 What Does *Benchmark* Mean?
A standard against which the performance of a security, mutual fund, or investment manager can be measured. Generally, broad market and market-segment stock and bond indexes are used for this purpose.

 Investopedia explains *Benchmark*
In evaluating the performance of any investment, it is important to compare it with an appropriate benchmark. In the financial field, there are dozens of indexes that analysts use to gauge the performance of any specific investment, including the S&P 500, the Dow Jones Industrial Average, and the Lehman Brothers Aggregate Bond Index.

RELATED TERMS:
- *Dow Jones Industrial Average*   • *Index*
- *Lehman Aggregate Bond Index*   • *Stock Market*
- *Standard & Poor's 500 Index*

BETA

 What Does *Beta* Mean?
A statistical measure of the volatility of an investment in relation to the market as a whole; also known as "beta coefficient" or "systematic risk."

Investopedia explains *Beta*

Beta is calculated by using regression analysis; one should think of beta as the tendency of a security's returns to respond to swings in the market. A beta of 1 indicates that the price of a security will move in tandem with the market; a beta less than 1 means that the security will be less volatile than the market. A beta more than 1 indicates that the security's price will be more volatile than the market. For example, if a stock's beta is 1.2, theoretically, it's 20% more volatile than the market. Many utilities stocks have a beta less than 1. Conversely, most high-flying tech stocks have a beta greater than 1, offering a chance for higher returns but with far greater risk.

RELATED TERMS:
- *Alpha*
- *R-Squared*
- *Unlevered Beta*
- *Capital Market Line—CML*
- *Swing Trading*

BID

 What Does *Bid* Mean?

(1) The price at which an offer is made by an investor, a trader, or a dealer to buy a security. The bid sets the price and the quantity to be purchased. (2) The price at which a market maker is willing to buy a security; market makers also display an ask price (both price and quantity) at which they are willing to sell.

 Investopedia explains *Bid*

Bid is the opposite of ask, which stipulates the price a seller is willing to accept for a security and the quantity of the security to be sold at that price. (1) An example of a bid in the market would be $23.53 × 1,000, which means that an investor wants to buy 1,000 shares at the price of $23.53. If a seller in the market is willing to sell that amount for that price, the transaction is completed. (2) Market makers are vital to the efficiency and liquidity of the marketplace. By quoting both bid and ask prices, they always allow investors to buy or sell a security if the investors need to.

RELATED TERMS:
- *Ask*
- *Market Maker*
- *Volume*
- *Bid-Ask Spread*
- *Spread*

BID-ASK SPREAD

What Does *Bid-Ask Spread* Mean?
The amount by which the ask price exceeds the bid price. Essentially, it is the difference between the highest price a buyer is willing to pay for an asset and the lowest price for which a seller is willing to sell it.

Investopedia explains *Bid-Ask Spread*
As an example, if the bid price is $20 and the ask price is $21, the bid-ask spread is $1. The size of the spread from one asset to another will vary with the liquidity of the asset. For example, currency is considered the most liquid asset in the world; thus, currency spreads are very narrow (one-hundredth of a percent). In contrast, less liquid assets such as a small-cap stock will have wider spreads, sometimes as high as 1 to 2% of the asset's value.

RELATED TERMS:
- *Ask*
- *Bid*
- *Market Maker*
- *Pink Sheets*
- *New York Stock Exchange—NYSE*

BLACK SCHOLES MODEL

What Does *Black Scholes Model* Mean?
A model of price variation over time in financial instruments such as stocks that often is used to calculate the price of a European call option. The model assumes that the price of heavily traded assets follows a geometric Brownian motion with constant drift and volatility. When applied to a stock option, the model incorporates the constant price variation of the stock, the time value of money, the option's strike price, and the time to the option's expiration. Also known as the Black-Scholes-Merton Model.

Investopedia explains *Black Scholes Model*
The Black Scholes Model is one of the most important concepts in modern financial theory. It was developed in 1973 by Fisher Black, Robert Merton, and Myron Scholes and is used widely today and regarded as one of the best formulas for determining option prices.

RELATED TERMS:
- *Exercise*
- *Option*
- *Standard Deviation*
- *Stock Option*
- *Strike Price*

BLUE-CHIP STOCK

What Does *Blue-Chip Stock* Mean?

The stock of a well-established and financially sound company that has demonstrated an ability to pay dividends in both good and bad times.

Investopedia explains *Blue-Chip Stock*

These stocks are usually less risky than other stocks. The stock price of a blue chip usually closely tracks the S&P 500 Index.

RELATED TERMS:
- *Dow Jones Industrial Average—DJIA*
- *New York Stock Exchange—NYSE*
- *Standard & Poor's 500 Index—S&P 500*
- *Large-Cap Stock*
- *Stock*

BOLLINGER BAND

What Does *Bollinger Band* Mean?

A band that is plotted two standard deviations away from a simple moving average. In the example below, the price of the stock is banded by an upper band and a lower band along with a 21-day simple moving average.

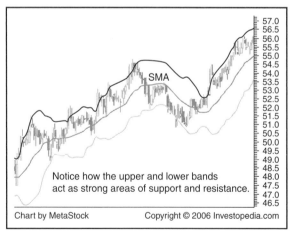

SMA

Notice how the upper and lower bands act as strong areas of support and resistance.

Chart by MetaStock   Copyright © 2006 Investopedia.com

Investopedia explains *Bollinger Band*

Because standard deviation is a measure of volatility, Bollinger bands adjust to changing market conditions. When markets become more volatile, the bands widen (move farther away from the average), and during less volatile periods, the bands contract (move closer to the average). A tightening of the bands often is used by technical traders as an early indication that volatility is about to increase sharply. This is one of the most popular technical analysis techniques. The closer prices move to the upper band, the more overbought the market is thought to be; the closer they move to the lower band, the more the market is considered oversold.

RELATED TERMS:
- Moving Average
- Technical Analysis
- Volatility
- Standard Deviation
- Trend Analysis

BOND

What Does *Bond* Mean?

A debt investment in which an investor lends money to an entity (corporate or government) that borrows the funds for a defined period at a fixed interest rate. Bonds are used by companies, municipalities, states, and U.S. and foreign governments to finance a variety of projects and activities. Bonds commonly are referred to as fixed-income securities and are one of the three main asset classes, along with stocks and cash equivalents.

Investopedia explains *Bond*

The indebted entity (issuer) issues a bond stipulating the stated interest rate (coupon) to be paid and a date when the loaned funds (bond principal) are to be returned (maturity date). Interest on bonds usually is paid every six months (semiannually); bond categories include corporate bonds, municipal bonds, and U.S. Treasury bonds, notes, and bills ("Treasuries"). Two features of a bond—credit quality and maturity—are the principal determinants of the interest rate of a bond. Bond maturities can range from a 90-day Treasury bill to a 30-year government bond. Corporate and municipal bonds typically go out 3 to 10 years.

RELATED TERMS:
- Callable Bond
- Corporate Bond
- Yield to Maturity
- Convertible Bond
- Junk Bond

BOND LADDER

What Does *Bond Ladder* mean?

A strategy for managing fixed-income investments by which the investor builds a ladder by dividing his or her investment dollars evenly among bonds or CDs that mature at regular intervals simultaneously (for example, every six months, once a year, or every two years).

Investopedia explains *Bond Ladder*

Advantages of bond ladders are consistent returns, low risk, and ongoing liquidity because every interval the investor has securities expiring. The bond ladder also protects the investor's bond portfolio from call risk: Since maturities are staggered, there is little chance that all the bonds in one portfolio will be called at once.

RELATED TERMS:
- Bond
- Interest Rate
- Yield to Maturity

- Corporate Bond
- Yield

BOND RATING

What Does *Bond Rating* Mean?

A grade assigned to a bond that indicates its credit quality; private rating services such as Standard & Poor's, Moody's, and Fitch evaluate a bond issuer's financial strength, or its ability to pay principal and interest in a timely fashion, and then give a bond a rating.

Investopedia explains *Bond Rating*

Bond ratings are expressed with letters ranging from AAA, which is the highest rating to C ("junk"), which is the lowest rating. Different rating services use the same letter grades but use various combinations of upper- and lowercase letters to differentiate themselves. Here's how the Standard & Poor's rating system works: AAA and AA: high credit-quality investment grade; AA and BBB: medium credit-quality investment grade; BB, B, CCC, CC, and C: low credit-quality (noninvestment grade), or "junk bonds"; D: bonds in default for nonpayment of principal and/or interest.

RELATED TERMS:
- Credit Rating
- Interest Rate
- Junk Bond

- High-Yield Bond
- Investment Grade

BOOK VALUE

What Does *Book Value* Mean?

(1) The value at which an asset is carried on a balance sheet; in other words, the cost of an asset minus accumulated depreciation. (2) The net asset value of a company, calculated as total assets minus intangible assets (patents, goodwill) and liabilities. (3) The initial outlay for an investment. This number may be net or gross of expenses such as trading costs, sales taxes, and service charges. In the United Kingdom book value is called net asset value.

Investopedia explains *Book Value*

Book value is the accounting value of a firm. It has three main uses: (1) It is the total value of the company's assets that shareholders theoretically would receive if a company were liquidated. (2) By comparing a company's book value with its market value, one sees whether its stock is under- or overpriced. (3) In personal finance, the book value of an investment is the price paid for a security or debt investment. When a stock is sold, the selling price minus the book value is the capital gain (or loss) from the investment.

RELATED TERMS:
- Depreciation
- Intrinsic Value
- Price-to-Book Ratio—P/B Ratio

- Intangible Asset
- Net Asset Value—NAV

BREAKPOINT

What Does *Breakpoint* Mean?

For a load mutual fund, the dollar amount for the purchase of the fund's shares that qualifies the investor for a reduced sales charge (load). The purchase may be made in a lump sum or by staggering payments within a prescribed period. The latter form of investment purchase in a fund must be documented by a letter of intent.

Investopedia explains *Breakpoint*
As an example, suppose an investor plans to invest $95,000 in a front-end load mutual fund and faces a sales charge of 6.25%, or $6,125. If a breakpoint of $100,000 exists with a lower sales charge of 5.5%, the investor should be advised to invest an additional $5,000. If the investor can add another $5,000 to the investment, he or she will benefit from a lower breakpoint sales charge of $5,500, for a savings of $625 on this transaction. Mutual funds are required to give a description of these breakpoints and the eligibility requirements in the fund prospectus. By reaching or surpassing a breakpoint, an investor will face a lower sales charge and save money. Any purchase of fund shares that occurs just below a breakpoint is considered unethical and in violation of NASD rules.

RELATED TERMS:
- *Broker-Dealer*
- *Front-End Load*
- *Total Return*
- *Expense Ratio*
- *Mutual Fund*

BROKER-DEALER

 What Does *Broker-Dealer* **Mean?**
A person or firm that is in the business of buying and selling securities and operating as both a broker and a dealer, depending on the transaction.

 Investopedia explains *Broker-Dealer*
Technically, a broker is only an agent to a transaction who executes orders on behalf of clients, whereas a dealer acts as a principal and trades (buys and sells) for his or her own account. Because most brokerages act as both brokers and principals, the term broker-dealer is used commonly to describe them.

RELATED TERMS:
- *FINRA*
- *Nasdaq*
- *Stock Market*
- *Market Maker*
- *New York Stock Exchange*

BULL MARKET

What Does *Bull Market* Mean?

A financial market condition in which security prices are rising or are expected to rise. The term most often is used to refer to the stock market but can be applied to anything that is traded, such as bonds, currencies, and commodities.

Investopedia explains *Bull Market*

Bull markets are characterized by optimism, investor confidence, and high expectations for a strong future. It is difficult to predict changes in the markets, especially when one considers investor psychology and speculation, which play a major role. The terms "bull" and "bear" come from the way each animal attacks its opponents. A bull thrusts its horns up into the air, whereas a bear swipes its paws down. These actions are metaphors for the movement in a market. When the trend is up, it's a bull market; when the trend is down, it's a bear market.

RELATED TERMS:
- *Bear Market*
- *Fundamental Analysis*
- *Uptrend*
- *Downtrend*
- *January Barometer*

BUSINESS CYCLE

What Does *Business Cycle* Mean?

The recurring and fluctuating levels of economic activity that an economy experiences over a long period; the five business cycles are growth (expansion), peak, recession (contraction), trough, and recovery. At one time business cycles were thought to occur on a regular and predictable basis, but today they are thought of as being more irregular, varying in frequency, magnitude, and duration.

Investopedia explains *Business Cycle*

Since World War II, most business cycles have lasted three to five years from peak to peak. The average duration of an expansion has been 44.8 months; the average duration of a recession has been 11 months. The Great Depression, which saw economic activity decline from 1929 to 1933, lasted 43 months.

RELATED TERMS:
- Asset Turnover
- Bull Market
- Recession
- Bear Market
- Law of Supply

BUY SIDE

What Does *Buy Side* Mean?

The institutional side of Wall Street that tends to buy large portions of securities for money-management purposes: mutual funds, pension funds, and insurance firms. The buy side is the opposite of the sell side; it provides research and recommendations for upgrades, downgrades, target prices, and opinions to the public market. Together, the buy side and the sell side make up the two sides of institutional Wall Street.

Investopedia explains *Buy Side*

As an example, a buy-side analyst typically works in a nonbrokerage firm (mutual fund or pension fund) and provides research and recommendations exclusively for the benefit of the company's own money managers (as opposed to individual investors). Unlike sell-side recommendations, which are meant for the public, buy-side recommendations are not available to anyone outside the firm. In fact, if a buy-side analyst stumbles upon a formula, vision, or approach that works, it is kept secret.

RELATED TERMS:
- Investment Bank
- No-Load Fund
- Security
- Mutual Fund
- Portfolio

BUY TO COVER

What Does *Buy to Cover* Mean?

A buy order placed on a stock or another listed security that closes out an existing short position. A short sale involves selling shares of a company that one does not own; since the shares are borrowed, they have to be returned (repaid) at some point. Buying back an equal number of shares that were borrowed "covers" the short sale, and the shares can be returned to the original lender. The lender is typically the investor's own broker-dealer, who in turn may have had to borrow the shares from a third party.

Investopedia explains *Buy to Cover*

These investors, who bet on a stock price's decline, hope to buy back the shares at a lower price than the price at which the shares were sold short. There is no time frame for short investors, who can wait as long as they wish to repurchase the shares. However, if a stock begins to rise above the price at which the shares were shorted, the investors' broker may force them to execute a buy to cover order to meet a margin call. To avoid margin calls, investors should keep enough buying power in their accounts to make a buy to cover trade, based on the current market price of the stock.

RELATED TERMS:
- *Maintenance Margin*
- *Short (or Short Position)*
- *Short Interest*
- *Naked Shorting*
- *Short Covering*

BUYBACK

What Does *Buyback* Mean?

The repurchase of outstanding shares (repurchase) by a company to reduce the number of shares outstanding in the market; companies buy back shares either to increase the value of available shares (reducing supply) or to eliminate threats by shareholders who may be planning a hostile takeover.

Investopedia explains *Buyback*

A buyback is a method for a company to invest in itself. Buybacks reduce the number of shares outstanding in the market, and that increases the proportion of shares the company owns. Buybacks can be carried out in two ways: (1) Shareholders may be given a tender offer by which they have the option to submit (or tender) a portion or all of their shares back to the company within a certain time frame and at a premium to the current market price. The premium is compensation for tendering their shares rather than holding on to them. (2) Companies buy back shares on the open market over an extended period.

RELATED TERMS:
- *Debt Financing*
- *Outstanding Shares*
- *Short Squeeze*
- *Dilution*
- *Short Covering*

copyright JackGuinan

"Some people take a top-down approach to investing. I prefer a bottoms-up one myself."

CALL

What Does *Call* Mean?
(1) The period of time between the opening and the closing of some future markets in which the prices are established through an auction process. (2) An option contract giving the owner the right (but not the obligation) to buy (call away) a specified amount of an underlying security at a specified price within a specified period.

Investopedia explains *Call*
(1) On some exchanges, the call period is an important time in which to match and execute a large number of orders before opening and closing. (2) A call becomes more valuable as the price of the underlying asset (stock) rises.

RELATED TERMS:
- Call Option
- Long (or Long Position)
- Put
- Callable Bond
- Open Interest

CALL OPTION

What Does *Call Option* Mean?
An investment contract that gives an investor the right (but not the obligation) to buy a stock, bond, commodity, or other instrument at a specified price within a specified time period.

Investopedia explains *Call Option*
A call option gives an investor the right to "call in" (buy) an asset. The investor profits on a call when the underlying asset increases in price above the call price.

RELATED TERMS:
- *Bull Market*
- *Long (or Long Position)*
- *Put Option*
- *Call*
- *Put*

CALLABLE BOND

What Does *Callable Bond* Mean?
A bond that can be redeemed (called) by the issuer before its maturity; usually a premium is paid to the bond owner when the bond is called. Also referred to as a redeemable bond.

Investopedia explains *Callable Bond*
The main reason a bond is called by an issuer is a decline in interest rates. If interest rates have declined since a company first issued its bonds, it probably will want to refinance the debt at a lower rate of interest. In this case, the company will call its current bonds and reissue new bonds at a lower rate of interest. This saves the issuer money by lowering the interest payments on the bonds.

RELATED TERMS:
- *Bond*
- *Debt*
- *Yield to Maturity*
- *Call*
- *Interest Rate*

CANDLESTICK

What Does *Candlestick* Mean?
A price chart that displays the daily high, low, open, and close for a security over a specified period.

Investopedia explains
Candlestick
Traders use candlestick
chart information to
execute many different
trading strategies.

RELATED TERMS:
• *Ask*
• *Bid*
• *Fundamental Analysis*
• *Technical Analysis*
• *Volume*

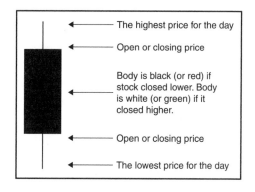

The highest price for the day

Open or closing price

Body is black (or red) if
stock closed lower. Body
is white (or green) if it
closed higher.

Open or closing price

The lowest price for the day

CAPITAL

 What Does *Capital* Mean?
(1) Financial assets or the financial value of assets, such as cash. (2)
The factories, machinery, and equipment owned by a business and
used for operations and production.

 Investopedia explains *Capital*
Capital is an extremely vague term, and its specific definition
depends on the context in which it is used. In general, it refers to
financial resources available for use: working capital.

RELATED TERMS:
• *Capital Asset Pricing Model—CAPM*   • *Capital Gain*
• *Capital Structure*   • *Depreciation*
• *Venture Capital*

CAPITAL ASSET PRICING MODEL (CAPM)

 What Does *Capital Asset Pricing Model (CAPM)* Mean?
A model that describes the relationship between risk and expected
return; it is used to price securities. The general idea behind CAPM
is that investors need to be compensated for investing their cash in
two ways: (1) time value of money and (2) risk. (1) The time value
of money is represented by the risk-free (rf) rate in the formula and
compensates investors for placing money in any investment over

a period of time. (2) Risk calculates the amount of compensation the investor needs for taking on additional risk. This is calculated by taking a risk measure (beta) that compares the returns of the asset to the market over a period of time and to the market premium (Rm-rf).

$$\overline{r}_a = r_f + \beta_a (\overline{r}_m - r_f)$$

Where:

r_f = Risk free rate

β_a = Beta of the security

$\overline{r}_m$ = Expected market return

 Investopedia explains *Capital Asset Pricing Model (CAPM)*
The CAPM states that the expected return of a security or a portfolio should equal the rate on a risk-free security (a U.S. Treasury bond) plus a risk premium. If this expected return does not meet or exceed the required return, the investment should not be undertaken. The security market line plots the results of the CAPM for all different risks (betas). Using the CAPM model with the following assumptions, one can compute the expected return of a stock: If the risk-free rate = 3%, the beta (risk measure) of the stock = 2, and the expected market return over the time period = 10%, the stock is expected to return 17% (3% + 2(10% −3%)).

RELATED TERMS:
- Beta
- Security Market Line—SML
- Treasury Bill—T-Bill
- Capital Market Line—CML
- Systematic Risk

CAPITAL GAIN

 What Does *Capital Gain* **Mean?**
(1) An increase in the value of a capital asset (investment or real estate) above its purchase price. The gain is not realized until the asset is sold. A capital gain may be short term (one year or less) or long term (more than one year) and must be reported for tax purposes. A capital loss is incurred when there is a decrease in the capital asset value below the purchase price of an asset. (2) The profit that results when the price of a security held in a mutual fund rises above its purchase price and the security is sold (realized gain). If the security continues to be held, the gain is unrealized. A capital loss occurs when the opposite takes place.

Investopedia explains *Capital Gain*
(1) Long-term capital gains usually are taxed at a lower rate than is regular income or dividends. This is done to encourage entrepreneurship and investment in the economy. (2) Tax-conscious mutual fund investors should check a mutual fund's unrealized accumulated capital gains, which are expressed as a percentage of its net assets, before investing in a fund that may have a significant unrealized capital gain component. This circumstance is referred to as a fund's capital gains exposure. When a fund distributes capital gains, the mutual fund's owners are liable for the tax.

RELATED TERMS:
- *Bull Market*
- *Capital Market Line—CML*
- *Stock*
- *Capital*
- *Return on Assets*

CAPITAL MARKET LINE (CML)

What Does *Capital Market Line (CML)* Mean?
A line used in the capital asset pricing model that plots the rates of return for efficient portfolios, depending on the risk-free rate of return and the level of risk (standard deviation) for a particular portfolio.

Investopedia explains *Capital Market Line (CML)*
The CML is derived by drawing a tangent line from the intercept point on the efficient frontier to the point where the expected return equals the risk-free rate of return. The CML is considered superior to the efficient frontier because it takes into account the inclusion of a risk-free asset in the portfolio. The capital asset pricing model (CAPM) demonstrates that the market portfolio is essentially the efficient frontier. This is represented visually by the security market line (SML).

RELATED TERMS:
- *Capital Asset Pricing Model—CAPM*
- *Efficient Market Hypothesis—EMH*
- *Modern Portfolio Theory—MPT*
- *Standard Deviation*
- *Volume*

CAPITAL STRUCTURE

What Does *Capital Structure* Mean?

The combination of a company's long-term debt, specific short-term debt, common equity, and preferred equity; the capital structure is the firm's various sources of funds used to finance its overall operations and growth. Debt comes in the form of bond issues or long-term notes payable, whereas equity is classified as common stock, preferred stock, or retained earnings. Short-term debt such as working capital requirements also is considered part of the capital structure.

Investopedia explains *Capital Structure*

The proportion of short-term and long-term debt is considered in analyzing a firm's capital structure. When people refer to capital structure, they most likely are talking about a firm's debt/equity ratio, which provides insight into how risky a company is. Usually a company financed heavily by debt poses greater risks because it is highly leveraged.

RELATED TERMS:
- Cost of Debt
- Long-Term Debt
- Shareholders' Equity
- Debt Financing
- Retained Earnings

CASH AND CASH EQUIVALENTS (CCE)

What Does *Cash and Cash Equivalents* (CCE) Mean?

An item on the balance sheet that reports the value of a company's assets that are cash or can be converted into cash immediately. Also called liquid assets.

Investopedia explains *Cash and Cash Equivalents* (CCE)

Examples of cash and cash equivalents are bank accounts, marketable securities, and Treasury bills (T-bills).

RELATED TERMS:
- Cash Conversion Cycle
- Current Assets
- Liquidity Ratios
- Cash Flow Statement
- Enterprise Value—EV

CASH CONVERSION CYCLE (CCC)

What Does *Cash Conversion Cycle (CCC)* Mean?

A metric that expresses the length of time in days that it takes for a company to convert resource inputs into cash flows. The cash conversion cycle attempts to measure the amount of time each net input dollar is tied up in the production and sales process before it is converted into cash through sales to customers. This metric looks at the amount of time needed to sell inventory, the amount of time needed to collect receivables, and the length of time the company is afforded to pay its bills without incurring penalties. Also known as the cash cycle. It is calculated as follows:

$$CCC = DIO + DSO - DPO$$

Where DIO represents days inventory outstanding, DSO represents days sales outstanding, and DPO represents days payable outstanding.

Investopedia explains *Cash Conversion Cycle (CCC)*

Usually a company acquires inventory on credit, which results in accounts payable. A company also can sell products on credit, which results in accounts receivable. Cash therefore is not involved until the company collects its accounts receivable and pays its accounts payable. The cash conversion cycle measures the time between the outlay of cash and cash recovery. This cycle is extremely important for retailers and similar businesses. CCC highlights how quickly a company can convert its products into cash through sales. The shorter the cycle is, the less time capital is tied up in the business process and thus the better it is for the company's balance sheet. Remember, cash is king.

RELATED TERMS:
- *Accounts Receivable*
- *Cash and Cash Equivalents—CCE*
- *Inventory*   • *Inventory Turnover*
- *Working Capital*

CASH FLOW

What Does *Cash Flow* Mean?

(1) A revenue or expense stream that changes a cash account over a specific period. Cash inflows usually arise from one of three activities—financing, operations, or investing—although they also

occur as a result of donations or gifts in the case of personal finance. Cash outflows result from expenses or investments. This holds true for both business and personal finance. (2) An accounting statement called the statement of cash flows shows the amount of cash generated and used by a company in a specific period. It is calculated by adding noncash charges (such as depreciation) to net income after taxes. Cash flow can be attributed to a specific project or to a business as a whole. Positive cash flow indicates a company's financial strength.

 Investopedia explains *Cash Flow*
(1) In business as in personal finance, cash flows are essential to solvency. They can represent past activities, such as the sale of a particular product, or forecast what a business or a person expects to take in and spend in the future. Cash flow is crucial to an entity's survival. Having ample cash on hand will ensure that creditors, employees. and others can be paid on time. If a person or business does not have enough cash to support its operations, it is said to be insolvent and a likely candidate for bankruptcy if the insolvency continues. (2) The statement of a business's cash flows often is used by analysts to gauge the business's financial performance. Companies with ample cash flow are able to invest the cash back into the business to generate more cash and profit.

RELATED TERMS:
- *Cash Conversion Cycle—CCC*
- *Discounted Cash Flow—DCF*
- *Net Income—NI*
- *Cash Flow Statement*
- *Free Cash Flow—FCF*

CASH FLOW STATEMENT

 What Does *Cash Flow Statement* **Mean?**
One of the quarterly financial reports a publicly traded company is required to disclose to the SEC and the public. It provides aggregate data regarding all cash inflows a company receives from both its ongoing operations and its external investment sources as well as all cash outflows that pay for business activities and investments during a specified quarter.

 Investopedia explains *Cash Flow Statement*
Because public companies tend to use accrual accounting, the income statements they release each quarter may not necessarily

reflect changes in their cash positions. For example, if a company lands a major contract, that contract will be recognized as revenue (and therefore income), but the company may not yet receive the cash from the contract until a later date. Although the company may be earning a profit in the eyes of accountants (and paying income taxes on it), the company may, during the quarter, end up with less cash than it had when it started. Even profitable companies can manage their cash flow inadequately. That is why the cash flow statement is important: It helps investors see if a company is having cash troubles.

RELATED TERMS:
- Accrual Accounting
- Cash and Cash Equivalents—CCE
- Generally Accepted Accounting Principles—GAAP
- Income Statement
- Balance Sheet

CERTIFICATE OF DEPOSIT (CD)

What Does *Certificate of Deposit (CD)* Mean?
A savings instrument that guarantees to pay to the purchaser interest and principal. A CD has a maturity date (one month to five years) and a specified fixed interest rate and is issued in several denominations. CDs generally are issued by commercial banks and are insured by the FDIC.

Investopedia explains *Certificate of Deposit (CD)*
A CD is a promissory note issued by a bank. It is a time deposit that restricts holders from withdrawing funds on demand. If one purchases a $10,000 CD with an interest rate of 5% compounded annually and a term of one year, at the year's end, the CD will have grown to $10,500 ($10,000 × 1.05). Although the holder can withdraw money before maturity, this action may result in a financial penalty. CDs of less than $100,000 are called small CDs; CDs of more than $100,000 are called large CDs or jumbo CDs. Almost all large CDs, as well as some small CDs, are negotiable.

RELATED TERMS:
- Banker's Acceptance—BA
- Interest Rate
- Money Market
- Commercial Paper
- Jumbo Loan

CHAPTER 11

What Does *Chapter 11* Mean?

Chapter 11 is a form of bankruptcy that involves a reorganization of a debtor's business affairs and assets. It generally is filed by corporations that require time to restructure their debts. Chapter 11 gives the debtor a fresh start, subject to the debtor's fulfillment of its obligations under its plan of reorganization.

Investopedia explains *Chapter 11*

A Chapter 11 reorganization is the most complex of all bankruptcy cases and generally the most expensive. Companies consider this only as a last resort and only after careful analysis and exploration of all other alternatives.

RELATED TERMS:
- Bankruptcy
- Debt Financing
- Recession
- Debt
- Dilution

CLOSED-END FUND

What Does *Closed-End Fund* Mean?

A closed-end fund is a publicly traded investment company that raises a fixed amount of capital through an initial public offering (IPO). The fund then issues shares that are listed and traded like a stock on a stock exchange. Also known as a closed-end investment or closed-end mutual fund.

Investopedia explains *Closed-End Fund*

Despite the similarity in name, a closed-end fund has little in common with a conventional mutual fund, which is technically known as an open-end fund. The former raises a prescribed amount of capital only once through an IPO by issuing a fixed amount of shares, which are purchased by investors in the closed-end fund as stock. Unlike regular stocks, a closed-end fund represents an interest in a specialized portfolio of securities that is managed actively by an investment advisor and typically concentrates on a specific industry, geographic region, or sector. The share price of a closed-end fund fluctuates in accordance with market forces (supply and demand) as well as the changing values of the securities in the fund's holdings.

Related Terms:
- Exchange Traded Fund
- Net Asset Value—NAV
- Stock
- Mutual Fund
- Open-End Fund

COEFFICIENT OF VARIATION (CV)

What Does *Coefficient of Variation (CV)* Mean?
A statistical measure of the dispersion of data points in a data series around the mean. It is calculated as follows:

$$\text{Coefficient of Variation} = \frac{\text{Standard Deviation}}{\text{Expected Return}}$$

The coefficient of variation represents the ratio of the standard deviation to the mean; it is a useful statistic for comparing the degree of variation from one data series to another even if the means are drastically different from each other.

Investopedia explains *Coefficient of Variation (CV)*
The coefficient of variation allows investors to determine how much volatility (risk) they are assuming in relation to the amount of expected return from an investment; the lower the ratio of standard deviation to the mean return is, the better the risk-return trade-off is. Note that if the expected return in the denominator of the calculation is negative or zero, the ratio will not make sense.

Related Terms:
- Beta
- Risk-Return Trade-Off
- Volatility
- Expected Return
- Standard Deviation

COLLATERAL

What Does *Collateral* Mean?
Properties or assets that secure a loan or another debt. Collateral becomes subject to seizure on default.

Investopedia explains *Collateral*
Collateral is a form of insurance to the lender in case the borrower fails to pay back the loan. For example, if a person gets a mortgage, the collateral would be the house. In margin stock trading, the securities in the account act as collateral against the margin loan.

RELATED TERMS:
- Asset
- Margin
- Regulation T
- Asset-Backed Security
- Margin Call

COLLATERALIZED DEBT OBLIGATION (CDO)

What Does *Collateralized Debt Obligation (CDO)* Mean?
An investment-grade security that is backed by a pool of bonds, loans, and other assets. CDOs represent various debt obligations but are often nonmortgage loans or bonds.

Investopedia explains *Collateralized Debt Obligation (CDO)*
Similar in structure to a collateralized mortgage obligation (CMO) or a collateralized bond obligation (CBO), CDOs are unique in that they represent different types of debt and credit risk. In the case of CDOs, these different types of debt often are referred to as tranches or slices. Each slice has a different maturity and risk associated with it. The higher the risk is, the more the CDO pays.

RELATED TERMS:
- Asset-Backed Security
- Collateralized Mortgage Obligation—CMO
- Debt
- Bond
- Tranches

COLLATERALIZED MORTGAGE OBLIGATION (CMO)

What Does *Collateralized Mortgage Obligation (CMO)* Mean?
A type of mortgage-backed security that creates separate pools of pass-through rates for different classes of bondholders with varying maturities, called tranches. The repayments from the pool of pass-through securities are used to retire the bonds in the precise order specified by the bonds' prospectus.

Investopedia explains *Collateralized Mortgage Obligation (CMO)*
CMOs work as follows: CMO investors are divided into three classes: class A, B, and C investors. Each class receives principal payments in a different order but receives interest payments until it is paid off completely. Class A investors are paid out first with prepayments and repayments until they are paid off. Next come class B investors,

followed by class C investors. In a situation like this, class A investors bear most of the prepayment risk and class C investors bear the least.

RELATED TERMS:
- Asset-Backed Security
- Collateralized Debt Obligation—CDO
- Mortgage-Backed Securities—MBS
- Mortgage
- Tranches

COMMERCIAL PAPER

What Does *Commercial Paper* Mean?

An unsecured, short-term debt instrument issued by a corporation, typically for the financing of accounts receivable, inventories, and short-term liabilities. Maturities on commercial paper rarely are longer than 270 days, and commercial paper usually is issued at a discount to prevailing market interest rates.

Investopedia explains *Commercial Paper*

Generally, commercial paper is not backed by any form of collateral; therefore, only firms with high-quality debt ratings will find buyers easily without having to offer a substantial discount (higher cost) for the debt issue. Commercial paper does not have to be registered with the Securities and Exchange Commission (SEC) as long as it matures before nine months (270 days), making it a very cost-effective means of financing. Monies from this type of financing can be used only on current assets (inventories), not on fixed assets, such as a new plant, without SEC involvement.

RELATED TERMS:
- Cash and Cash Equivalents
- Certificate of Deposit—CD
- Money Market
- Banker's Acceptance—BA
- Interest Rate

COMMODITY

What Does *Commodity* Mean?

(1) A basic good used in commerce that is interchangeable with other commodities of the same type. Commodities most often are used as inputs in the production of other goods or services. The quality of a commodity may differ slightly, but it is essentially uniform across producers. Commodities traded on an exchange must

meet specified minimum standards, also known as a basis grade. (2) Any good exchanged during commerce, including goods traded on a commodity exchange.

 Investopedia explains *Commodity*
(1) Basically, there is little difference in a commodity from one producer to another; for example, a barrel of oil is a barrel of oil regardless of the producer. In contrast, electronic equipment is not a commodity, and the quality can be completely different, depending on the producer. Familiar commodities are grains, gold, beef, oil, and natural gas. More recently, financial products such as foreign currencies and indexes have been called commodities. Closer to home, cell phone minutes and bandwidth are becoming commodities. (2) The sale and purchase of commodities usually are carried out through futures contracts on exchanges that standardize the quantity and minimum quality of the commodities being traded. For example, the Chicago Board of Trade stipulates that one wheat contract must be for 5,000 bushels and a stated grade (e.g., No. 2 Northern Spring).

RELATED TERMS:
- *Futures*
- *Hedge*
- *Over the Counter*

- *Futures Contract*
- *Net Tangible Assets*

COMMON STOCK

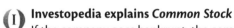 **What Does** *Common Stock* **Mean?**
A security that represents ownership in a corporation; holders of common stock exercise control by electing a board of directors and voting on corporate policy. Common stockholders are on the bottom of the priority ladder if a company fails. In the case of liquidation, common shareholders get paid after bondholders, preferred shareholders, and other debtholders. In the United Kingdom, common stock is called ordinary shares.

 Investopedia explains *Common Stock*
If the company goes bankrupt, the common stockholders will not receive their money until the creditors and preferred shareholders have received their respective shares of the leftover assets. In the event of liquidation, this makes common stock riskier than debt or

preferred shares. However, historically, common stock has outperformed bonds and preferred shares in the long run.

RELATED TERMS:
- Equity
- Marketable Security
- Shareholders' Equity

- Initial Public offering—IPO
- Preferred Stock

COMPOUND ANNUAL GROWTH RATE (CAGR)

What Does *Compound Annual Growth Rate (CAGR)* Mean?
The year-over-year growth rate of an investment over a specified
period; calculated by taking the (N)th root of the total percentage
growth rate, where (N) is the
number of years in the period
being considered. It is expressed
as follows:

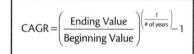

$$CAGR = \left(\frac{\text{Ending Value}}{\text{Beginning Value}} \right)^{\left(\frac{1}{\#\text{ of years}} \right)} - 1$$

Investopedia explains *Compound Annual Growth Rate (CAGR)*
In reality, CAGR is not the actual return but an imaginary number
that describes the rate at which an investment would have grown
if it had grown at a steady rate. CAGR can be thought of as a way
to smooth out returns. This concept may seem fuzzy, and CAGR is
better defined by example. Suppose you invest $10,000 in a port-
folio on January 1, 2005, and it grows to $13,000 by January 1, 2006,
then to $14,000 by 2007, and finally to $19,500 by 2008. Your CAGR
would be the ratio of your ending value to your beginning value
($19,500/$10,000 = 1.95) raised to the power of 1/3 (since 1/number
of years = 1/3). Then 1 is subtracted from the resulting number: 1.95
raised to 1/3 power = 1.2493. (This could be written as 1.95^0.3333.)
1.2493 − 1 = 0.2493. Another way of writing 0.2493 is 24.93%. The
CAGR for your three-year investment is equal to 24.93%, representing the smoothed-out annualized gain earned over the time frame
of the investment.

RELATED TERMS:
- Compounding
- Growth Stock
- Yield

- Duration
- Interest Rate

COMPOUNDING

What Does *Compounding* Mean?

The ability of an asset to generate earnings, which then are reinvested to generate their own earnings. In other words, compounding refers to generating earnings from previous earnings. Also known as compound interest.

Investopedia explains *Compounding*

Suppose you invest $10,000 in Cory's Tequila Company. The first year, the shares rise 20%. The investment is now worth $12,000. In year 2, the shares appreciate another 20% so that your $12,000 grows to $14,400. Rather than your shares appreciating an additional $2,000 (20%) as they did in the first year, they appreciate an additional $400 because the $2,000 you gained in the first year grew by 20% as well. If you extrapolate the process, the numbers can start to get very big as your previous earnings earn returns of their own. In fact, $10,000 invested at 20% annually for 25 years would grow to nearly $1,000,000 without your having invested another dime! Albert Einstein was rumored to have called compounding the eighth wonder of the world.

RELATED TERMS:
- *Annual Percentage Yield—APY*
- *Compound Annual Growth Rate—CAGR*
- *Dividend*
- *Money Market Account*
- *Interest Rate*

CONSUMER PRICE INDEX (CPI)

What Does *Consumer Price Index (CPI)* Mean?

A measure that examines the weighted average of prices of a basket of consumer goods and services such as transportation, food, and medical care. CPI is calculated by taking price changes for each item in the predetermined basket of goods and averaging them; the goods are weighted according to their importance. Changes in CPI are used to assess price changes associated with the cost of living. Sometimes referred to as headline inflation.

Investopedia explains *Consumer Price Index (CPI)*

The U.S. Bureau of Labor Statistics measures two kinds of CPI statistics: (1) CPI for urban wage earners and clerical workers (CPI-W) and

(2) chained CPI for all urban consumers (C-CPI-U). Of the CPI-U is more representative of the general public because it encompasses 87% of the population. CPI is one of the most frequently used statistics for identifying periods of inflation or deflation. This is the case because large rises in CPI during a short period typically denote periods of inflation, whereas large drops in CPI during a short period usually mark periods of deflation.

RELATED TERMS:
- Bear Market
- Inflation
- Treasury Inflation Protected Securities—TIPS
- Hyperinflation
- Market Economy

CONSUMER STAPLES

What Does *Consumer Staples* Mean?
A category of companies that manufacture and sell food and beverages, tobacco, prescription drugs, and household products; generally they are goods and services that people buy regardless of economic conditions.

Investopedia explains *Consumer Staples*
Consumer staple companies produce products that people purchase in good and bad economic times. Examples are soaps, healthcare products, food, and some types of clothing. Consumer staple products are the opposite of consumer discretionary products, which are items purchased at the discretion of the consumer, such as luxury goods.

RELATED TERMS:
- Bear Market
- Business Cycle
- Recession
- Bull Market
- Inflation

CONTRIBUTION MARGIN

What Does *Contribution Margin* Mean?
A cost accounting method that allows a company to determine the profitability of individual products. It is calculated as follows:

$$\frac{\text{Product Revenue} - \text{Product Variable Costs}}{\text{Product Revenue}}$$

The phrase "contribution margin" also refers to a per unit measure of a product's gross operating margin; it is calculated simply as the product's price minus its total variable costs.

 Investopedia explains *Contribution Margin*
Consider a situation in which a business manager determines that a particular product has a 35% contribution margin, which happens to be less than that of other products in the company's product line. This figure can help determine whether variable costs for that product can be reduced or the price of the end product can be increased. If both options are unattractive, the manager can drop the unprofitable product and produce an alternative product with a higher contribution margin.

RELATED TERMS:
- Accrual Accounting
- Margin
- Revenue
- Income Statement
- Operating Margin

CONVERTIBLE BOND

 What Does *Convertible Bond* Mean?
A bond that can be converted into a predetermined amount of equity at certain times during its life, usually at the discretion of the bondholder; convertibles sometimes are called CVs.

 Investopedia explains *Convertible Bond*
Issuing convertible bonds is one way for a company to minimize negative investor sentiment toward its corporate actions. For example, if a public company chooses to issue stock, the market usually interprets it as a sign that the company's share price is somewhat overvalued. To avoid this negative impression, the company may choose to issue convertible bonds, which bondholders probably will convert to equity anyway if the company continues to do well. From the investor's perspective, a convertible bond has a value-added component built into it because it is essentially a bond but with a stock option hidden inside. However, it tends to offer a lower rate of return in exchange for the value of the option to convert the bond into stock.

RELATED TERMS:
- Bond
- Dilution
- Shareholders' Equity

- Convertible Preferred Stock
- Fully Diluted Shares

CONVERTIBLE PREFERRED STOCK

What Does *Convertible Preferred Stock* Mean?
Preferred stock that allows the holder to convert the preferred shares into a fixed number of common shares, usually any time after a predetermined date. Also known as convertible preferred shares.

Investopedia explains *Convertible Preferred Stock*
Most convertible preferred stock is exchanged at the request of the shareholder, but sometimes there is a provision that allows the company (or issuer) to force conversion. The value of convertible common stock ultimately is based on the performance (or lack of performance) of the common stock.

RELATED TERMS:
- Common Stock
- Dividend
- Premium

- Convertible Bond
- Preferred Stock

CORPORATE BOND

What Does *Corporate Bond* Mean?
A debt security issued by a corporation and sold to investors. The bond is backed by the company's ability to pay interest and principal, which typically comes from money earned from future operations. In some cases, the company's physical assets may be used as collateral for bonds. Corporate bonds are considered higher risk than government bonds. As a result, interest rates are almost always higher on corporate bonds, even for top-flight credit quality companies.

Investopedia explains *Corporate Bond*
Corporate bonds are issued in blocks of $1,000 in par value (face value) and usually have a standard coupon payment structure. Corporate bonds also may contain call provisions to allow for early

prepayment if prevailing rates change. Corporate bonds, that is, debt financing, along with equity and bank loans/lines of credit, are a major source of capital for businesses. In general, a company should exhibit consistent earnings potential to be able to offer debt securities to the public at a favorable coupon rate. The higher a company's perceived credit quality is, the easier it becomes to issue debt at lower interest rates and issue higher amounts of debt. Most corporate bonds are taxable and have maturities of more than one year. Corporate debt that matures in less than one year typically is called commercial paper.

RELATED TERMS:
- Bond
- Municipal Bond
- Yield to maturity—YTM
- Debt Financing
- Yield

CORRELATION

What Does *Correlation* Mean?
In the investment world, correlation is a statistical measure of how two securities move in relation to each other. Correlations are used in advanced portfolio management.

Investopedia explains *Correlation*
Correlation is expressed as the correlation coefficient, which ranges between −1 and +1. Perfect positive correlation (a correlation coefficient of +1) means that as one security moves up or down, the other security will move lockstep in the same direction. Perfect negative correlation means that when one security moves in one direction, the other security will move by an equal amount in the opposite direction. If the correlation is 0, the movements of the securities are said to have no correlation; they are completely random. In real life, one rarely finds perfectly correlated securities but rather securities with degrees of correlation.

RELATED TERMS:
- Asset Allocation
- Correlation
- Diversification
- Modern Portfolio Theory—MPT
- Standard Deviation

COST OF CAPITAL

What Does *Cost of Capital* Mean?

The required rate of return necessary to make a capital budgeting expenditure, such as building a new factory, worthwhile. Cost of capital includes the cost of debt and the cost of equity.

Investopedia explains *Cost of Capital*

The cost of capital influences the ways in which a company can raise money (through issuing stock or bonds or a mix of the two). Cost of capital is essentially the rate of return that a firm would receive if it invested in a different vehicle with similar risk.

RELATED TERMS:
- *Capital Asset Pricing Model—CAPM*
- *Opportunity Cost*
- *Unlevered Beta*
- *Cost of Debt*
- *Risk*

COST OF DEBT

What Does *Cost of Debt* Mean?

The effective rate that a company pays on its current debt; it can be measured as either before-tax or after-tax returns; however, because interest expense is deductible, the after-tax cost is seen most often. This is one part of the company's capital structure, which also includes the cost of equity.

Investopedia explains *Cost of Debt*

Companies use bonds, loans, and other forms of debt for capital; this measure is useful because it indicates the overall rate being used for debt financing. It also gives investors an idea of how risky a company can be; riskier companies generally have a higher cost of debt. To get the after-tax rate, multiply the before-tax rate by 1 minus the marginal tax rate (before-tax rate $\times$ (1 – marginal tax)). For example, if a company's only debt was a single bond in which it paid 5%, the before-tax cost of debt would be 5%. If, however, the company's marginal tax rate was 40%, the company's after-tax cost of debt would be only 3% (5% $\times$ (1 –40%)).

RELATED TERMS:
- *Capital Structure*
- *Debt Financing*
- *Interest Rate*
- *Cost of Capital*
- *Discounted Cash Flow—DCF*

COST OF GOODS SOLD (COGS)

What Does *Cost of Goods Sold* Mean?

The direct costs incurred in the production of the goods sold by a company; it includes the cost of the materials and direct labor costs. Indirect expenses such as distribution costs and sales force costs are not part of COGS. COGS appears on the income statement and can be deducted from revenue to calculate a company's gross margin. Also referred to as cost of sales.

Investopedia explains *Cost of Goods Sold*

COGS consists of the costs that go into creating the products that a company sells; therefore, the only costs included in the measure are those which are tied directly to the production of the products. For example, the COGS for an automaker would include the material costs for the parts that go into making the car along with the labor costs used to put the car together. The cost of sending the cars to dealerships and the cost of the labor used to sell the car would be excluded. COGS differs from one industry to another. COGS is considered an expense. There are several ways to calculate COGS; one of the more basic ways is to start with the beginning inventory for the period and add the total amount of purchases made during the period and then deduct the ending inventory. This gives the total amount of inventory, specifically, the cost of the inventory sold by the company during the period. If a company begins with $10 million in inventory, makes $2 million in purchases, and ends the period with $9 million in inventory, the company's COGS would be $3 million ($10 million + $2 million − $9 million).

RELATED TERMS:
- Accounts Payable
- Gross Margin
- Operating Income
- Accrual Accounting
- Inventory

COUNTERPARTY RISK

What Does *Counterparty Risk* Mean?

The risk inherent to each party to a contract that the counterparty will not live up to its contractual obligations.

Investopedia explains *Counterparty Risk*
In most financial contracts, counterparty risk is known as default risk.

RELATED TERMS:
- Beta
- Risk-Return Trade-Off
- Unsystematic Risk
- Risk
- Systematic Risk

COUPON

 What Does *Coupon* Mean?
The interest rate stated on a bond when it is issued. The coupon typically is paid semiannually. This also is referred to as the coupon rate or coupon percent rate.

 Investopedia explains *Coupon*
For example, a $1,000 bond with a coupon of 7% will pay $70 a year. It is called a coupon because some bonds literally have coupons attached to them. Holders receive interest by stripping off the coupons and redeeming them. This is less common today as more records are kept electronically.

RELATED TERMS:
- Bond
- Premium
- Zero-Coupon Bond
- Interest Rate
- Yield

COVARIANCE

 What Does *Covariance* Mean?
A measure of the degree by which the returns on two risky assets move in tandem. A positive covariance means that asset returns move together; a negative covariance means the returns move inversely. One method of calculating covariance is by looking at return surprises (deviations from expected return) in each scenario. Another method is to multiply the correlation between the two variables by the standard deviation of each variable.

Investopedia explains *Covariance*

Financial assets that have a high covariance with each other will not provide very much diversification. For example, if stock A's return is high whenever stock B's return is high or low when B's is also low, these stocks are said to have a positive covariance. An investor seeking diversified earnings should pick financial assets that have low covariance to each other.

RELATED TERMS:
- Correlation
- Efficient Market Hypothesis—EMH
- Modern Portfolio Theory—MPT
- Diversification
- Technical Analysis

COVERED CALL

What Does *Covered Call* Mean?

An options strategy in which an investor holds a long position in an asset and writes (sells) call options on that asset in an attempt to generate increased income from the asset. This strategy often is employed when an investor's short-term view of the asset is neutral. When an asset is bought long and an option is sold against the stock, the investor receives income from receiving the option premium. This is known as a buy-write.

Investopedia explains *Covered Call*

For example, let's say that you own shares in the TSJ Sports Conglomerate and are bullish about the company's and the stock's long-term prospects; however, in the short term you think the stock will trade relatively flat, perhaps within a few dollars of its current market price, say, $25. If you sell a call option on TSJ for $26, you earn the premium from the option sale but cap your upside potential at $26. One of three scenarios will play out: (1) TSJ shares trade flat (below the $26 strike price); the option expires worthless, and you keep the premium from the option. In this case, by using the buy-write strategy you have outperformed the stock. (2) TSJ share price drops; the option expires worthless, and you keep the premium. Again, you outperform the stock. (3) TSJ shares rise above $26; the option is exercised, and your upside is capped at $26, plus the option premium that you received. In this case, if the stock price exceeds $26 plus the premium that you received, your buy-write strategy has underperformed the TSJ shares.

RELATED TERMS:
- *Call Option*
- *Long (or Long Position)*
- *Strike Price*
- *Common Stock*
- *Stock Option*

CREDIT CRUNCH

What Does *Credit Crunch* Mean?

An economic condition characterized by extreme difficulty in obtaining capital. Banks and investors become wary of lending funds to corporations, and that drives up the price of debt products for borrowers.

Investopedia explains *Credit Crunch*

Credit crunches usually occur during recessions. A credit crunch makes it nearly impossible for companies to borrow money because lenders are scared of bankruptcies or defaults and charge higher interest rates because of that fear. The result is a slowdown in growth that leads to a prolonged recession (or slower recovery), which is compounded as banks hold tight to the banking reserves.

RELATED TERMS:
- *Bankruptcy*
- *Debt*
- *Subprime Meltdown*
- *Bear Market*
- *Recession*

CREDIT DEFAULT SWAP (CDS)

What Does *Credit Default Swap* (CDS) Mean?

A swap designed to transfer the credit exposure of fixed-income products between parties.

Investopedia explains *Credit Default Swap* (CDS)

The buyer of a credit swap receives credit protection, whereas the seller of the swap guarantees the creditworthiness of the product. When this is done, the risk of default is transferred from the holder of the fixed-income security to the seller of the swap. For example, the buyer of a credit swap still is entitled to the par value of the bond from the seller of the swap if the bond defaults in its coupon payments.

RELATED TERMS:
- Bond
- Fixed Income Security
- Swap
- Credit Derivative
- Interest Rate Swap

CREDIT DERIVATIVE

What Does *Credit Derivative* Mean?

Privately held negotiable bilateral contracts that enable their users to manage their exposure to credit risk. Credit derivatives are financial assets like forward contracts, swaps, and options for which the price is driven by the credit risk of economic agents (private investors or governments).

Investopedia explains *Credit Derivative*

As an example, a bank concerned that one of its customers may not be able to repay a loan can protect itself against loss from default by transferring the credit risk to another party while keeping the loan on its books.

RELATED TERMS:
- Credit Default Swap
- Derivative
- Yield
- Credit Rating
- Securitization

CREDIT RATING

What Does *Credit Rating* Mean?

An assessment of the creditworthiness of individuals and corporations. It is based on the history of borrowing and repayment as well as the availability of assets and the extent of liabilities.

Investopedia explains *Credit Rating*

Credit is important because individuals and corporations with poor credit will have difficulty finding financing and most likely will have to pay more because of the risk of default. Credit ratings are a tool used by lenders to determine the types of loans and rate of interest that can be extended to a potential borrower.

RELATED TERMS:
- Bond
- Debt Financing
- Risk

- Bond Rating
- Interest Rate

CREDIT SPREAD

What Does *Credit Spread* Mean?
(1) The spread between Treasury securities and non-Treasury securities that are identical in all respects except for the quality rating.
(2) An options strategy in which a high-premium option is sold and a low-premium option is bought on the same underlying security.

Investopedia explains *Credit Spread*
(1) For instance, the yields on Treasuries are lower than the yields on single A-rated industrial bonds because the Treasuries are backed by the full-faith and credit of the government and are rated higher; the Industrial bond is not. (2) An option credit spread example would be buying a Jan 50 call on ABC for $2 and writing a Jan 45 call on ABC for $5. The net amount received (credit) is $3. The investor will profit if the spread narrows. This also can be called a credit spread option or credit risk option.

RELATED TERMS:
- Bond
- Treasury Bond—T-Bill
- Yield Curve

- Premium
- Yield

CURRENCY FORWARD

What Does *Currency Forward* Mean?
A forward contract in the forex market that locks in the price at which an entity can buy or sell a currency on a future date. Also known as an outright forward currency transaction, forward outright, or FX forward.

Investopedia explains *Currency Forward*
In currency forward contracts, the contract holders are obligated to buy or sell the currency at a specified price, at a specified quantity, and on a specified future date. These contracts are not transferrable.

RELATED TERMS:
- Currency Swap
- Forward Contract
- Option
- Forex—FX
- Hedge

CURRENCY SWAP

What Does *Currency Swap* Mean?

A swap that involves the exchange of the principal and interest in one currency for the principal and interest in another currency; it is considered a foreign exchange transaction and is not required by law to be shown on the balance sheet.

Investopedia explains *Currency Swap*

As an example, suppose a U.S.-based company needs to acquire Swiss francs and a Swiss-based company needs to acquire U.S. dollars. The two companies could arrange to swap currencies by establishing an interest rate, an agreed-upon amount, and a common maturity date for the exchange. Currency swap maturities are negotiable for at least 10 years, making them a very flexible method of foreign exchange. Currency swaps originally were used to get around exchange controls.

RELATED TERMS:
- Currency Forward
- Interest Rate Swap
- Swap
- Interest Rate
- Spread

CURRENT ASSETS

What Does *Current Assets* Mean?

(1) A balance sheet account that represents the value of all assets that can reasonably be expected to be converted into cash within one year in the normal course of business. Current assets include cash, accounts receivable, inventory, marketable securities, prepaid expenses, and other liquid assets that can be converted readily to cash. (2) In personal finance, current assets are all assets that a person can convert readily to cash to pay outstanding debts and

cover liabilities without having to sell fixed assets. In the United Kingdom, current assets are also known as current accounts.

Investopedia explains *Current Assets*
(1) Current assets are important to businesses because they are the assets that are used to fund day-to-day operations and pay ongoing expenses. Depending on the nature of the business, current assets can range from barrels of crude oil, to baked goods, to foreign currency. (2) In personal finance, current assets include cash on hand, bank accounts, and marketable securities that are not tied up in long-term investments. In other words, current assets have value and can be converted to cash rather quickly (highly liquid).

RELATED TERMS:
- *Acid-Test Ratio*
- *Cash and Cash Equivalents—CCE*
- *Working Capital*
- *Balance Sheet*
- *Current Liabilities*

CURRENT LIABILITIES

What Does *Current Liabilities* Mean?
A company's debts or obligations payable within one year. Current liabilities appear on the company's balance sheet and include short-term debt, accounts payable, accrued liabilities, and other debts.

Investopedia explains *Current Liabilities*
Essentially, these are bills that are due to creditors and suppliers within a short time. Normally, companies withdraw cash or liquidate current assets to pay their current liabilities. Analysts and creditors often use the current ratio, (which divides current assets by current liabilities), or the quick ratio (which divides current assets minus inventories by current liabilities) to discern whether a company has the ability to pay off its current liabilities.

RELATED TERMS:
- *Accounts Payable—AP*
- *Current Ratio*
- *Working Capital*
- *Current Assets*
- *Quick Ratio*

CURRENT RATIO

What Does *Current Ratio* Mean?

Also known as liquidity ratio, cash asset ratio, and cash ratio; a liquidity ratio that measures a company's ability to pay short-term obligations. It is calculated as follows:

$$\text{Current Ratio} = \frac{\text{Current Assets}}{\text{Current Liabilities}}$$

Investopedia explains *Current Ratio*

The current ratio is used primarily to ascertain a company's ability to pay back its short-term liabilities (debt and payables) with its short-term assets (cash, inventory, receivables). The higher the current ratio, the better the company's ability to pay its obligations. A ratio under 1 suggests that the company would be unable to pay off its obligations if they came due at that point. Although this may indicate that the company is not in good financial health, it does not necessarily mean that it will go bankrupt—there are many ways to access financing—but it is definitely not a good sign. The current ratio can give a sense of the efficiency of a company's operating cycle or its ability to turn its product into cash. Companies that have trouble collecting their receivables or have long inventory turnover can run into liquidity problems. Since businesses differ by industry, it is best to use this ratio to compare companies within the same industry. This ratio is similar to the acid-test ratio except that the acid-test ratio does not consider inventory and prepaids as liquid assets. The components of the current ratio (current assets and current liabilities) can be used to derive working capital (difference between current assets and current liabilities). Working capital frequently is used to calculate the working capital ratio, which is working capital as a ratio of sales.

RELATED TERMS:

- *Current Assets*
- *Inventory Turnover*
- *Receivables Turnover Ratio*
- *Current Liabilities*
- *Liquidity Ratios*

CURRENT YIELD

What Does *Current Yield* Mean?

Annual income (interest or dividends) divided by the current price of a security. This measure considers the current price of a bond instead of its face value and reflects the return an investor would expect if he or she purchased the bond and held it for one year; it is not an accurate measure of the actual return that an investor will receive in all cases because bond and stock prices change constantly as a result of market factors. Also referred to as bond yield or, in the case of stocks, dividend yield.

$$\text{Current Yield} = \frac{\text{Annual Cash Inflows}}{\text{Market Price}}$$

 Investopedia explains *Current Yield*
As an example, if a bond is priced at $95.75 and has an annual coupon of $5.10, the current yield of the bond will be 5.33%. If the bond is a 10-year bond with 9 years remaining until maturity and you were planning to hold it for only 1 year, you would receive the $5.10, but your actual return would depend on the bond's price when you sold it. If, during this period, interest rates rose and the price of the bond fell to $87.34, your actual return for your holding period would be –3.5% (–$3.31/$95.75) because although you gained $5.10 in dividends, your capital loss was $8.41.

RELATED TERMS:
- Bond
- Dividend
- Yield to Maturity—YTM
- Coupon
- Yield

CUSIP NUMBER

 What Does *CUSIP Number* **Mean?**
An identification number assigned to all stocks and registered bonds. The Committee on Uniform Securities Identification Procedures (CUSIP) oversees the entire CUSIP system.

 Investopedia explains *CUSIP Number*
This system is used in the United States and Canada. Foreign securities have a similar number called the CINS number.

RELATED TERMS:
- Common Stock
- New York Stock Exchange—NYSE
- Stock Market
- Marketable Security
- Stock

copyright JackGuinan

"They passed me up for the promotion down at the bank; they said I lacked interest."

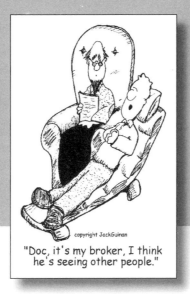

"Doc, it's my broker, I think he's seeing other people."

copyright JackGuinan

DEAD CAT BOUNCE

What Does *Dead Cat Bounce* Mean?
A temporary recovery that occurs during a prolonged decline (bear market); after the bounce, the market continues to fall.

Investopedia explains *Dead Cat Bounce*
Remember the following saying: "Even a dead cat will bounce if dropped from high enough!"

RELATED TERMS:
- *Bear Market*
- *Fundamental Analysis*
- *Trend Analysis*
- *Bull Market*
- *Quantitative Analysis*

DEBENTURE

What Does *Debenture* Mean?
A debt instrument that is not secured by a physical asset or collateral. Debentures are backed only by the general creditworthiness and reputation of the issuer. Both corporations and governments frequently issue this type of bond to secure capital. Like other types of bonds, debentures are documented in an indenture.

Investopedia explains *Debenture*
Debentures have no collateral. Bond buyers generally purchase debentures when they believe that the bond issuer is unlikely to default on the repayment. An example of a government debenture would be any government-issued Treasury bond (T-bond) or Treasury bill (T-bill); these generally are considered risk-free because governments, at worst, can print more money or raise taxes to pay these types of debts.

RELATED TERMS:
- Bond
- Corporate Bond
- Liability
- Convertible Bond
- Debt

DEBT

 What Does *Debt* Mean?
An amount of money borrowed by one party from another. Many corporations and individuals use debt as a method for making large purchases that they otherwise could not afford at the time of purchase. A debt arrangement gives the borrowing party permission to borrow money under the condition that it is to be paid back at a later date, usually with interest.

 Investopedia explains *Debt*
Bonds, loans, and commercial paper are examples of debt. For example, a company may look to borrow $1 million so that it can buy a certain piece of equipment. In this case, the debt of $1 million will have to be paid back (with interest owing) to the creditor at a later date.

RELATED TERMS:
- Credit Rating
- Debt Financing
- Liability
- Debenture
- Interest Rate

DEBT FINANCING

 What Does *Debt Financing* Mean?
When a firm raises money for working capital or capital expenditures by selling bonds, bills, or notes to individual and/or

institutional investors. As a result of lending the money, the individuals or institutions become creditors and fully expect to be repaid on the principal and interest.

 Investopedia explains Debt Financing
Besides debt financing, the other way to raise capital is to issue shares of stock in a public offering. This is called equity financing.

RELATED TERMS:
- Bond
- Commercial Paper
- Deleverage
- Capital Structure
- Credit Spread

DEBT RATIO

What Does Debt Ratio Mean?
A ratio indicating the proportion of debt a company has relative to its assets; it gives a general idea of the leverage of the company along with the potential risks the company faces in terms of its debt load.

$$\text{Debt Ratio} = \frac{\text{Total Debt}}{\text{Total Assets}}$$

 Investopedia explains Debt Ratio
A debt ratio greater than 1 indicates that a company has more debt than assets; a debt ratio less than 1 indicates that a company has more assets than debt. Used in conjunction with other measures of financial health, the debt ratio helps investors determine a company's level of risk.

RELATED TERMS:
- Acid-Test Ratio
- Debt/Equity Ratio
- Leverage Ratio
- Capital Structure
- Leverage

DEBT/EQUITY RATIO

What Does Debt/Equity Ratio Mean?
A measure of a company's financial leverage calculated by dividing its total liabilities by its stockholders' equity; it indicates what proportion of equity and debt the company is using to finance its assets.

$$= \frac{\text{Total Liabilities}}{\text{Shareholders' Equity}}$$

Note: Sometimes only interest-bearing, long-term debt is used instead of total liabilities in the calculation.

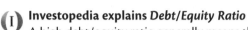 **Investopedia explains *Debt/Equity Ratio***
A high debt/equity ratio generally means that a company has been aggressive in financing its growth with debt. This can result in volatile earnings as a result of the additional interest expense. If a lot of debt is used to finance increased operations (high debt to equity), the company could generate more earnings than it would have without outside financing. If this increases earnings by a greater amount than the debt cost (interest), the shareholders benefit as more earnings are being spread among the same amount of shareholders. However, when the cost of the debt financing outweighs the return that the company generates on the debt, this could spell trouble for the company, leading to possible bankruptcy, which would leave shareholders with nothing. The debt/equity ratio also depends on the industry in which the company operates. For example, capital-intensive industries such as automobiles tend to have a debt/equity ratio above 2, whereas personal computer companies have a debt/equity ratio under 0.5.

RELATED TERMS:
- Acid-Test Ratio
- Leverage
- Shareholders' Equity
- Debt-to-Capital Ratio
- Long-Term Debt

DEBT-TO-CAPITAL RATIO

 What Does *Debt-to-Capital Ratio* Mean?
A measure of a company's financial leverage calculated by dividing the company's total capital by its debt. Debt includes all short-term and long-term obligations. Total capital includes the company's debt and shareholders' equity, which includes common stock, preferred stock, minority interest, and net debt. It is calculated as follows:

$$\text{Debt-to-Capital Ratio} = \frac{\text{Debt}}{\text{Shareholders' Equity} + \text{Debt}}$$

 **Investopedia explains *Debt-to-Capital Ratio***
Companies finance their operations through either debt or equity. The debt-to-capital ratio reveals a company's financial structure, the way it is financing its operations, and its overall financial strength.

The higher the debt-to-capital ratio, the more debt the company has compared to its equity. This tells investors whether a company is more prone to using debt financing or equity financing. A company with high debt-to-capital ratios compared with its industry peers shows weak financial strength because the cost of those debts may weigh on the company and increase its risk of default. Because this is a non-GAAP measure, in practice, there are many variations of this ratio. Therefore, it is important to pay close attention when reading what is or is not included in the ratio on a company's financial statements.

RELATED TERMS:
- Acid-Test Ratio
- Debt/Equity Ratio
- Long-Term Debt
- Capital Structure
- Leverage

DEFINED-BENEFIT PLAN

What Does *Defined-Benefit Plan* **Mean?**
An employer-sponsored retirement plan in which employee benefits are sorted out on the basis of a formula, using factors such as salary history and duration of employment. Investment risk and portfolio management are entirely under the control of the company. There are also restrictions on when and how an employee can withdraw funds without incurring penalties. Also known as a qualified benefit plan or nonqualified benefit plan.

Investopedia explains *Defined-Benefit Plan*
This type of fund is different from many pension funds in which payouts are somewhat dependent on the return of the invested funds. Therefore, employers sometimes need to dip into the company's earnings when the fund's investment returns result in a funding shortfall. The payouts made to retiring employees participating in defined-benefit plans are determined by factors such as age and length of employment. A tax-qualified benefit plan has the same characteristics as a defined-benefit plan but can provide the beneficiary of the plan with added tax incentives, which are not afforded under nonqualified plans.

RELATED TERMS:
- *Defined-Contribution Plan*
- *Mutual Fund*
- *Tax Deferred*
- *Inflation*
- *Net Worth*

DEFINED-CONTRIBUTION PLAN

What Does *Defined-Contribution Plan* Mean?
A retirement plan in which a certain amount or percentage of money is set aside each year by a company for the benefit of the employee. There are restrictions on when and how the employee can withdraw these funds without penalties.

Investopedia explains *Defined-Contribution Plan*
There is no way to know how much the plan ultimately will give the employee upon retirement. The amount contributed is fixed, but the benefit is not.

RELATED TERMS:
- *401(k) Plan*
- *Individual Retirement Account—IRA*
- *Qualified Retirement Plan*
- *Defined-Benefit Plan*
- *Roth IRA*

DEFLATION

What Does *Deflation* Mean?
A general decline in prices often caused by a reduction in the money supply or credit; it also may result from a decrease in government, personal, or investment spending. The opposite of inflation, deflation has the side effect of increased unemployment since there is a lower level of demand in the economy, which can lead to an economic depression.

Investopedia explains *Deflation*
Declining prices, if they persist, generally create a vicious negative spiral of falling profits, closing factories, shrinking employment and incomes, and increasing defaults on loans by companies and individuals. To counter deflation, the Federal Reserve (the Fed) can use monetary policy to increase the money supply and deliberately induce higher prices and inflation. Rising prices provide an essential

lubricant for a sustained recovery because businesses increase profits and take some of the depressive pressures off wages and debtors of every kind.

RELATED TERMS:
- Consumer Price Index—CPI
- Inflation
- Stagflation
- Hyperinflation
- Monetary Policy

DELEVERAGE

What Does *Deleverage* Mean?
A company's attempt to decrease its financial leverage. The best way for a company to delever is to pay off any existing debt on its balance sheet immediately. If it is unable to do this, the company will be in significant default risk.

Investopedia explains *Deleverage*
Companies often take on excessive amounts of debt to finance growth. However, leverage substantially increases a firm's risk because if the leverage does not foster growth as planned, the debt risk can become too much for the company to bear. When this happens, all the firm can do is delever by paying off debt. Any sign of deleverage shown by a company is a red flag to investors who require growth in the companies in which they invest.

RELATED TERMS:
- Capital
- Leverage Ratio
- Unlevered Beta
- Debt/Equity Ratio
- Leveraged Buyout—LBO

DELTA

What Does *Delta* Mean?
The ratio that compares the change in the price of an underlying asset to the corresponding change in the price of a derivative; sometimes referred to as the hedge ratio.

Investopedia explains *Delta*
As an example, with respect to call options, a delta of 0.7 means that for every $1 increase in the underlying stock, the call option

will increase by $0.70. Put option deltas, in contrast, will be negative, because as the underlying security increases, the value of the option decreases. Thus, a put option with a delta of −0.7 will decrease by $0.70 for every $1 increase in the stock price. As an in-the-money call option nears expiration, it will approach a delta of 1.00, and as an in-the-money put option nears expiration, it will approach a delta of −1.00.

RELATED TERMS:
- Call Option
- Derivative
- Put Option
- Delta Hedging
- Gamma

DELTA HEDGING

What Does *Delta Hedging* Mean?

An options strategy that aims to reduce (hedge) the risk associated with price movements in the underlying asset by offsetting long and short positions. For example, a long call position may be delta hedged by shorting the underlying stock. This strategy is based on the change in premium (the price of the option) caused by a change in the price of the underlying security. The change in premium for each basis-point change in the price of the underlying is the delta, and the relationship between the two movements is the hedge ratio.

Investopedia explains *Delta Hedging*

As an example, the price of a call option with a hedge ratio of 40 will rise 40% (of the stock-price move) if the price of the underlying stock increases. Typically, options with high hedge ratios are usually more profitable to buy than to write because the greater the percentage movement relative to the price of the underlying stock and the corresponding little time-value erosion, the greater the leverage. The opposite is true for options with a low hedge ratio.

RELATED TERMS:
- Call Option
- Delta
- Hedge
- Common Stock
- Gamma

DEMAND

What Does *Demand* Mean?

An economic principle that describes a consumer's desire and willingness to pay a price for a specific good or service; all things being equal, the price of a good or service increases as its demand increases and vice versa.

Investopedia explains *Demand*

One can think of demand as a person's willingness to go out and buy a certain product. For example, market demand is the total of what everybody in the market wants and is willing to pay for. Businesses often spend a considerable amount of money to determine the amount of demand that the public has for its products and services. Underestimating demand can result in money left on the table, whereas overestimating can lead to large inventories and losses.

RELATED TERMS:
- *Inelastic*
- *Law of Supply*
- *Market Value*
- *Law of Demand*
- *Market Economy*

DEPRECIATION

What Does *Depreciation* Mean?

(1) In accounting, an expense recorded to allocate a tangible asset's cost over its useful life. Because depreciation is a noncash expense, it increases free cash flow while decreasing reported earnings. (2) A decrease in the value of a particular currency relative to other currencies.

Investopedia explains *Depreciation*

(1) Depreciation is used in accounting to try to match the expense of an asset to the asset's income. For example, if a company buys a piece of equipment for $1 million and expects it to have a useful life of 10 years, it will be depreciated over 10 years. Every accounting year, the company will expense $100,000 (assuming straight-line depreciation, $1 million/10), which will be matched with the money that the equipment helps to make each year. (2) Examples of currency depreciation would be the Russian ruble crisis in 1998, which saw the ruble lose 25% of its value in a single day.

RELATED TERMS:
- *Accrual Accounting*
- *Asset*
- *Tangible Asset*
- *Amortization*
- *Book Value*

DERIVATIVE

What Does *Derivative* Mean?

In finance, a security whose price is dependent on or derived from one or more underlying assets. The derivative itself is merely a contract between two or more parties, with a value determined by fluctuations in the underlying asset, which could be stocks, bonds, commodities, currencies, interest rates, and market indexes. Most derivatives are characterized by high leverage.

Investopedia explains *Derivative*

Futures contracts, forward contracts, options, and swaps are the most common types of derivatives. Since derivatives are contracts, almost anything can be used as a derivative's underlying asset. There are even derivatives based on weather data, such as the amount of rain or the number of sunny days in a particular region. Derivatives generally are used to hedge risk but also can be used for speculative purposes. For example, a European investor purchasing shares of an American company on a foreign exchange (using American dollars to do so) would be exposed to exchange-rate risk while holding that stock. To hedge that risk, the investor could purchase currency futures to lock in a specified exchange rate for the future stock sale and conversion back into the foreign currency.

RELATED TERMS:
- *Credit Derivative*
- *Hedge*
- *Stock Option*
- *Forward Contract*
- *Option*

DILUTED EARNINGS PER SHARE (DILUTED EPS)

What Does *Diluted Earnings per Share (Diluted EPS)* Mean?

A performance metric used to gauge the quality of a company's earnings per share (EPS) if all convertible securities were exercised. Convertible securities refer to all outstanding convertible preferred shares, convertible debentures, stock options (primarily employee-based), and warrants. Unless the company has no additional potential shares outstanding (a relatively rare circumstance), the diluted EPS will always be lower than the simple EPS.

 Investopedia explains *Diluted Earnings per Share (Diluted EPS)*
Earnings per share (EPS) is calculated by dividing a company's earnings by the number of shares outstanding. Warrants, stock options, convertible preferred shares, and the like, all serve to increase the number of shares outstanding. For a shareholder, this is a bad thing because the larger the denominator in the equation (shares outstanding) is, the more the EPS will be reduced. This is a conservative metric because it indicates somewhat of a worst-case scenario. People holding options, warrants, convertible preferred shares, and so on, are unlikely to convert their shares all at once. At the same time, if things go well, there is a good chance that many option and convertible shareholders will convert their holdings into common stock. A big difference between a company's EPS and diluted EPS can indicate high potential dilution for the company's shares, an attribute almost unanimously disfavored by analysts and investors alike.

RELATED TERMS:
- *Dilution*
- *Earnings per Share—EPS*
- *Outstanding Shares*
- *Earnings*
- *Fully Diluted Shares*

DILUTION

 What Does *Dilution* **mean?**
A reduction in earnings per share of common stock that occurs as a result of an issuance of additional shares or through the conversion of convertible securities into additional common shares.

 Investopedia explains *Dilution*
Adding to the number of shares outstanding reduces the value of the holdings of existing shareholders.

RELATED TERMS:
- *Convertible Bond*
- *Diluted Earnings per Share—Diluted EPS*
- *Outstanding Shares*
- *Convertible Preferred Stock*
- *Shareholders' Equity*

DISCOUNT BROKER

What Does *Discount Broker* Mean?

A brokerage company that carries out buy and sell orders at a reduced commission compared with a full-service broker but provides no investment advice.

Investopedia explains *Discount Broker*

It used to be that only the wealthy could afford a broker and invest in the stock market. However, in the mid-1970s, the brokerage industry was deregulated and brokerage commissions became extremely cheap. The arrival of the Internet created an explosion of online discount brokers. However, it is important to remember that discount brokers do not provide personalized investment advice. Because of discount brokers, nearly anybody can afford to invest in the market. For those who wish to do their own research or do not want to invest a lot of money, a discount broker is an excellent way to invest.

Related Terms:
- Broker-Dealer
- Market Maker
- National Association of Securities Dealers—NASD
- Securities and Exchange Commission—SEC
- Stock Market

DISCOUNT RATE

What Does *Discount Rate* Mean?

(1) The interest rate that an eligible depository institution is charged to borrow short-term funds directly from a Federal Reserve Bank.
(2) The interest rate used in determining the present value of future cash flows.

Investopedia explains *Discount Rate*

(1) This type of borrowing from the Fed is fairly limited. Institutions often seek other means of meeting short-term liquidity needs. The Federal funds discount rate is one of two interest rates the Fed sets, the other being the overnight lending rate, or the Fed funds rate.
(2) Let's say you expect $1,000 in one year's time. To determine the present value of this $1,000 (what it is worth to you today), you would need to discount it by a particular rate of interest (often the risk-free rate but not always). Assuming a discount rate of 10%, the

$1,000 in a year's time would be the equivalent of $909.09 to you today (1,000/[1.00 + 0.10]).

RELATED TERMS:
- *Federal Funds Rate*
- *Federal Open Market Committee*
- *Monetary Policy*

- *Interest Rate*
- *Prime Rate*

DISCOUNTED CASH FLOW (DCF)

What Does *Discounted Cash Flow (DCF)* Mean?
A valuation method used to estimate the attractiveness of an investment opportunity. DCF analysis uses future free cash flow projections and discounts them (most often by using the weighted average cost of capital method) to arrive at a present value, which is used to evaluate the investment's potential. If the value arrived at through DCF analysis is higher than the current cost of the investment, the opportunity may be a good one. It is calculated as follows:

$$DCF = \frac{CF_1}{(1+r)^1} + \frac{CF_2}{(1+r)^2} + \cdots + \frac{CF_n}{(1+r)^n}$$

$CF = $ Cash Flow

$r = $ discount rate (WACC)

Investopedia explains *Discounted Cash Flow (DCF)*
There are many variations in what can be used for cash flows and the discount rate in a DCF analysis. Despite the complexity of the calculations involved, the purpose of DCF analysis is simply to estimate the money one would receive from an investment, adjusting for the time value of money. DCF models are valuable tools, but they have shortcomings. DCF is merely a mechanical valuation tool, which makes it subject to the axiom "garbage in, garbage out." Small changes in inputs can result in large changes in the value of a company. Instead of trying to project the cash flows to infinity, a terminal value approach often is used. A simple annuity is used to estimate the terminal value past 10 years, for example. This is done because it is harder to come to a realistic estimate of the cash flows as time goes on.

RELATED TERMS:
- *Cash Flow*
- *Free Cash Flow—FCF*
- *Net Present Value—NPV*

- *Cash Flow Statement*
- *Internal Rate of Return—IRR*

DIVERSIFICATION

What Does *Diversification* Mean?

A risk management investment strategy in which a wide variety of investments are mixed within a portfolio; the rationale is that a portfolio of different investments will, on average, yield higher returns and pose a lower risk than any individual investment within the portfolio. Diversification strives to smooth out unsystematic risk in a portfolio so that the positive performance of some investments will neutralize the negative performance of others. Therefore, the benefits of diversification will hold only if the securities in the portfolio are not correlated.

Investopedia explains *Diversification*

Studies and mathematical models have shown that maintaining a well-diversified portfolio of 25 to 30 stocks will yield the most cost-effective level of risk reduction. Investing in more securities will yield further diversification benefits, but to a drastically smaller degree. Further diversification benefits can be gained by investing in foreign securities because they tend to be less closely correlated with domestic investments. For example, an economic downturn in the U.S. economy may not affect Japan's economy; therefore, Japanese investments could do well when domestic investments perform poorly. The average person may not have enough money to diversify properly, but buying shares in a mutual fund can help provide investors with an inexpensive way to diversify. This may explain why mutual fund investing is so popular.

RELATED TERMS:
- Asset Allocation
- Modern Portfolio Theory—MPT
- Systematic Risk
- Correlation
- Mutual Fund

DIVIDEND

What Does *Dividend* Mean?

(1) A distribution of a portion of a company's earnings paid out to shareholders. The dividend most often is quoted in terms of the dollar amount each share receives (dividends per share). It also can be quoted in terms of a percentage of the current market price, referred

to as dividend yield. Also referred to as dividend per share (DPS). (2) Mandatory distributions of income and realized capital gains made to mutual fund investors.

 Investopedia explains *Dividend*
(1) Dividends may be in the form of cash, stock, or property. Most secure and stable companies offer dividends to their stockholders. Their share prices may not move much, but the dividend is used in an attempt to make up for this. High-growth companies rarely offer dividends because they reinvest their profits back into the company to help sustain higher-than-average growth. (2) Mutual funds pay out interest and dividend income received from their portfolio holdings as dividends to fund shareholders.

RELATED TERMS:
- *Dividend Discount Model—DDM*
- *Ex-Date*
- *Record Date*
- *Dividend Yield*
- *Ex-Dividend*

DIVIDEND DISCOUNT MODEL (DDM)

 What Does *Dividend Discount Model (DDM)* Mean?
A procedure for valuing the price of a stock by using predicted dividends and discounting them back to present value; if the value obtained from the DDM is higher than what the shares are currently trading at, the stock is undervalued.

$$\text{Value of Stock} = \frac{\text{Dividend per Share}}{\text{Discount Rate} - \text{Dividend Growth Rate}}$$

 Investopedia explains *Dividend Discount Model (DDM)*
This procedure has many variations, but it will not work for companies that do not pay out dividends.

RELATED TERMS:
- *Discount Rate*
- *Dividend Payout Ratio*
- *Gordon Growth Model*
- *Dividend*
- *Dividend Yield*

DIVIDEND PAYOUT RATIO

What Does *Dividend Payout Ratio* Mean?
The percentage of earnings paid to shareholders in dividends. It is calculated as follows:

Investopedia explains *Dividend Payout Ratio*
The payout ratio provides an idea of how well earnings support the dividend pay-

$$= \frac{\text{Yearly Dividend per Share}}{\text{Earnings per Share}}$$

or equivalently:

$$= \frac{\text{Dividends}}{\text{Net Income}}$$

ments. More mature companies tend to have a higher payout ratio. In the United Kingdom there is a similar ratio that is known as dividend cover. It is calculated as earnings per share divided by dividends per share.

RELATED TERMS:
- Dividend
- Ex-Date
- Record Date
- Earnings per Share—EPS
- Ex-Dividend

DIVIDEND REINVESTMENT PLAN (DRIP)

What Does *Dividend Reinvestment Plan (DRIP)* Mean?
A plan offered by a corporation that allows investors to reinvest their cash dividends back into the company by purchasing additional shares or fractional shares on the dividend payment date.

Investopedia explains *Dividend Reinvestment Plan (DRIP)*
A DRIP is an excellent way to increase the value of an investment. Most DRIPs allow an investor to buy shares commission-free and at a significant discount to the current share price. Most DRIPS do not allow reinvestments much lower than $10. This term sometimes is abbreviated as DRP.

RELATED TERMS:
- Common Stock
- Dividend
- Dollar-Cost Averaging—DCA
- Compounding
- Dividend Yield

DIVIDEND YIELD

What Does *Dividend Yield* Mean?

A financial ratio that shows how much a company pays out in dividends each year relative to its share price. In the absence of any capital gains, the dividend yield is the return on investment for a stock. Dividend yield is calculated as follows:

$$= \frac{\text{Annual Dividends per Share}}{\text{Price per Share}}$$

Investopedia explains *Dividend Yield*

Dividend yield is a way to measure how much cash flow an investor is getting for each dollar invested in an equity position, in other words, how much "bang for the buck" the investor is getting from dividends. Investors who require a minimum stream of cash flow from their investment portfolios can secure this cash flow by investing in stocks paying relatively high, stable dividend yields. For example, if two companies both pay annual dividends of $1 per share, but ABC Company's stock is trading at $20 and XYZ Company's stock is trading at $40, ABC has a dividend yield of 5% and XYZ is yielding only 2.5%. Thus, assuming all other factors are equivalent, an investor looking to supplement his or her income probably would prefer ABC's stock over that of XYZ.

RELATED TERMS:

- Current Yield
- Return on Assets—ROA
- Yield
- Dividend
- Return on Investments—ROI

DOLLAR-COST AVERAGING (DCA)

What Does *Dollar-Cost Averaging (DCA)* Mean?

The technique of buying a fixed dollar amount of a particular investment on a regular schedule regardless of the share price. By using DCA, an investor is continually buying shares, some when the stock price is down and some when the stock price is up, with the goal of averaging out the price of all shares purchased. Also referred to as a constant dollar plan.

Investopedia explains *Dollar-Cost Averaging (DCA)*

Eventually, the average cost per share of the security will become smaller and smaller. Dollar-cost averaging lessens the risk of investing a large amount in a single investment at the wrong time. For example, consider a $100 purchase of XYZ each month for three months. In January, XYZ is worth $33, and so the investor buys three shares. In February, XYZ is worth $25, and so the investor buys four additional shares. Finally, in March, XYZ is worth $20, and so the investor buys five shares. In total, the investor winds up purchasing 12 shares for an average price of approximately $25 each. In the United Kingdom, this is called pound-cost averaging.

RELATED TERMS:
- Common Stock
- Dividend Reinvestment Plan—DRIP
- Mutual Fund
- Compounding
- Net Asset Value

DOW JONES INDUSTRIAL AVERAGE (DJIA)

What Does *Dow Jones Industrial Average* Mean?
The Dow Jones Industrial Average is a price-weighted average of 30 stocks traded on the New York Stock Exchange and the Nasdaq. The DJIA was invented by Charles Dow in 1896.

Investopedia explains *Dow Jones Industrial Average*
Often referred to as "the Dow," the DJIA is the oldest and most watched index in the world. The DJIA includes companies such as General Electric, Disney, Exxon, and Microsoft. When the TV networks say that "the market is up today," they generally are referring to the Dow.

RELATED TERMS:
- Benchmark
- New York Stock Exchange—NYSE
- Standard & Poor's 500 Index—S&P 500
- Stock Market
- Nasdaq

DOWNTREND

What Does *Downtrend* Mean?
Describes the price movement of a financial asset when the overall direction is downward. A formal downtrend occurs when each successive peak and trough is lower than the ones found earlier in the trend.

Copyright © 2006 Investopedia.com

Notice how each successive peak and trough is lower than the previous one. For example, the low at point 3 is lower than the low at point 1. The downtrend will be deemed broken once the price closes above the high at point 4. A downtrend is the opposite of an uptrend.

Investopedia explains *Downtrend*
Many traders seek to avoid downtrends because they can affect the value of any investment drastically. A downtrend can last for minutes, days, weeks, months, or even years, and so identifying a downtrend early is very important. Once a downtrend has been established (series of lower peaks), a trader should be very cautious about entering into new long positions.

RELATED TERMS:
- *Average Directional Index—ADX*
- *Business Cycle*
- *Uptrend*
- *Bear Market*
- *Trend Analysis*

DUE DILIGENCE (DD)

What Does *Due Diligence (DD)* **Mean?**
(1) An investigation or audit of a potential investment. Due diligence serves to confirm all material facts in regard to a sale.
(2) Generally, due diligence refers to the care a reasonable person should take to obtain all the material facts before entering into an agreement or transaction with another party.

Investopedia explains *Due Diligence (DD)*
(1) Offers to purchase an asset are usually dependent on the results of due diligence analysis. This includes reviewing all financial records plus anything else deemed material to the sale. Sellers also can perform a due diligence analysis on the buyer. Items that may be considered include the buyer's ability to purchase as well as other items that would affect the purchased entity or the seller after the sale has been completed. (2) Due diligence is a way of preventing surprises that could unnecessarily harm either party involved in a transaction.

RELATED TERMS:
- *10-K*
- *Balance Sheet*
- *Generally Accepted Accounting Principles—GAAP*
- *Technical Analysis*
- *Accrual Accounting*

DURATION

What Does *Duration* Mean?

A measure of the price sensitivity (the value of principal) of a fixed-income investment to a change in interest rates; duration is expressed in number of years. Rising interest rates mean falling bond prices, whereas declining interest rates mean rising bond prices. The bigger the duration number, the greater the interest rate risk or reward for bond prices.

Investopedia explains *Duration*

The duration number is a complicated calculation involving present value, yield, coupon, final maturity, and call features. Fortunately for investors, this indicator is a standard data point provided in the presentation of comprehensive bond and bond mutual fund information. It is a common misconception among nonprofessional investors that bonds and bond funds are risk-free. They are not. Investors need to be aware of two main risks that can affect a bond's investment value: (1) credit risk (default) and (2) interest rate risk (rate fluctuations). The duration indicator addresses interest rate risk. Short-term, intermediate-term, and long-term bond funds all have different durations or maturities. For example, Vanguard's short-, intermediate,- and long-term bond index funds have durations of around 3 years, 6 years, and 11 years, respectively.

RELATED TERMS:

- *Accrual Accounting*
- *Basis Point—BPS*
- *Zero-Coupon Bond*
- *Bond*
- *Modified Duration*

"I don't think
he's the right Buffett."

EARNINGS

What Does *Earnings* Mean?

The amount of profit a company produces during a specific period; usually presented on a quarterly (three calendar months) or annual basis. Earnings typically refers to after-tax net income. Ultimately, a business's earnings are the main determinant of its share price, because earnings and the circumstances relating to them can indicate whether the business will be profitable and successful in the long run.

Investopedia explains *Earnings*

Earnings are perhaps the single most studied number in a company's financial statements because earnings reveal a company's profitability. A business's quarterly and annual earnings typically are compared with the company's and analysts' estimates. In most cases, when earnings do not meet either of those estimates, the company's stock price will drop. In contrast, when they beat estimates, the share price can surge.

RELATED TERMS:
- *Balance Sheet*
- *Earnings before Interest, Taxes, Depreciation, and Amortization—EBITDA*
- *Earnings per Share—EPS*
- *Net Income—NI*
- *Pro Forma*

EARNINGS BEFORE INTEREST, TAXES, DEPRECIATION, AND AMORTIZATION (EBITDA)

What Does *Earnings before Interest, Taxes, Depreciation, and Amortization (EBITDA)* Mean?

A measurement of a company's financial performance. It is calculated as follows:

EBITDA = Revenue – Expenses (excluding tax, interest, depreciation, and amortization)

EBITDA can be used to analyze and compare profitability between companies and industries because it eliminates the effects of financing and accounting decisions. However, this is a non-GAAP measure that allows for greater discretion in terms of what is (and is not) included in the calculation. This also means that companies often change the items included in their EBITDA calculation from one reporting period to the next.

Investopedia explains *Earnings before Interest, Taxes, Depreciation, and Amortization (EBITDA)*

EBITDA came on the scene during the leveraged buyout boom of the 1980s, when it was used to indicate the ability of a company to service debt. As time passed, it became popular in industries with expensive assets that had to be written down over long periods. EBITDA now is quoted commonly by many companies, especially in the tech sector, even when it is not warranted. A common misconception is that EBITDA represents cash earnings. EBITDA is a good metric to evaluate profitability but not cash flow. EBITDA also leaves out the cash required to fund working capital and the replacement of old equipment, which can be significant. Consequently, EBITDA often is used as an accounting gimmick to dress up a company's earnings. Investors should not look at EBITDA alone but also look at other performance measures to help identify whether a company is hiding something in its EBITDA results.

Related Terms:
- Amortization
- Depreciation
- Generally Accepted Accounting Principles—GAAP
- Net Income
- Operating Income

EARNINGS PER SHARE (EPS)

What Does *Earnings per Share (EPS)* Mean?

The portion of a company's profit allocated to each outstanding share of common stock. EPS serves as an indicator of a company's profitability. It is calculated as follows:

$$= \frac{\text{Net Income} - \text{Dividends on Preferred Stock}}{\text{Average Outstanding Shares}}$$

In the EPS calculation, it is more accurate to use a weighted average number of shares outstanding over the reporting term, because the number of shares outstanding can change over time. However, data sources sometimes simplify the calculation by using the number of shares outstanding at the end of the period. Diluted EPS expands on basic EPS by including the shares of convertibles or warrants outstanding in the outstanding shares number.

Investopedia explains *Earnings per Share (EPS)*

Earnings per share generally is considered the single most important variable in determining a share's price. It is also a major component of the price-to-earnings valuation ratio. For example, assume that a company has a net income of $25 million. If the company pays out $1 million in preferred dividends and has 10 million shares for half of the year and 15 million shares for the other half, the EPS will be $1.92 (24/12.5). First, the $1 million is deducted from the net income to get $24 million, and then a weighted average is taken to find the number of shares outstanding (0.5 × 10M + 0.5 × 15M = 12.5M). An important component of EPS that often is ignored is the capital that is required to generate the earnings (net income) in the calculation. Two companies could generate the same EPS, but the one that could do so with less equity (investment) would be more efficient at using its capital to generate income and, all other things equal, would be a "better" company. Investors also need to be aware of earnings manipulation that may distort EPS. Therefore, do not rely on any one financial measure; use statement analysis and other measures as well.

RELATED TERMS:
- Diluted Earnings per Share—Diluted EPS
- Outstanding Shares
- Price-Earnings Ratio—P/E Ratio
- Earnings
- Weighted Average

ECONOMIC PROFIT (OR LOSS)

What Does *Economic Profit (or Loss)* Mean?
The difference between the revenue received from the sale of an output and the opportunity cost of the inputs used. Sometimes referred to as economic value added (EVA).

Investopedia explains *Economic Profit (or Loss)*
This should not be confused with accounting profit, which is what most people mean when they refer to profit. In calculating economic profit, opportunity costs are deducted from revenues earned. Opportunity costs are the returns not realized by using the chosen inputs. As a result, there can be a significant accounting profit with little to no economic profit. For example, say you invest $100,000 to start a business and in that year earn $120,000 in profits. Your accounting profit would be $20,000. However, say that in the same year, instead of starting the business, you could have worked for someone else and earned $45,000. Therefore, you have an economic loss of $25,000 (120,000 − 100,000 − 45,000).

RELATED TERMS:
- Economic Value Added—EVA
- Opportunity Cost
- Revenue
- Economies of Scale
- Profit Margin

ECONOMIC VALUE ADDED (EVA)

What Does *Economic Value Added (EVA)* Mean?
A measure of a company's financial performance that is based on the residual wealth calculated by deducting cost of capital from its operating profit (adjusted for taxes on a cash basis). Also called economic profit. The formula for calculating EVA is as follows: EVA = Net Operating Profit after Taxes (NOPAT) − (Capital × Cost of Capital).

Investopedia explains *Economic Value Added (EVA)*
This measure was devised by Stern Stewart & Co. and is used as a way to ascertain the true economic profit of a company.

RELATED TERMS:
- Equity
- Net Operating Profit after Tax—NOPAT
- Return on Equity
- Market Value
- Return on Net Assets

ECONOMIES OF SCALE

What Does *Economies of Scale* **Mean?**

The increase in the efficiency of production as the number of goods being produced increases. Typically, a company that achieves economies of scale lowers the average cost per unit by increasing output, which spreads fixed costs over an increased number of goods produced. There are two types of economies of scale: (1) External economies—the cost per unit depends on the size of the industry, not that of the firm; and (2) Internal economies—the cost per unit depends on the size of the individual firm.

Investopedia explains *Economies of Scale*

Economies of scale give big companies access to a larger market by allowing them to operate with a greater geographic reach. For more traditional (small to medium) companies, however, size does have its limits. After a point, an increase in size (output) actually causes an increase in production costs. This is called diseconomies of scale.

RELATED TERMS:
- *Economic Profit*
- *Law of Demand*
- *Market Economy*
- *Economic Value Added—EVA*
- *Law of Supply*

EFFECTIVE ANNUAL INTEREST RATE

What Does *Effective Annual Interest Rate* **Mean?**

The annual rate of interest of an investment when compounding occurs more often than once a year. It is calculated as follows:

$$= \left(1 + \frac{i}{n}\right)^{n} - 1$$

i = stated annual interest rate

n = number of compounding periods

Investopedia explains *Effective Annual Interest Rate*

Consider a stated annual rate of 10%. Compounded yearly, this rate will turn $1,000 into $1,100. However, if compounding occurs monthly, $1,000 will grow to $1,104.70 by the end of the year, for an effective annual interest rate of 10.47%. Basically, the effective annual rate is the annual rate of interest that accounts for compounding.

RELATED TERMS:
- *Annual Percentage Yield*
- *Coupon*
- *Interest Rate*
- *Compounding*
- *Fixed-Income Security*

EFFICIENT FRONTIER

What Does *Efficient Frontier* Mean?

A line created from the risk-reward graph, composed of optimal portfolios that reflect various portfolio diversification strategies ranging from a most conservative all-cash portfolio to a most aggressive all-equity portfolio.

Investopedia explains *Efficient Frontier*

The optimal portfolios plotted along the curve have the highest expected return possible for the given amount of risk.

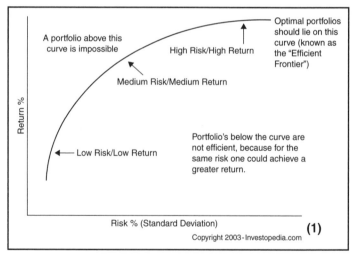

RELATED TERMS:
- *Asset Allocation*
- *Modern Portfolio Theory—MPT*
- *Risk-Return Trade-Off*
- *Diversification*
- *Risk*

EFFICIENCY RATIO

What Does *Efficiency Ratio* Mean?

A ratio used to calculate a bank's efficiency. Not all banks calculate the efficiency ratio the same way. The ratio can be calculated one of four ways: (1) noninterest expense divided by total revenue less interest expense, (2) noninterest expense divided by net interest income before provision for loan losses, (3) noninterest expense divided by revenue, (4) operating expenses divided by fee income plus tax equivalent net interest income. In all four methods, an increase means the company is losing a larger percentage of its income to expenses. If the efficiency ratio is getting lower, it is good for the bank and its shareholders. Also referred to as the overhead burden or overhead efficiency ratio.

Investopedia explains *Efficiency Ratio*

Regardless of which ratio calculation method is used, the efficiency ratio's purpose is to evaluate the overhead structure of a financial institution. Banking is no different from any mature industry: Companies that survive keep their costs down. The efficiency ratio measures how effectively a bank is operating and how profitable it is.

RELATED TERMS:
- Cash and Cash Equivalents
- Net Income—NI
- Operating Expense
- Expense Ratio
- Net Operating Income—NOI

EFFICIENT MARKET HYPOTHESIS (EMH)

What Does *Efficient Market Hypothesis (EMH)* Mean?

An investment theory that postulates that it is impossible to "beat the market" because stock market efficiency causes stock prices to incorporate and reflect all relevant information in all cases. According to the EMH, stocks always trade at their fair market value on stock exchanges, making it impossible for investors to purchase undervalued stocks or sell stocks for inflated prices. Consequently, it should be impossible to outperform the overall market through market timing, and the only way investors can obtain higher returns is by purchasing riskier investments.

Investopedia explains *Efficient Market Hypothesis (EMH)*
Although considered the cornerstone of modern financial theory, the EMH is highly controversial and often is disputed. Supporters argue that it is pointless to search for undervalued stocks or try to predict trends in the market through either fundamental or technical analysis. Detractors such as Warren Buffett consistently have beaten the market over long periods, which according to EMH is virtually impossible. EMH detractors point to major events, such as the 1987 stock market crash when the Dow Jones Industrial Average (DJIA) fell by over 20% in a single day, and the wild market swings of late 2008 as evidence that stock prices can deviate seriously from their fair values.

RELATED TERMS:
- *Arbitrage*
- *Fundamental Analysis*
- *Technical Analysis*
- *Behavioral Finance*
- *Systematic Risk*

ELECTRONIC COMMUNICATION NETWORK (ECN)

 What Does *Electronic Communication Network (ECN)* **Mean?**
An electronic trading system that attempts to eliminate the role of a third party in the execution of orders entered by an exchange market maker or an over-the-counter market maker and permits such orders to be executed entirely or partly.

 Investopedia explains *Electronic Communication Network (ECN)*
An ECN connects major brokerages and individual traders so that they can trade directly among themselves without having to go through a middle man.

RELATED TERMS:
- *Broker-Dealer*
- *Over the Counter—OTC*
- *Stock Market*
- *Market Maker*
- *Nasdaq*

ENTERPRISE VALUE (EV)

What Does *Enterprise Value (EV)* **Mean?**
A measure of a company's value that often is used as an alternative to straightforward market capitalization. EV is calculated as market

cap plus debt, minority interest, and preferred shares, minus total cash and cash equivalents.

 Investopedia explains *Enterprise Value (EV)*
One should think of enterprise value as the theoretical takeover price. In the event of a buyout, an acquirer would have to take on the company's debt but would pocket its cash. EV differs significantly from simple market capitalization in several ways, and many consider it a more accurate representation of a firm's value. The amount of a firm's debt, for example, would have to be paid by the buyer when taking over a company; thus EV provides a much more accurate takeover valuation because it includes debt in its value calculation.

RELATED TERMS:
- Book Value
- Fair Value
- Total Enterprise Value—TEV
- Cash and Cash Equivalents
- Market Value

EQUILIBRIUM

 What Does *Equilibrium* **Mean?**
The state in which market supply and market demand balance each other out, resulting in stable market prices. Generally, when there is too much supply for goods or services, the price goes down, which results in higher demand. The balancing effect of supply and demand results in a state of equilibrium.

 Investopedia explains *Equilibrium*
The equilibrium price occurs where the supply of goods matches the demand for goods. When a major index experiences a period of consolidation or sideways momentum, it can be said that the forces of supply and demand are relatively equal and that the market is in a state of equilibrium.

RELATED TERMS:
- Demand
- Market Economy
- Technical Analysis
- Efficient Market Hypothesis
- Quantitative Analysis

EQUITY

What Does *Equity* Mean?

(1) A stock or any other security representing an ownership interest. (2) On a company's balance sheet, the amount of the funds contributed by the owners (the stockholders) plus the retained earnings (or losses). Also referred to as shareholders' equity. (3) In the context of margin trading, the value of securities in a margin account minus what has been borrowed from the brokerage. (4) In the context of real estate, the difference between the current market value of a property and the amount the owner still owes on the mortgage. It is the amount that the owner would receive after selling the property and paying off the mortgage. (5) In terms of investment strategies, equity (stocks) is one of the principal asset classes. The other two are fixed-income (bonds) and cash/cash equivalents. These are used in asset allocation planning to structure a desired risk and return profile for an investor's portfolio.

Investopedia explains *Equity*

The meaning of equity depends very much on the context. In general, one can think of equity as ownership in any asset after all the debts associated with that asset are paid off. For example, a car or house with no outstanding debt is considered the owner's equity because he or she can sell the item readily for cash. Stocks are equity because they represent ownership in a company.

RELATED TERMS:
- Asset
- Common Stock
- Shareholders' Equity
- Balance Sheet
- Private Equity

EQUITY MULTIPLIER

What Does *Equity Multiplier* Mean?

A measure of financial leverage calculated as Total Assets/Total Stockholders' Equity. Like all debt management ratios, the equity multiplier is a way of examining how a company uses debt to finance its assets. Also known as the financial leverage ratio or leverage ratio.

Investopedia explains *Equity Multiplier*
In other words, this ratio shows a company's total assets per dollar of stockholders' equity. A higher equity multiplier indicates higher financial leverage, which means the company is relying more on debt to finance its assets.

RELATED TERMS:
- Asset
- Debt/Equity Ratio
- Shareholders' Equity
- Current Ratio
- Leverage

EQUITY RISK PREMIUM

 What Does *Equity Risk Premium* Mean?
The return provided by an individual stock or the overall stock market in excess of the risk-free rate. This excess return compensates investors for taking on the relatively higher risk of the equity market. The size of the risk premium will vary as the risk in a particular stock, or in the stock market as a whole, changes; high-risk investments are compensated with a higher premium. Also referred to as the equity premium.

 Investopedia explains *Equity Risk Premium*
The risk premium is the result of the risk-return trade-off, in which investors require a higher rate of return on riskier investments. The risk-free rate in the market often is quoted as the rate on longer-term U.S. government bonds, which are considered risk-free because of the unlikelihood that the government will default on its loans. Compare that with securities that offer no or little guarantees. Remember, companies regularly experience downturns and go out of business. If the return on a stock is 15% and the risk-free rate over the same period is 7%, the equity-risk premium is 8% for this stock over that period.

RELATED TERMS:
- Equity
- Premium
- Risk-Return Trade-Off
- Gordon Growth Model
- Risk

EURO LIBOR

What Does *Euro LIBOR* Mean?

The London Interbank Offer Rate denominated in euros. This is the interest rate that banks offer one another for large short-term loans in euros. The rate is fixed once a day by a small group of large London banks but fluctuates throughout the day. This market makes it easier for banks to maintain liquidity requirements because they are able to borrow quickly from other banks that have surpluses.

Investopedia explains *Euro LIBOR*

The Euro LIBOR is based on the average lending rates of 16 banks. These bank rates are available to the public through the British Bankers' Association. Euro LIBOR exists mainly for continuity purposes in swap contracts dating back to preeuro times and is not used very commonly.

RELATED TERMS:
- *Debt*
- *Money Market*
- *London Interbank Offer Rate—LIBOR*
- *Singapore Interbank Offered Rate—SIBOR*
- *Interest Rate*

EXCHANGE-TRADED FUND (ETF)

What Does *Exchange-Traded Fund (ETF)* Mean?

A type of closed-end mutual fund that trades like a stock on an exchange; ETFs usually are constructed to track an index, a commodity, or a basket of assets like an index fund. ETFs fluctuate in price during the trading day as they are bought and sold on an exchange just like a stock.

Investopedia explains *Exchange-Traded Fund (ETF)*

Because it trades like a stock, an ETF does not have its net asset value (NAV) calculated every day the way an open-end mutual fund does. By owning an ETF, an investor gets the diversification of an index fund as well as the ability to sell short, buy on margin, and purchase as little as one share (like a stock). Another advantage is that the expense ratios for most ETFs are lower than those of the average mutual fund. When buying and selling ETFs, one pays a brokerage commission, just as one would for a stock. The most widely recognized ETF is called the Spiders (SPDR), which tracks the S&P 500 index and trades under the symbol SPY.

RELATED TERMS:
- Closed-End Fund
- Expense Ratio
- Spiders—SPDR
- Diversification
- Index Fund

EX-DATE

What Does *Ex-Date* Mean?
The date on which or the date after a security trades without its previously declared dividend or distribution. After the ex-date, a stock is said to trade ex-dividend.

Investopedia explains *Ex-Date*
This is the date when the seller of a stock—not the buyer—will be entitled to receive a recently declared dividend. The ex-date is usually two business days before the record date. The ex-dividend date in stock listings is designated with an x.

RELATED TERMS:
- Dividend
- Preferred Stock
- Yield
- Ex-Dividend
- Record Date

EX-DIVIDEND

What Does *Ex-Dividend* Mean?
A classification assigned to stock when a declared dividend belongs to the seller rather than the buyer at the time of a trade. A stock is given ex-dividend status if a person has been confirmed by the company to receive the dividend payment.

Investopedia explains *Ex-Dividend*
A stock trades ex-dividend on or after the ex-dividend date (ex-date). At this point, the person who owns the security on the ex-dividend date will be awarded the payment regardless of who currently holds the stock. After the ex-date has been declared, the stock usually drops in price by the amount of the expected dividend; the stock is trading without the dividend.

RELATED TERMS:
- Dividend
- Preferred Stock
- Stock
- Ex-Date
- Record Date

EXERCISE

What Does *Exercise* Mean?
An action taken by a stockholder in response to a certain privilege offered by a company or another financial institution. This includes warrants, options, and other exotic financial instruments.

Investopedia explains *Exercise*
When an investor exercises a stock option, that investor "trades in" his or her options for the actual stock.

RELATED TERMS:
- Call Option
- Put Option
- Warrant
- Expiration Date
- Strike Price

EXPECTED RETURN

What Does *Expected Return* Mean?
The average of a probability distribution of possible returns. It is calculated by using the following formula:

$$E(R)=\sum_{i=1}^{n}P_i\times R_i$$

Investopedia explains *Expected Return*
One calculates the average of a probability distribution by taking the probability of each possible return outcome and multiplying it by the return outcome itself. For example, if one knew a given investment had a 50% chance of earning a 10% return, a 25% chance of earning 20%, and a 25% chance of earning −10%, the expected return would be equal to 7.5%: Expected Return = (0.5) (0.1) + (0.25) (0.2) + (0.25) (−0.1). Although this is what one would expect the return to be, there is no guarantee that it will be the actual return.

RELATED TERMS:
- Coefficient of Variation
- Return on Assets
- Total Return
- Equity Premium
- Return on Equity

EXPENSE RATIO

What Does *Expense Ratio* Mean?

The amount it costs an investment company to operate a mutual fund. An expense ratio is determined through an annual calculation in which a fund's operating expenses are divided by the average dollar value of its assets under management. Operating expenses are taken out of a fund's assets and lower the return to a fund's investors. Also known as management expense ratio (MER).

Investopedia explains *Expense Ratio*

Depending on the type of fund, operating expenses vary widely. The largest component of operating expenses is the fee paid to a fund's investment manager/advisor. Other costs include recordkeeping, custodial services, taxes, legal expenses, and accounting and auditing fees. Some funds have a marketing cost referred to as a 12b-1 fee, which also would be included in operating expenses. A fund's trading activity—the buying and selling of portfolio securities—is not included in the calculation of the expense ratio. Costs associated with mutual funds but not included in operating expenses are loads and redemption fees, which, if they apply, are paid directly by fund investors.

RELATED TERMS:
- *Exchange-Traded Fund—ETF*
- *Mutual Fund*
- *Turnover Ratio*
- *Internal Rate of Return*
- *Operating Expense*

EXPIRATION DATE

What Does *Expiration Date* Mean?

The day on which an option or futures contract is no longer valid and therefore ceases to exist.

Investopedia explains *Expiration Date*

The expiration date for all listed stock options in the United States is the third Friday of the expiration month (except when it falls on a holiday, in which case it is on Thursday).

RELATED TERMS:
- *Common Stock*
- *Option*
- *Strike Price*
- *Maturity*
- *Stock Option*

copyright JackGuinan

"Recently, I've discovered
that while my happiness isn't tied
to the stock market, my misery
is joined at its hip."

My broker tells me that I should buy and hold.

I should speak with your broker. Mine tells me to buy and pray.

copyright JackGusman

FACE VALUE

What Does *Face Value* Mean?

The nominal or dollar value of a security at the time it is issued. For stocks, it is the original cost of the stock shown on the certificate. For bonds, it is the amount paid to the holder at maturity (generally $1,000). Also known as par value or par.

Investopedia explains *Face Value*

In bond investing, face value, or par value, commonly refers to the amount paid to a bondholder at the maturity date, assuming the issuer does not default. However, bond prices on the secondary market fluctuate with interest rates. For example, if interest rates are higher than a bond's coupon rate, the bond is sold at a discount (below par). Conversely, if interest rates are lower than the bond's coupon rate, the bond is sold at a premium (above par).

RELATED TERMS:
- *Bond*
- *Market Value*
- *Premium*
- *Fair Value*
- *Par Value*

FAIR VALUE

What Does *Fair Value* Mean?

(1) The estimated value of all assets and liabilities of an acquired company used to consolidate the financial statements of both companies. (2) In the futures market, the equilibrium price for a futures contract. This is equal to the spot price after taking into account compounded interest (and dividends lost because the investor owns the futures contract rather than the physical stocks) over a certain period.

Investopedia explains *Fair Value*

The "fair value" quoted on TV refers to the relationship between the futures contract on a market index and the actual value of the index. When futures trade above fair value, this means that traders are betting that the market index will go higher; the opposite is true if futures are trading below fair value.

RELATED TERMS:
- *Ask*
- *Market Value*
- *Premium*
- *Face Value*
- *Par Value*

FANNIE MAE—FEDERAL NATIONAL MORTGAGE ASSOCIATION (FNMA)

What Does *Fannie Mae—Federal National Mortgage Association (FNMA)* Mean?

A government-sponsored enterprise (GSE) that was created in 1938 to expand the flow of mortgage money by creating a secondary mortgage market. Fannie Mae is a publicly traded company that operates under a congressional charter that directs it to channel its efforts into increasing the availability of affordable home ownership for low-, moderate-, and middle-income Americans.

Investopedia explains *Fannie Mae—Federal National Mortgage Association (FNMA)*

Fannie Mae purchases and guarantees mortgages that meet its funding criteria. Through this process it secures mortgages to form mortgage-backed securities (MBSs). The market for Fannie Mae's MBSs is extremely large. Pension funds, insurance companies, and foreign governments are among the investors in Fannie Mae's MBSs. To promote home ownership, Fannie Mae also holds a large portfolio

of its own and other institutions' MBSs, known as its retained portfolio. To fund this portfolio, Fannie Mae issues debt known in the
marketplace as agency debt. Fannie Mae's "little brother" is Freddie
Mac. Together, Fannie Mae and Freddie Mac purchase or guarantee
40 to 60% of all mortgages originated annually in the United States,
depending on market conditions and consumer trends.

RELATED TERMS:
• *Freddie Mac—Federal Home Loan Mortgage Corp.*
• *Ginnie Mae—Government National Mortgage Association (GNMA)*
• *Mortgage*   • *Subprime Loan*
• *Subprime Meltdown*

FEDERAL FUNDS RATE

What Does *Federal Funds Rate* Mean?
The interest rate at which a depository institution lends immediately
available funds (balances at the Federal Reserve) to another depository institution overnight; sometimes referred to as the overnight
funds rate.

Investopedia explains *Federal Funds Rate*
This is what news reports are referring to when they talk about
the Fed changing interest rates. In fact, the Federal Open Market
Committee sets a target for this rate but not the actual rate itself
(because it is determined by the open market).

RELATED TERMS:
• *Discount Rate*
• *Federal Open Market Committee—FOMC*
• *Fiscal Policy*   • *Interest Rate*
• *Monetary Policy*

FEDERAL OPEN MARKET COMMITTEE (FOMC)

What Does *Federal Open Market Committee (FOMC)* Mean?
The branch of the Federal Reserve Board that sets the direction of
monetary policy. The FOMC is composed of the Board of Governors,
which has seven members, and five reserve bank presidents. The
president of the Federal Reserve Bank of New York serves continuously, and the presidents of the other reserve banks rotate in their
service of one-year terms.

Investopedia explains *Federal Open Market Committee* (FOMC)
The FOMC meets eight times a year to set key interest rates, such
as the discount rate, and decide whether to increase or decrease
the money supply, which the Fed does through buying and selling
government securities. For example, to tighten the money supply,
or decrease the amount of money available in the banking system,
the Fed sells government securities. The meetings of the committee,
which are secret, are the subject of much speculation on Wall Street
as analysts try to guess whether the Fed will tighten or loosen the
money supply, causing interest rates to rise or fall.

RELATED TERMS:
- *Discount Rate*
- *Federal Funds Rate*
- *Prime Rate*
- *Fiscal Policy*
- *Monetary Policy*

FINANCIAL INDUSTRY REGULATORY AUTHORITY (FINRA)

 What Does *Financial Industry Regulatory Authority* (FINRA) Mean?
A regulatory body created after the merger of the National Association of Securities Dealers and the New York Stock Exchange's
regulation committee. The Financial Industry Regulatory Authority
is responsible for governing business between brokers, dealers, and
the investing public. By consolidating these two regulators, FINRA
aims to eliminate regulatory overlap and cost inefficiencies.

 Investopedia explains *Financial Industry Regulatory Authority* (FINRA)
Originally, FINRA was known as SIRA, the Securities Industry Regulatory Authority. However, complaints were made about the name,
noting that it sounded very similar to the Arabic term "Sirah," the
traditional term for biographical texts about Muhammad.

RELATED TERMS:
- *Broker-Dealer*
- *National Association of Securities Dealers—NASD*
- *New York Stock Exchange—NYSE*
- *Securities and Exchange Commission—SEC*
- *Series 7*

FIRST IN, FIRST OUT (FIFO)

What Does *First In, First Out (FIFO)* mean?

An asset-management and accounting valuation method in which the assets produced or acquired first are sold, used, or disposed of first. FIFO may be used by an individual or a corporation.

Investopedia explains *First In, First Out (FIFO)*

For taxation purposes, FIFO assumes that the assets that are remaining in inventory are matched to the assets that are purchased or produced most recently. Because of this assumption, a number of tax minimization strategies are associated with using the FIFO asset-management and valuation method. In selling shares, FIFO can be used to determine one's cost basis so that sales are matched to share purchases that result in a more favorable tax treatment.

RELATED TERMS:

- Asset
- Generally Accepted Accounting Principles—GAAP
- Inventory
- Asset Turnover
- Inventory Turnover

FISCAL POLICY

What Does *Fiscal Policy* Mean?

Government spending policies that influence macroeconomic conditions. These policies are used to influence the overall economy by manipulating tax rates, interest rates, and government spending.

Investopedia explains *Fiscal Policy*

Since the 1980s, most western countries have followed a "tight" policy, limiting public expenditure.

RELATED TERMS:

- Efficient Market Hypothesis—EMH
- Macroeconomics
- Monetary Policy
- Interest Rates
- Microeconomics

FIXED ANNUITY

What Does *Fixed Annuity* Mean?

An insurance contract in which the insurance company makes fixed dollar payments to the annuitant for the term of the contract, usually until the annuitant dies. The insurance company guarantees both earnings and principal.

Investopedia explains *Fixed Annuity*
A fairly good financial instrument for those seeking fixed investment income; this is particularly attractive to retirees.

RELATED TERMS:
- *Annuity*
- *Income Statement*
- *Individual Retirement Account—IRA*
- *Mutual Fund*
- *Defined-Benefit Plan*

FIXED-INCOME SECURITY

What Does *Fixed-Income Security* **Mean?**
An investment that provides income in the form of fixed periodic payments and the eventual return of principal at maturity. Unlike a variable-income security, in which payments change on the basis of an underlying measure such as short-term interest rates, the payments of a fixed-income security are known in advance and do not change.

Investopedia explains *Fixed-Income Security*
An example of a fixed-income security would be a 5% fixed-rate government bond in which a $1,000 investment would result in an annual $50 payment until maturity, at which time the investor would receive the $1,000 back. Generally, these types of assets offer a lower return on investment because they guarantee a fixed rate of income.

RELATED TERMS:
- *Annuity*
- *Coupon*
- *Yield*
- *Bond*
- *Interest rate*

FLOAT

What Does *Float* **Mean?**
The total number of a company's shares that are publicly owned and available for trading. The float is calculated by subtracting restricted shares from outstanding shares. Also known as free float.

Investopedia explains *Float*

As an example, a company may have 10 million outstanding shares, but only 7 million are trading on the stock market. Therefore, this company's float would be 7 million. Stocks with small floats of less than 7 million shares tend to be a lot more volatile than others.

RELATED TERMS:
- Dilution
- Outstanding Shares
- Volatility
- Market Capitalization
- Shareholders' Equity

FOREX (FX)

 What Does *Forex (FX)* Mean?

The currency exchange marketplace; the forex market is the largest, most liquid market in the world, with average trading values in the billions each day, and includes all the currencies in the world.

 Investopedia explains *Forex (FX)*

There is no central marketplace for currency exchange; trade is conducted over the counter. The Forex market is open 24 hours a day, five days a week, and currencies are traded worldwide among the major financial centers of London, New York, Tokyo, Frankfurt, Hong Kong, Singapore, Paris, Sydney, and others. The forex is the largest market in the world in terms of the total cash value traded, and any person, firm, or country may participate in this market.

RELATED TERMS:
- Arbitrage
- Currency Swap
- Over-the-Counter—OTC
- Currency Forward
- Euro LIBOR

FORWARD CONTRACT

 What Does *Forward Contract* Mean?

A cash market transaction in which delivery of the commodity is deferred until after the contract has been made. Although the delivery is made in the future, the price is determined on the initial trade date.

Investopedia explains *Forward Contract*
Most forward contracts do not have standards and are not traded on exchanges. A farmer would use a forward contract to "lock in" a price for his or her grain for the upcoming fall harvest.

RELATED TERMS:
- *Cash and Cash Equivalents—CCE*
- *Commodity*
- *Derivative*
- *Money Market*
- *Currency Forward*

FORWARD PRICE TO EARNINGS (FORWARD P/E)

 What Does *Forward Price to Earnings (Forward P/E)* Mean?
A measure of the price-to-earnings ratio (P/E) that uses forecasted earnings to calculate the P/E. Although the earnings used in the calculation are just estimates and thus are not as reliable as current earnings data, there is still a benefit in forward P/E analysis. The forecasted earnings used in the formula can be for the next 12 months or for the next full-year fiscal period. It is calculated as follows:

$$\text{Forward P/E} = \frac{\text{Market Price per Share}}{\text{Expected Earnings per Share}}$$

Also referred to as estimated price to earnings.

 Investopedia explains *Forward Price to Earnings (Forward P/E)*
The estimated forward P/E of a company often is used to compare current earnings to estimated future earnings. If earnings are expected to grow in the future, the estimated P/E will be lower than the current P/E. This measure also is used to compare one company to another with a forward-looking focus.

RELATED TERMS:
- *Earnings*
- *Gearing Ratio*
- *Price-Earnings Ratio—P/E Ratio*
- *Price/Earnings to Growth Ratio—PEG Ratio*
- *Earning per Share—EPS*

FREDDIE MAC—FEDERAL HOME LOAN MORTGAGE CORP. (FHLMC)

What Does *Freddie Mac—Federal Home Loan Mortgage Corp. (FHLMC)* **Mean?**

A stockholder-owned, government-sponsored enterprise (GSE) chartered by Congress in 1970 that makes money easily available to mortgage lenders to promote affordable home ownership for middle-income Americans. The FHLMC purchases, guarantees, and securitizes mortgages into what are called mortgage-backed securities. The mortgage-backed securities trade like stocks and are purchased by institutions and other public investors.

Investopedia explains *Freddie Mac—Federal Home Loan Mortgage Corp. (FHLMC)*

Freddie Mac has come under criticism because as a government enterprise, it can borrow money at interest rates lower than those available to non-GSE financial institutions. With this funding advantage, it issues large amounts of debt (known in the marketplace as agency debt or agencies) and in turn purchases and holds a huge portfolio of mortgages known as its retained portfolio. It was the size of this retained portfolio that contributed to the systemic mortgage bank financial crisis of 2008.

RELATED TERMS:
- *Fannie Mae—Federal National Mortgage Association (FNMA)*
- *Ginnie Mae—Government National Mortgage Association (GNMA)*
- *Mortgage*
- *Real Estate Investment Trust—REIT*
- *Subprime Meltdown*

FREE CASH FLOW (FCF)

What Does *Free Cash Flow (FCF)* **Mean?**

A measure of financial performance calculated as operating cash flow minus capital expenditures. Free cash flow represents the cash that a company is able to generate after laying out the money required to maintain or expand its asset base. Free cash flow is important because it allows a company to pursue opportunities that enhance shareholder value. Without cash, it is tough to develop new products, make acquisitions, pay dividends, and reduce debt. FCF is calculated as follows:

It also can be calculated by taking operating cash flow and subtracting capital expenditures.

Net Income
+Amortization/Depreciation
− Changes in Working Capital
− Capital Expenditures
=Free Cash Flow

 Investopedia explains *Free Cash Flow (FCF)*

Some people believe that Wall Street focuses too much on earnings while ignoring the "real" cash that a firm generates. Earnings often can be clouded by accounting gimmicks, but it is tougher to fake cash flow. For this reason, some investors believe that FCF gives a much clearer view of a company's ability to grow and generate cash (and thus profits). It is important to note that negative free cash flow is not necessarily a bad thing. If free cash flow is negative, it could be a sign that a company is making large investments. If these investments earn a high return, the strategy has the potential to pay off in the long run.

RELATED TERMS:
- *Cash Flow Statement*
- *Free Cash Flow Yield*
- *Operating Cash Flow Ratio*
- *Free Cash Flow to Equity—FCFE*
- *Operating Cash Flow—OCF*

FREE CASH FLOW TO EQUITY (FCFE)

 What Does *Free Cash Flow to Equity (FCFE)* **Mean?**

This is a measure of how much cash can be paid to a company's equity shareholders after accounting for all expenses, reinvestment, and debt repayment. It is calculated as follows: FCFE = Net Income – Net – Change in Net Working Capital + New Debt – Debt Repayment

 Investopedia explains *Free Cash Flow to Equity (FCFE)*

FCFE is one method analysts use to determine the value of a company. FCFE valuation gained popularity as the usefulness of the dividend discount model became increasingly questionable.

RELATED TERMS:
- *Cash Flow*
- *Dividend Discount Model—DDM*
- *Free Cash Flow Yield*
- *Discounted Cash Flow—DCF*
- *Free Cash Flow—FCF*

FREE CASH FLOW YIELD

What Does *Free Cash Flow Yield* Mean?

An overall return evaluation ratio on a stock that standardizes the free cash flow per share that a company expects to earn against its market price per share. The ratio is calculated by taking the free cash flow per share divided by the share price. It is calculated as follows:

$$\text{Free Cash Flow Yield} = \frac{\text{Free Cash Flow per Share}}{\text{Current Market Price per Share}}$$

Investopedia explains *Free Cash Flow Yield*

Free cash flow yield is similar to the earnings yield metric, which is a measure of GAAP earnings per share divided by share price. Generally, the lower the ratio is, the less attractive the investment is, and vice versa. Logically, investors want to pay as little as possible for more earnings. Some investors regard free cash flow (which takes into account capital expenditures and other ongoing costs of business) as a more accurate representation of a company and thus prefer free cash flow yield as a valuation metric over earnings yield.

RELATED TERMS:

- *Cash Flow Statement*
- *Free Cash Flow—FCF*
- *Free Cash Flow to Equity—FCFE*
- *Earnings per Share—EPS*
- *Yield*

FRONT-END LOAD

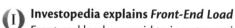

What Does *Front-End Load* Mean?

A commission or sales charge applied at the time of the initial purchase for an investment instrument, usually a mutual fund or insurance policy. The load is deducted from the investment amount, which reduces the actual amount invested.

Investopedia explains *Front-End Load*

Front-end loads are paid to investment intermediaries (financial planners, brokers, investment advisors) as sales commissions. Thus, these sales charges are not part of a mutual fund's operating expenses. It is argued that a load is a cost that investors incur for obtaining an investment intermediary's expertise in selecting appropriate funds for clients. It is a matter of record that load funds do not outperform no-load funds. Generally, the sales charge on a load mutual fund will

be waived if such a fund is included as an investment option in a
retirement plan such as a 401(k).

RELATED TERMS:
- *Closed-End Fund*
- *Mutual Fund*
- *No-Load Fund*
- *Load Fund*
- *Net Asset Value—NAV*

FULLY DILUTED SHARES

What Does *Fully Diluted Shares* Mean?
The total number of shares that would be outstanding if all possible
sources of conversion, such as convertible bonds and stock options,
were exercised. Companies often release specific financial figures
in terms of fully diluted shares outstanding (such as the company's
profits reported on a fully diluted per share basis) to help investors
properly assess a company's financial situation.

Investopedia explains *Fully Diluted Shares*
An investor should consider carefully the fully diluted share figure
because it can cause a company's share price to plummet significantly if a large number of option holders or convertible bond holders decide to claim their stock. For example, let's say that XYZ Corp.
is priced at $5 and has 1 million shares outstanding and 1 million
options outstanding (assuming each option gives the right to buy
one share). If all the investors decide to exercise their options, there
will be 2 million shares outstanding and the share price probably will
drop to $2.50.

RELATED TERMS:
- *Convertible Bond*
- *Diluted Earnings per Share—Diluted EPS*
- *Float*
- *Convertible Preferred Stock*
- *Outstanding Shares*

FUNDAMENTAL ANALYSIS

What Does *Fundamental Analysis* Mean?
A valuation method that measures the intrinsic value of a security
by examining related economic, financial, and other qualitative and
quantitative factors. Fundamental analysts study everything that

could possibly affect a security's value, including macroeconomic factors (such as the overall economy and industry conditions) and specific factors (such as the financial condition and management of companies). The end goal of fundamental analysis is to produce a value that an investor can compare with a security's current price in an attempt to figure out whether the security is underpriced or overpriced. Fundamental analysis is the opposite of technical analysis.

 Investopedia explains *Fundamental Analysis*
Fundamental analysis employs real data to evaluate the value of a security. Although most analysts use fundamental analysis to value stocks, this method of valuation can be used for almost any type of security. For example, an investor can perform fundamental analysis on a bond's value by looking at economic factors, such as interest rates and the overall state of the economy, along with information about the bond issuer, such as potential changes in its credit ratings. With stocks, this method can consider revenues, earnings, future growth, return on equity, profit margins, and other data to determine a company's underlying value and potential growth. Fundamental analysis is used to look deeply into a company's financial statements. Warren Buffett, the Oracle of Omaha, is a well-known fundamental analyst.

RELATED TERMS:
- *Balance Sheet*
- *Intrinsic Value*
- *Technical Analysis*

- *Income Statement*
- *Quantitative Analysis*

FUTURE VALUE (FV)

 What Does *Future Value (FV)* **Mean?**
The future value of an asset or cash expressed in terms of its equivalent value to a specified sum today. There are two ways to calculate FV: (1) for an asset with simple annual interest = Original Investment × (1+ (Interest Rate × Number of Years)); (2) for an asset with interest compounded annually = Original Investment × ((1 + Interest Rate) ^ Number of Years).

Investopedia explains *Future Value (FV)*
Consider the following examples: (1) $1,000 invested for 5 years
with simple annual interest of 10% would have a future value of
$1,500.00; (2) $1,000 invested for 5 years at 10%, compounded annually has a future value of $1,610.51.

RELATED TERMS:
- Compounding
- Inflation
- Time Value of Money
- Discount Rate
- Present Value

FUTURES

 ### What Does *Futures* Mean?

Futures involve a financial contract that requires the buyer to
purchase an asset (or the seller to sell an asset), such as a physical
commodity or a financial instrument, at a specific price on a predetermined date in the future. Futures contracts detail the quality and
quantity of the underlying asset; they are standardized to facilitate
trading on a futures exchange. Some futures contracts may call for
physical delivery of the asset, and others are settled in cash. The
futures markets are characterized by the ability to use very high
leverage relative to stock markets. Futures can be used either to
hedge or to speculate on the price movement of the underlying
asset. For example, a producer of corn could use futures to lock in
a certain price and reduce risk (hedge). However, anybody could
speculate on the price movement of corn by going long or short
using futures.

 Investopedia explains *Futures*
The primary difference between options and futures is that options
give the holder the right, not the obligation, to buy or sell the underlying asset until expiration, whereas the holder of a futures contract
is obligated to fulfill the terms of the contract. In reality, most futures
contract holders do not hold the contract to expiration. In addition,
if an investor were long in a futures contract, that investor could go
short the same type of contract to offset his or her position. This
serves to exit the position, much like selling a stock in the equity markets would close a trade.

RELATED TERMS:
- Commodity
- Leverage
- Short (or Short Position)

- Hedge
- Option

FUTURES CONTRACT

What Does *Futures Contract* Mean?
A contractual agreement, generally made on the trading floor of a futures exchange, to buy or sell a particular commodity or financial instrument at a predetermined price in the future. Futures contracts detail the quality and quantity of the underlying asset; they are standardized to facilitate trading on a futures exchange. Some futures contracts may call for physical delivery of the asset, whereas others are settled in cash.

Investopedia explains *Futures Contract*
The terms "futures contract" and "futures" refer to essentially the same thing. For example, one might hear somebody say he or she bought "oil futures," which means the same thing as an "oil futures contract." To get really specific, one could say that a futures contract refers only to the specific characteristics of the underlying asset, whereas "futures" is more general and also can refer to the overall market, as in "He's a futures trader."

RELATED TERMS:
- Commodity
- Forward Contract
- Hedge

- Derivative
- Futures

"Keep in mind, your losses
shown here are not actual size."

"I bought call options for my portfolio in case the market goes up, and flowers and chocolates for my wife in case it doesn't."

GAMMA

What Does *Gamma* Mean?

The rate of change for delta with respect to the price of the underlying asset.

Investopedia explains *Gamma*

Mathematically, gamma is the first derivative of delta and is used when one is trying to gauge the price of an option relative to how much it is in or out of the money. When the option being measured is deeply in or out of the money, gamma is small. When the option is near the money, gamma is large.

RELATED TERMS:
- *Alpha*
- *Delta*
- *Stock Option*
- *Beta*
- *In the Money*

GEARING RATIO

What Does *Gearing Ratio* Mean?

A term describing a financial ratio that compares some form of owner's equity (or capital) to borrowed funds. Gearing is a measure of financial leverage, demonstrating the degree to which a firm's activities are funded by owner's funds versus creditor's funds.

Investopedia explains *Gearing Ratio*
The more leverage a company has, the riskier that company may be. As with most ratios, the acceptable level of leverage is determined by comparing ratios of like companies in the same industry. The best examples of gearing ratios include the debt-to-equity ratio (total debt/total equity), times interest earned (EBIT/total interest), equity ratio (equity/assets), and debt ratio (total debt /total assets). A company with high gearing (high leverage) is more vulnerable to downturns in the business cycle because it must continue to service its debt regardless of how bad sales are. A larger proportion of equity provides a cushion and is seen as a measure of financial strength.

RELATED TERMS:
- *Business Cycle*
- *Debt/Equity Ratio*
- *Leverage*
- *Debt Ratio*
- *Equity*

GENERALLY ACCEPTED ACCOUNTING PRINCIPLES (GAAP)

 What Does *Generally Accepted Accounting Principles (GAAP)* Mean?
The overriding accounting principles, standards, and procedures that companies follow when compiling their financial statements. GAAP is a combination of authoritative standards (set by policy boards) and the commonly accepted ways of recording and reporting accounting information.

 Investopedia explains *Generally Accepted Accounting Principles (GAAP)*
Companies use GAAP to standardize their financial statements so that investors can better use those statements to analyze a company for investment purposes. GAAP covers things such as revenue recognition, balance sheet item classification, and outstanding share measurements. Companies are expected to follow GAAP rules when reporting their financial data in their financial statements. If a financial statement is not prepared using GAAP principles, investors should be very wary! That said, GAAP is only a set of guidelines, and that leaves plenty of room for interpretation by unscrupulous accountants to distort figures. Thus, even with GAAP, one should not put complete faith in the numbers companies report.

RELATED TERMS:
- *Accrual Accounting*
- *Cash Flow Statement*
- *First In, First Out—FIFO*
- *Balance Sheet*
- *Income Statement*

GINNIE MAE—GOVERNMENT NATIONAL MORTGAGE ASSOCIATION (GNMA)

What Does *Ginnie Mae—Government National Mortgage Association (GNMA)* Mean?

A U.S. government corporation within the U.S. Department of Housing and Urban Development (HUD). Ginnie May aims to (1) ensure liquidity for government-insured mortgages, including those insured by the Federal Housing Administration (FHA), the Veterans Administration (VA), and the Rural Housing Administration (RHA) and (2) draw investor capital in the market so that the issuers have the means to issue more. Most of the mortgages securitized as Ginnie Mae mortgage-backed securities (MBSs) are those guaranteed by FHA, which are typically mortgages for first-time home buyers and low-income borrowers.

Investopedia explains *Ginnie Mae—Government National Mortgage Association (GNMA)*

Ginnie Mae does not issue, sell, or buy pass-through mortgage-backed securities or purchase mortgage loans. It simply guarantees (insures) the timely payment of principal and interest from approved issuers (such as mortgage bankers, savings and loans, and commercial banks) of qualifying loans, such as those issued by the FHA and RHA. Unlike its cousins Freddie Mac, Fannie Mae, and Sallie Mae, Ginnie Mae is not a publicly traded company. An investor in a GNMA security will not know who the underlying issuer of the mortgages is, only that the security is guaranteed by GNMA, which is backed by the full faith and credit of the U.S. government, just like U.S. Treasuries.

RELATED TERMS:
- *Fannie Mae—Federal National Mortgage Association (FNMA)*
- *Freddie Mac—Federal Home Loan Mortgage Corp.*
- *Mortgage*
- *Mortgage-Backed Securities—MBSs*
- *Securitization*

GLASS-STEAGALL ACT

What Does *Glass-Steagall Act* Mean?

An act passed by Congress in 1933 that prohibited commercial banks from collaborating with full-service brokerage firms or participating in investment banking activities.

Investopedia explains *Glass-Steagall Act*

The Glass-Steagall Act was enacted during the Great Depression to help protect depositors from the additional risks associated with security transactions. The act was dismantled in 1999. Consequently, the distinction between commercial banks and brokerage firms has blurred. Today, for better or worse, many banks own brokerage firms and provide investment services.

RELATED TERMS:
- Bear Market
- Common Stock
- Underwriting
- Broker-Dealer
- Investment Bank

GLOBAL DEPOSITARY RECEIPT (GDR)

What Does *Global Depositary Receipt (GDR)* Mean?

(1) A bank certificate representing shares in a foreign country and issued in more than one country. The shares are held by a foreign branch of an international bank. The shares trade as domestic shares but are offered for sale globally through the various bank branches.
(2) A financial instrument used by private markets to raise capital denominated in either U.S. dollars or foreign currencies.

Investopedia explains *Global Depositary Receipt (GDR)*

(1) A GDR is very similar to an American Depositary Receipt.
(2) These instruments are called EDRs when private markets are attempting to obtain euros.

RELATED TERMS:
- American Depositary Receipt—ADR
- American Stock Exchange—AMEX
- Common Stock
- Exchange-Traded Fund
- Mutual Fund

GOODWILL

What Does *Goodwill* Mean?

An account recorded in the assets portion of a company's balance sheet. Goodwill often arises when one company is purchased by another company. In an acquisition, the amount paid for the company over book value usually accounts for the target firm's intangible assets.

Investopedia explains *Goodwill*

Goodwill is seen as an intangible asset on the balance sheet because it is not a physical asset such as buildings and equipment. Goodwill typically reflects the value of intangible assets such as a strong brand name, good customer relations, good employee relations, and patents or proprietary technology.

RELATED TERMS:
- Balance Sheet
- Book Value
- Generally Accepted Accounting Principles—GAAP
- Intangible Asset
- Tangible Asset

GORDON GROWTH MODEL

What Does *Gordon Growth Model* Mean?

A model for determining the intrinsic value of a stock on the basis of a future series of dividends that grow at a constant rate. Given a dividend per share that is payable in one year and the assumption that the dividend grows at a constant rate in perpetuity, the model solves for the present value of the infinite series of future dividends. It is calculated as follows:

$$\text{Stock Value (P)} = \frac{D}{k-G}$$

Where D = expected dividend per share one year from now; k = required rate of return for equity investor; G = growth rate in dividends (in perpetuity).

Investopedia explains *Gordon Growth Model*

Because the model simplistically assumes a constant rate of growth, it generally is used only for mature companies (or broad market indices) with low to moderate growth rates.

RELATED TERMS:
- *Discount Rate*
- *Dividend Discount Model—DDM*
- *Present Value—PV*
- *Intrinsic Value*
- *Required Rate of Return*

GOVERNMENT SECURITY

 What Does *Government Security* Mean?
A government debt obligation (local or national) backed by the credit and taxing power of a country; as a result, there is very little risk of default.

 Investopedia explains *Government Security*
This includes short-term Treasury bills, medium-term Treasury notes, and long-term Treasury bonds.

RELATED TERMS:
- *Bond*
- *Treasury Bill—T-Bill*
- *U.S. Treasury*
- *Risk-Free Rate of Return*
- *Treasury Bond—T-Bond*

GROSS DOMESTIC PRODUCT (GDP)

What Does *Gross Domestic Product (GDP)* Mean?
The monetary value of all the finished goods and services produced within a country's borders in a specific period; GDP usually is calculated on an annual basis and includes all private and public consumption, government outlays, investments, and exports less imports that occur within a defined territory. GDP = C + G + I + NX (where C = all private consumption, or consumer spending, in a nation's economy; G = the sum of government spending; I = the sum of all the country's business spending on capital; NX = the nation's total net exports, calculated as total exports minus total imports).

Investopedia explains *Gross Domestic Product (GDP)*
GDP is used commonly as an indicator of the economic health of a country as well as to gauge a country's standard of living. Critics of GDP contend that the statistic does not take into account the underground economy: transactions that for whatever reason are not reported to the government. Others say that GDP is not intended to gauge material well-being but serves as a measure of a nation's productivity, which is unrelated.

RELATED TERMS:
- Bear Market
- Consumer Price Index—CPI
- Nominal GDP
- Bull Market
- Inflation

GROSS INCOME

What Does *Gross Income* Mean?
(1) An individual's total personal income before taking taxes or deductions into account. (2) A company's revenue minus cost of goods sold. Also called gross margin and gross profit.

Investopedia explains *Gross Income*
(1) Your gross income is how much you make before taxes. If someone asks you how much money you gross a month, this is the figure that you would give. (2) This is an important number when one is analyzing a company; it indicates how efficiently management uses labor and supplies in the production process. One must keep in mind that gross income varies significantly from industry to industry.

RELATED TERMS:
- Cost of Goods Sold—COGS
- Net Income—NI
- Revenue
- Income Statement
- Operating Income

GROSS MARGIN

What Does *Gross Margin* Mean?
A company's total sales revenue minus its cost of goods sold (COGS), divided by the total sales revenue, expressed as a percentage. The gross margin represents the percentage of total sales revenue that the company retains after incurring the direct costs associated with producing the goods and services it sells. The higher the percentage is, the more the company retains on each dollar of sales to service its other costs and obligations. It is calculated as follows:

$$\text{Gross Margin (\%)} = \frac{\text{Revenue} - \text{Cost of Goods Sold}}{\text{Revenue}}$$

Investopedia explains *Gross Margin*

This number represents the proportion of each dollar of revenue that the company retains as gross profit. For example, if a company's gross margin for the most recent quarter was 35%, it would retain $0.35 from each dollar of revenue generated. This money could be used to pay off selling, general, and administrative expenses; interest expenses; and distributions to shareholders. The levels of gross margin can vary drastically from one industry to another. For example, a software company generally has a higher gross margin than does a manufacturing firm.

RELATED TERMS:
- Gross Profit Margin
- Operating Leverage
- Return on Sales—ROS
- Net Income—NI
- Profit Margin

GROSS PROFIT MARGIN

 What Does *Gross Profit Margin* **Mean?**

A financial metric used to assess a firm's financial health by revealing the proportion of revenues left over after accounting for the cost of goods sold. Gross profit margin serves as the source for paying additional expenses and future savings. Also known as gross margin. It is calculated as follows:

$$\text{Gross Profit Margin} = \frac{\text{Revenue} - \text{COGS}}{\text{Revenue}}$$

Where COGS = cost of goods sold.

 Investopedia explains *Gross Profit Margin*

As an example, suppose ABC Corp. earned $20 million in revenue from producing widgets and incurred $10 million in COGS-related expense. ABC's gross profit margin would be 50%. This means that for every dollar that ABC earned, its profits were $0.50 at the end of the day. This metric is useful in comparing like companies, and companies that are operating more efficiently usually show higher profit margins.

RELATED TERMS:
- Contribution Margin
- Gross Margin
- Revenue
- Cost of Goods Sold—COGS
- Operating Income

GROWTH STOCK

What Does *Growth Stock* Mean?

Shares of a company whose earnings are expected to grow at an above-average rate relative to the market. Also known as a glamor stock.

Investopedia explains *Growth Stock*

A growth stock usually does not pay a dividend, as the company would prefer to reinvest its retained earnings back into capital projects for the company. Most technology companies are considered growth stocks. They reinvest earnings back into research and development for future growth. Note that a growth company's stock is not always classified as growth stock. In fact, a growth company's stock is often overvalued.

RELATED TERMS:

- *Equity*
- *Price-Earnings Ratio—P/E Ratio*
- *Value Stock*
- *Large Cap*
- *Small Cap*

"I know your investment performance has been lousy, but our policy against whining is quite clear in the prospectus."

copyright JackGuinan

"In a land where cash is king,
I'd like you to meet my husband,
one of the serfs."

HAIRCUT

What Does *Haircut* Mean?
(1) The difference between the prices at which a market maker can buy and sell a security. (2) The percentage by which an asset's market value is reduced for the purpose of calculating capital requirement, margin, and collateral levels.

Investopedia explains *Haircut*
(1) The term "haircut" comes from the fact that market makers can trade at such a thin spread. (2) When securities are used as collateral, they generally are devalued since a cushion is required by the lending parties in case the market value falls.

RELATED TERMS:
- *Initial Public Offering—IPO*
- *Margin*
- *Market Value*
- *Investment Bank*
- *Market Maker*

HEAD AND SHOULDERS PATTERN

What Does *Head and Shoulders Pattern* Mean?
A technical analysis term used to describe a chart formation in which a stock's price (1) rises to a peak and subsequently declines; (2) then rises above the former peak and again declines; and (3) rises again,

but not to the second peak, and declines once more. The first and third peaks are shoulders, and the second peak forms the head.

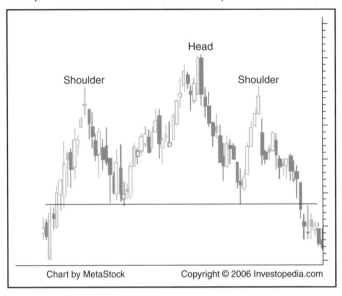

Chart by MetaStock   Copyright © 2006 Investopedia.com

 Investopedia explains *Head and Shoulders Pattern*
The head and shoulders pattern is considered the most reliable trend-reversal pattern.

RELATED TERMS:
- *Bear Market*
- *Quantitative Analysis*
- *Trend Analysis*
- *Bull Market*
- *Technical Analysis*

HEDGE

What Does *Hedge* Mean?
An investment that is used in an attempt to reduce the risk of adverse price movements in an asset. Normally, a hedge consists of taking an offsetting position in a related security, such as a futures contract.

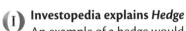 **Investopedia explains *Hedge***
An example of a hedge would be if an investor owned a stock and then sold a futures contract that allows him or her to sell that stock at a set price on a future date regardless of what the market price of

the stock is on that future date. Investors use this strategy to combat uncertainty in the market.

RELATED TERMS:
- Delta
- Hedge
- Naked Shorting
- Delta Hedging
- Hedge Fund

HEDGE FUND

What Does *Hedge Fund* Mean?
An aggressively managed portfolio of investments that uses advanced investment strategies such as leverage and long, short, and derivative positions in both domestic and international markets with the goal of generating high returns either in an absolute sense or relative to a specified market benchmark. Legally, hedge funds most often are set up as private investment partnerships that are open to a limited number of investors and require a very large initial minimum investment. Investments in hedge funds are illiquid as they often require investors to keep their money in the fund for at least one year.

Investopedia explains *Hedge Fund*
For the most part, hedge funds (unlike mutual funds) are unregulated because they cater to sophisticated and ultrawealthy investors. In the United States, laws require that the majority of investors in a hedge fund be accredited. That is, they must earn a minimum amount of money annually and have a net worth of more than $1 million. One can think of hedge funds as mutual funds for the superrich. They are similar to mutual funds in that investments are pooled and professionally managed but differ in that a hedge fund has far more flexibility in its investment strategies. It is important to note that hedging is actually the practice of attempting to reduce risk, but the goal of most hedge funds is to maximize return on investment by maximizing risk. The name is mostly historical, as the first hedge funds tried to hedge against the downside risk of a bear market by shorting the market (mutual funds generally cannot enter into short positions as one of their primary goals). Today, hedge funds do not actually "hedge risk." In fact, because hedge fund managers make speculative investments, these funds tend to carry more risk than the overall market.

RELATED TERMS:
- Hedge
- Margin
- Short Sale

- Leverage
- Risk

HIGH-YIELD BOND

What Does *High-Yield Bond* **Mean?**

A bond that has a low credit rating and thus pays out a high rate of interest. Because they have a higher risk of default than investment-grade bonds, high-yield bonds pay a higher yield. In the two main credit rating agencies, high-yield bonds carry a rating of BBB or lower from S&P and Baa or lower from Moody's. Bonds with ratings above these levels are considered investment-grade. Credit ratings can be as low as D (currently in default), and most bonds with C ratings or lower carry a high risk of default; to compensate for this risk, yields typically are very high. Also known as junk bonds.

Investopedia explains *High-Yield Bond*

The term "junk bonds" aside, high-yield bonds are widely held by investors worldwide, although most participate through the use of mutual funds or exchange-traded funds. The yield spread between investment-grade and high-yield bonds fluctuates over time, depending on the state of the economy, as well as company- and sector-specific events. Generally, investors in high-yield bonds can expect a yield that is at least 150 to 300 basis points higher than the yield on an investment-grade bond. Mutual funds provide a good way to gain exposure without the undue risk of investing in only one issuer's junk bonds.

RELATED TERMS:
- Basis Point
- Interest Rate
- Junk Bond

- Coupon
- Investment Grade

HISTORICAL COST

What Does *Historical Cost* **Mean?**

A measure of value used in accounting in which the price of an asset on the balance sheet is based on its nominal or original cost when it was acquired by the company. The historical-cost method is used for assets in the United States under generally accepted accounting principles (GAAP).

 Investopedia explains *Historical Cost*
Based on the historical-cost principle, under U.S. GAAP, most assets held on the balance sheet are to be recorded at their historical cost even if they have changed significantly in value over time. For example, say the main headquarters of a company, which includes the land and building, was bought for $100,000 in 1925, and its expected market value today is $20 million. The asset is still recorded on the balance sheet at $100,000. Not all assets are held at historical cost. For example, marketable securities are held at market value on the balance sheet.

RELATED TERMS
- *Accrual Accounting*
- *Balance Sheet*
- *Dollar-Cost Averaging*
- *First In, First Out—FIFO*
- *Generally Accepted Accounting Principles—GAAP*

HOSTILE TAKEOVER

 What Does *Hostile Takeover* **Mean?**
A takeover attempt that is resisted strongly by the targeted company.

 Investopedia explains *Hostile Takeover*
Hostile takeovers are usually bad news for both companies, as the target company's employees' morale and attitude can turn quickly to animosity toward the acquiring firm.

RELATED TERMS:
- *Leverage Buyout*
- *Merger*
- *Mergers and Acquisitions—M&A*
- *Poison Pill*
- *Takeover*

HYPERINFLATION

What Does *Hyperinflation* **Mean?**
Extremely rapid or out-of-control inflation. There is no precise numerical definition of hyperinflation. Hyperinflation is a situation in which the price increases are so out of control that the concept of inflation is meaningless.

Investopedia explains *Hyperinflation*

When associated with depressions, hyperinflation often occurs when there is a large increase in the money supply that is not supported by gross domestic product (GDP) growth, resulting in an imbalance in the supply and demand for the money. Left unchecked, this causes prices to increase as the currency loses its value. When associated with wars, hyperinflation often occurs when there is a loss of confidence in the ability of a currency to maintain its value in the aftermath. Because of this, sellers demand a risk premium to accept the currency, and they do this by raising their prices. One of the most famous examples of hyperinflation occurred in Germany between January 1922 and November 1923. By some estimates, the average price level increased by a factor of 20 billion, doubling every 28 hours.

RELATED TERMS:
- *Behavioral Finance*
- *Deflation*
- *Stagflation*
- *Consumer Price Index—CPI*
- *Inflation*

copyright JackGuinan

"My stock in the cloning
company split again and again
and again and again and ..."

ILLIQUID

What Does *Illiquid* Mean?

The state of a security or another asset when it cannot be sold or exchanged easily for cash without a substantial loss in value. Illiquid assets also cannot be sold quickly because of a lack of ready and willing investors or speculators. The lack of ready buyers also leads to larger spreads between the ask price (from the seller) and the bid price (from a buyer) than would be found in an orderly market with daily trading activity.

Investopedia explains *Illiquid*

Illiquid assets include houses, cars, antiques, private company interests, and some types of debt instruments. On the other end of the spectrum, most listed securities traded on major exchanges, such as stocks, funds, bonds, and commodities, are very liquid and can be sold instantaneously during regular market hours at the fair market price. Illiquid securities carry higher risks than do liquid ones; this occurs during times of market turmoil when the ratio of buyers to sellers is out of balance. During these times, holders of illiquid securities may find themselves unable to unload them at all or unable to do so without losing a lot of money.

RELATED TERMS:
- Intrinsic Value
- Law of Supply
- Marketable Securities
- Law of Demand
- Liquidity

IMPLIED VOLATILITY (IV)

What Does *Implied Volatility* Mean?
The estimated volatility of the price of a security.

Investopedia explains *Implied Volatility*
In general, implied volatility increases when the market is bearish and decreases when the market is bullish. This is due to the common belief that bearish markets are more risky than bullish markets. In addition to known factors such as market price, interest rate, expiration date, and strike price, implied volatility is used in calculating an option's premium. IV can be derived from a model such as the Black Scholes Model. Implied volatility sometimes is referred to as vols.

RELATED TERMS:
- Beta
- Options
- Volatility
- Black Scholes Model
- Stock Option

IN THE MONEY

What Does *In the Money* Mean?
The state of a call option when its strike price is below the market price of the underlying asset. For put options, it is the state when the strike price is above the market price of the underlying asset.

Investopedia explains *In the Money*
In other words, this is when a stock option is worth money and the investor can turn around and sell or exercise it for a profit.

RELATED TERMS:
- Call Option
- Premium
- Strike Price
- Common Stock
- Put Option

INCOME STATEMENT

What Does *Income Statement* Mean?
A financial statement that measures a company's financial performance over a specific accounting period. Financial performance is assessed by summarizing how the business incurs its revenues and expenses through both operating and nonoperating activities. It also shows the net profit or loss incurred over a specific accounting period, typically a fiscal quarter or year. Also referred to as the profit and loss statement or statement of revenue and expense.

Investopedia explains *Income Statement*
The income statement is one of the three major financial statements. The other two are the balance sheet and the statement of cash flows. The income statement is divided into two parts: the operating and nonoperating sections. The portion of the income statement that deals with operating items is interesting to investors and analysts alike because this section discloses information about revenues and expenses that are a direct result of the regular business operations. For example, if a business creates sports equipment, the operating items section will talk about the revenues and expenses involved in the production of sports equipment. The nonoperating items section discloses revenue and expense information about activities that are not tied directly to a company's regular operations. For example, if the sport equipment company sold a factory and some old plant equipment, this information would be in the nonoperating items section.

RELATED TERMS:
- *Accrual Accounting*
- *Generally Accepted Accounting Principles—GAAP*
- *Net Income*   • *Profit Margin*
- *Revenue*

INDEX

What Does *Index* Mean?
A statistical measure of change in an economy or a securities market. In the case of financial markets, an index is a portfolio of securities that represent a particular market or a portion of a market. Each index has its own calculation methodology and usually is expressed in terms of a change from a base value. Thus, the percentage change

is more important than the actual numeric value. Some stock and bond market indexes are used to construct index mutual funds and exchange-traded funds (ETFs) whose portfolios mirror the components of the index.

 Investopedia explains *Index*
The Standard & Poor's 500 Index is one of the world's best known indexes and is the most commonly used benchmark for the overall stock market. Other prominent indexes include the DJ Wilshire 5000 (total stock market), the MSCI EAFE (foreign stocks in Europe, Australasia, and the Far East), and the Lehman Aggregate Bond Index (total bond market). Technically, one cannot buy an index, but one can purchase index mutual funds and exchange-traded funds that allow investors to invest in securities representing broad market indexes.

RELATED TERMS:
- *Benchmark*
- *Dow Jones Industrial Average—DJIA*
- *Index Fund*　　　　　　　　　　・ *Index Futures*
- *Standard & Poor's 500 Index—S&P 500*

INDEX FUND

What Does *Index Fund* **Mean?**
A type of mutual fund with a portfolio constructed to match or track the components of a market index such as the Standard & Poor's 500 Index (S&P 500). An index mutual fund is said to provide broad market exposure, low operating expenses, and low portfolio turnover.

Investopedia explains *Index Fund*
Indexing is a passive form of fund management that some argue outperforms most actively managed mutual funds. The most popular index funds track the S&P 500, but a number of other indexes, including the Russell 2000 (small companies), the DJ Wilshire 5000 (total stock market), the MSCI EAFE (foreign stocks in Europe, Australasia, and the Far East), and the Lehman Aggregate Bond Index (total bond market), are followed widely by investors. Investing in an index fund is a form of passive investing. The primary advantage is the lower management expense ratio. Many actively managed mutual funds fail to beat broad market indexes because their returns are reduced by higher expense ratios.

RELATED TERMS:
- *Benchmark*
- *MSCI—Emerging Markets Index*
- *Standard & Poor's 500 Index—S&P 500*
- *Expense Ratio*
- *Mutual Fund*

INDEX FUTURES

What Does *Index Futures* Mean?
This term refers to a futures contract on a stock or financial index. For each index there may be a different multiple for determining the price of the futures contract.

Investopedia explains *Index Futures*
As an example, the S&P 500 Index is one of the most widely traded index futures contracts in the United States. Stock portfolio managers who want to hedge risk over a certain period of time often use S&P 500 futures for that purpose. By shorting these contracts, stock portfolio managers can protect themselves from the downside price risk of the broader market. However, there is a trade-off: When this hedging strategy is used, the manager's portfolio will not participate in any gains on the index; instead, the portfolio will lock in gains equivalent to the risk-free rate of interest. Alternatively, stock portfolio managers can use index futures to increase their exposure to movements in a particular index, essentially leveraging their portfolios.

RELATED TERMS:
- *Derivative*
- *Futures Contract*
- *Index*
- *Futures*
- *Hedge*

INDIVIDUAL RETIREMENT ACCOUNT (IRA)

What Does *Individual Retirement Account (IRA)* Mean?
An investing tool used by individuals to save for retirement. There are several types of IRAs: Traditional IRAs, Roth IRAs, SIMPLE IRAs, and SEP IRAs. Traditional and Roth IRAs are established by individuals, who are allowed to contribute 100% of compensation (self-employment income for sole proprietors and partners) up to a set maximum dollar amount. Contributions to the Traditional IRA may be tax-deductible, depending on the taxpayer's income, tax filing

status, and coverage by an employer-sponsored retirement plan. Roth IRA contributions are not tax-deductible. SEPs and SIMPLEs are retirement plans established by employers. Individual participant contributions are made to SEP IRAs and SIMPLE IRAs. Also referred to as individual retirement arrangements.

Investopedia explains *Individual Retirement Account (IRA)*
With the exception of Roth IRAs, in which eligible distributions are tax-free, all IRA withdrawals are taxed as income. Because income is likely to be lower during retirement, the tax rate may be lower at that time. In addition to the potential tax savings from deductible contributions and nontaxable growth, IRAs can be very valuable tax management tools for individuals, and depending on income, an individual may be able to fit into a lower tax bracket with tax-deductible contributions during his or her working years and still enjoy a low tax bracket during retirement.

RELATED TERMS:
- 401(k) Plan
- Roth IRA
- Traditional IRA
- Mutual Fund
- Tax Deferred

INELASTIC

What Does *Inelastic* **Mean?**
An economic term used to describe the situation in which the supply and demand for a good or service are not affected when the price of that good or service changes.

Investopedia explains *Inelastic*
When a price change has no effect on the supply and demand of a good or service, that good or service is considered perfectly inelastic. An example of perfectly inelastic demand would be a lifesaving drug that people will pay any price to obtain. If the price of the drug increased dramatically, the quantity demanded would remain the same.

RELATED TERMS:
- Bear Market
- Demand
- Inventory
- Bull Market
- Inflation

INFLATION

What Does *Inflation* Mean?
The rate at which the general level of prices for goods and services rises and, subsequently, purchasing power falls; investors can track the direction of inflation by monitoring the Consumer Price Index (CPI).

Investopedia explains *Inflation*
As inflation rises, every dollar will buy a smaller percentage of a good. For example, if the inflation rate is 2%, a $1 pack of gum will cost $1.02 in a year. Most countries' central banks try to sustain an inflation rate of 2 to 3%.

RELATED TERMS:
- Consumer Price Index—CPI
- Deflation
- Hyperinflation
- Stagflation
- Treasury Inflation Protected Securities (TIPS)

INITIAL PUBLIC OFFERING (IPO)

What Does *Initial Public Offering (IPO)* Mean?
The initial selling of stock by a company to the public to raise capital; IPOs often are issued by smaller, younger companies seeking the capital to expand but also can be issued by large privately owned companies looking to become publicly traded. In an IPO, the issuer obtains the assistance of an underwriting firm, which helps it determine what type of security to issue (common or preferred), the best offering price, and the time to bring it to market. Also referred to as a public offering.

Investopedia explains *Initial Public Offering (IPO)*
An IPO can be a risky investment. For the individual investor, it is difficult to predict what the stock will do on its initial day of trading or in the future because there is often little historical performance data with which to analyze the company. Also, many IPOs are issued by companies going through a transitory growth period and are subject to additional uncertainty about their future values.

RELATED TERMS:
- Equity
- Investment Bank
- Private Equity
- Stock
- Underwriter

INTANGIBLE ASSET

What Does *Intangible Asset* Mean?

A company's nonphysical assets, such as intellectual property (items such as patents, trademarks, copyrights, and business methodologies), goodwill, and brand recognition; an intangible asset can be classified as either indefinite or definite. A company's brand name is considered an indefinite asset, as it stays with the company as long as the company continues operations. However, if a company entered into a legal agreement to operate under another company's patent, with no plans for extending the agreement, it would have a limited life and would be classified as a definite asset.

Investopedia explains *Intangible Asset*

Although intangible assets do not have the obvious physical value of a factory or equipment, they can prove very valuable and can be critical to a company's long-term success. For example, a company such as Coca-Cola would not be nearly as successful without the high value obtained through its brand-name recognition. Although brand recognition is not a tangible asset that one can see or touch, its positive effects on bottom-line profits can prove extremely valuable to firms such as Coca-Cola, whose brand strength drives global sales year after year.

RELATED TERMS:
- Asset
- Balance Sheet
- Generally Accepted Accounting Principles—GAAP
- Goodwill
- Tangible Asset

INTERBANK RATE

What Does *Interbank Rate* Mean?

The rate of interest charged on short-term loans made between banks. Banks borrow and lend money in the interbank market to manage liquidity and meet their regulatory requirements. The interest rate charged depends on the availability of money in the market, prevailing rates, and the specific terms of the contract, such as term length.

Investopedia explains *Interbank Rate*

Banks are required to hold an adequate amount of liquid assets on reserve, such as cash, to manage potential withdrawals by their clients. If a bank cannot meet these liquidity requirements, it has to borrow money, and the interbank market helps cover the shortfall.

Some banks, in contrast, have excess liquid assets above and beyond the liquidity requirements. These banks will lend money in the interbank market, receiving interest on the assets. There is a wide range of published interbank rates, including the LIBOR, which is set daily, based on the average rates on loans made within the London interbank market.

RELATED TERMS:
- Euro LIBOR
- London Interbank Offered Rate—LIBOR
- Federal Funds Rate
- Singapore Interbank Offered Rate—SIBOR
- Interest Rate

INTEREST COVERAGE RATIO

What Does *Interest Coverage Ratio* Mean?
A ratio used to determine how easily a company can pay interest on outstanding debt. The interest coverage ratio is calculated by dividing a company's earnings before interest and taxes (EBIT) for one period by the company's interest expenses for the same period. It is calculated as follows:

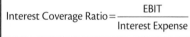

$$\text{Interest Coverage Ratio} = \frac{\text{EBIT}}{\text{Interest Expense}}$$

Investopedia explains *Interest Coverage Ratio*
The lower the ratio is, the more a company is burdened by its debt expense. When a company's interest coverage ratio is 1.5 or less, its ability to meet its interest expenses may be questionable. An interest coverage ratio below 1 indicates that a company is not generating sufficient revenues to satisfy interest expenses and should raise a red flag for investors.

RELATED TERMS:
- Cash and Cash Equivalents—CCE
- Fixed-Income Security
- Junk Bond
- Debt
- Interest Rate

INTEREST RATE

What Does *Interest Rate* Mean?
The rate charged by lenders, expressed as a percentage of the principal, to borrowers for the use of assets. Interest rates typically are

quoted on an annualized basis known as the annual percentage rate (APR). The assets borrowed could include cash, consumer goods, and large assets such as a vehicle or building. Interest is essentially a rental, or leasing charge, to the borrower for the asset's use. In the case of a large asset such as a vehicle or building, the interest rate sometimes is called the lease rate. When one opens a bank account, one basically is lending the bank his or her money. In return, the investor charges the bank interest, which is what the bank pays the investor.

(I) **Investopedia explains *Interest Rate***
Interest is charged by lenders as compensation for the loss of an asset's use. In the case of lending money, the lender could have invested the funds instead of lending them out. When lending a large asset, the lender may forgo income from the asset that would have resulted if the investor had decided to use it himself or herself. Using the simple interest formula—Simple Interest = P (principal) × I (annual interest rate) × N (years)—borrowing $1,000 at a 6% annual interest rate for 8 months means that the borrower would owe $40 in interest (1000 × 6% × 8/12). Using the compound interest formula—Compound Interest = P (principal) × [(1 + I(interest rate)^N (months)) − 1]—borrowing $1,000 at a 6% annual interest rate for 8 months means that the borrower would owe $40.70. Compounded interest nets higher amounts because interest has been charged monthly on the principal plus accrued interest from the previous months. For shorter time frames, the calculation is similar for both methods. As the lending time increases, though, the disparity between the two types of interest calculations grows.

Related Terms:
- Bond
- Interest Rate Swap
- Premium
- Coupon
- Money Market Account

INTEREST RATE SWAP

What Does *Interest Rate Swap* Mean?
An agreement between two parties (known as counterparties) in which one stream of future interest payments is exchanged for another stream, based on a specified principal amount. Interest rate swaps often involve exchanging a fixed payment for a floating payment, which is linked to an interest rate (most often the LIBOR).

A company typically uses interest rate swaps to limit or manage its exposure to fluctuations in interest rates or to obtain a marginally lower interest rate than it would have been able to get without the swap.

 Investopedia explains *Interest Rate Swap*
Interest rate swaps are the exchange of one set of cash flows (based on interest rate specifications) for another. Because they trade over the counter (OTC), they are really contracts set up between two or more parties and thus can be customized in a number of ways. Generally, swaps are sought by firms that desire a type of interest rate structure that another firm can provide less expensively. For example, let's say Cory's Tequila Company (CTC) is seeking to lend funds at a fixed interest rate, but Tom's Sports Inc. (TSI) has access to marginally cheaper fixed-rate funds. Tom's Sports can issue debt to investors at its low fixed rate and then trade the fixed-rate cash flow obligations to CTC for floating-rate obligations issued by TSI. Even though TSI may have a higher floating rate than CTC, by swapping the interest structures it is best able to obtain inexpensively, the combined costs are decreased, a benefit that can be shared by both parties.

RELATED TERMS:
- *Bond*
- *Interest Rate*
- *Swap*
- *Debt*
- *Notional Value*

INTERNAL RATE OF RETURN (IRR)

 What Does *Internal Rate of Return* **Mean?**
The discount rate often used in capital budgeting that makes the net present value of all cash flows from a particular project equal to zero. Generally, the higher a project's internal rate of return is, the more desirable it is to undertake. Thus, IRR can be used to rank potential projects. Assuming all factors are equal, the project with the highest IRR probably would be considered the best and would be undertaken first. IRR sometimes is referred to as the economic rate of return (ERR).

 Investopedia explains *Internal Rate of Return*
One can think of IRR as the rate of growth a project is expected to generate. Although the actual result may differ from the estimated IRR rate, a project with a substantially higher IRR value than other available options still will provide a much better chance for strong

growth. IRRs also can be compared against prevailing rates of return in the securities market. If a firm cannot find any projects with IRRs greater than the returns that can be generated in the financial markets, it may choose to invest its retained earnings in the market.

RELATED TERMS:
- Discount Rate
- Interest Rate
- Modified Internal Rate of Return—MIRR
- Present Value Interest Factor—PVIF
- Discounted Cash Flow—DCF

INTRINSIC VALUE

What Does *Intrinsic Value* Mean?
(1) The actual value of a company or an asset, based on an underlying perception of its true value, including all aspects of the business, in terms of both tangible and intangible factors. This value may differ from the current market value. Value investors use a variety of analytical techniques to estimate the intrinsic value of securities in hopes of finding investments in which the true value of the investment exceeds its current market value. (2) For call options, the difference between the underlying stock's price and the strike price. For put options, the difference between the strike price and the underlying stock's price. In the case of both puts and calls, if the respective difference is negative, the intrinsic value is stated as zero.

Investopedia explains *Intrinsic Value*
(1) For example, value investors that use fundamental analysis look at both qualitative (business model, governance, target market factors, etc.) and quantitative (ratios, financial statement analysis, etc.) aspects of a business to see if that business is currently out of favor with the market and potentially worth much more than its current valuation. (2) An option's intrinsic value is the in-the-money portion of that option's premium. For example, if a call option's strike price is $15 and the underlying stock's market price is at $25, the intrinsic value of the call option is $10. An option is usually never worth less than what an option holder can receive if the option is exercised.

RELATED TERMS:
- Book Value
- Future Value
- Market Value
- Fundamental Analysis
- In the Money

INVENTORY

What Does *Inventory* Mean?

The raw materials, work-in-process goods, or completely finished goods that are currently or soon will be available for sale. Inventory represents one of the most important assets most businesses possess; inventory turnover is one of the primary sources of revenue generation and subsequent earnings for the company's shareholders.

Investopedia explains *Inventory*

Possessing a high amount of inventory for long periods is not usually good for a business because it carries inventory storage, obsolescence, and spoilage costs. However, possessing too little inventory is not good either, because the business runs the risk of not filling customers' orders and losing potential sales and thus market share as well. Inventory management techniques such as a just-in-time inventory system can help minimize inventory costs because goods are created or received as inventory only when needed.

RELATED TERMS:
- Accounts Payable—AP
- Cash Conversion Cycle—CCC
- Inventory Turnover
- Accounts Receivable—AR
- First In, First Out—FIFO

INVENTORY TURNOVER

What Does *Inventory Turnover* Mean?

A ratio showing how many times a company's inventory is sold and replaced over a certain period. It is calculated as follows:

Generally calculated as:

$$= \frac{\text{Sales}}{\text{Inventory}}$$

However, it may also be calculated as:

$$= \frac{\text{Cost of Goods Sold}}{\text{Average Inventory}}$$

Investopedia explains *Inventory Turnover*

Although the first calculation is used more frequently, COGS (cost of goods sold) may be substituted because sales are recorded at market value, whereas inventories usually are recorded at cost. Also, average inventory may be used instead of ending inventory to minimize seasonal factors. A low turnover ratio implies poor sales and therefore excess inventory. A high ratio implies either strong sales or ineffective buying. High inventory levels are unhealthy because they represent an investment with a rate of return of zero. This also opens up the company to trouble if prices begin to fall.

RELATED TERMS:
- *Accrual Accounting*
- *Cost of Goods Sold—COGS*
- *Inventory*
- *Asset Turnover*
- *Gross Profit Margin*

INVERTED YIELD CURVE

What Does *Inverted Yield Curve* Mean?

An interest rate environment in which long-term debt instruments have lower yields than do short-term debt instruments of the same credit quality. This type of yield curve is the rarest of the three main curve types and is considered a predictor of economic recession.

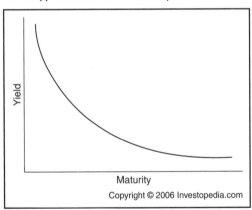

Copyright © 2006 Investopedia.com

Partial inversion occurs when only some of the short-term Treasuries (5 or 10 years) have higher yields than the 30-year Treasuries; an inverted yield curve sometimes is referred to as a negative yield curve.

Investopedia explains *Inverted Yield Curve*

Historically, inversions of the yield curve have preceded many U.S. recessions. Because of this historical correlation, the yield curve often is seen as an accurate indicator of the turning points of the business cycle. An inverse yield curve predicts lower interest rates in the future as longer-term bonds are being demanded, sending the yields down.

RELATED TERMS:
- Interest Rate
- Treasury Bond—T-Bond
- Yield Curve
- Treasury Bill—T-Bill
- Treasury Note

INVESTMENT BANK (IB)

What Does *Investment Bank (IB)* Mean?
A financial intermediary that performs a variety of investment services, including underwriting, acting as an intermediary between an issuer of securities and the investing public, facilitating mergers and other corporate reorganizations and also acting as a broker for institutional clients.

Investopedia explains *Investment Bank (IB)*
The role of an investment bank begins with preunderwriting counseling and continues after the distribution of securities in the form of advice.

RELATED TERMS:
- Capital
- Private Equity
- Underwriting
- Initial Public Offering—IPO
- Syndicate

INVESTMENT GRADE

What Does *Investment Grade* Mean?
A rating that is assigned to a municipal or corporate bond that indicates its creditworthiness and likelihood of default. Bond rating firms such as Standard & Poor's, use different designations consisting of the uppercase and lowercase letters A and B to identify a bond's credit quality rating. AAA and AA (high credit quality) and A and BBB (medium credit quality) are considered investment grade. Credit ratings for bonds below these designations (BB, B, CCC, etc.) are considered low credit quality and thus are referred to commonly as junk bonds.

Investopedia explains *Investment Grade*
Investors should note that government bonds, or Treasuries, are not subject to credit quality ratings because they are considered to have the very highest credit quality. In the case of municipal and

corporate bond funds, a fund prospectus and independent investment research reports will report an "average credit quality" for a fund's portfolio as a whole. Investors should be aware that an agency downgrade of a company's bonds from BBB to BB reclassifies the company's debt from investment-grade to junk status with just a one-step drop in quality. The repercussions of such an event can be highly problematic for the issuer and also adversely affect bond prices for investors. Safety-conscious fund investors should pay attention to a bond fund's portfolio credit quality breakdown.

RELATED TERMS:
- Bond
- Credit Rating
- Junk Bond
- Bond Rating
- Fundamental Analysis

IRREVOCABLE TRUST

 What Does *Irrevocable Trust* Mean?
A trust that cannot be modified or terminated without the permission of the beneficiary; the grantor, having transferred assets into the trust, effectively relinquishes all rights of ownership to the assets and the trust. This is the opposite of a revocable trust, which allows the grantor to modify the trust.

 Investopedia explains *Irrevocable Trust*
The main reason for setting up an irrevocable trust is estate and tax considerations. The benefit of this type of trust for estate assets is that it removes all incidents of ownership, effectively removing the trust's assets from the grantor's taxable estate. The grantor also is relieved of the tax liability on the income generated by the assets. Although the tax rules vary among jurisdictions, in most cases the grantor cannot receive those benefits if he or she is the trustee of the trust. The assets held in the trust can include but are not limited to a business, investment assets, cash, and life insurance policies.

RELATED TERMS:
- Annuity
- Mutual Fund
- Investment Bank
- Money Market Account
- Private Equity

copyright JackGuinan

"Honey, good news, I don't
see any signs of insider trading."

JANUARY BAROMETER

What Does *January Barometer* Mean?

A theory stating that the movement of the S&P 500 during the month
of January sets the direction of the stock market for the year (as measured by the S&P 500). In other words, if the S&P 500 was up at the
end of January compared with the beginning of the month, propo-
nents would expect the stock market to rise during the rest of the year.

Investopedia explains *January Barometer*

If an investor believes in the ability of the January barometer to
predict the equity market's performance, he or she will invest in
the market only in the years when the barometer predicts that
the market will rise and stay out of the market when it forecasts a
market pullback. Although the January barometer has been seen to
produce better than 50% accuracy rates during 20-year periods, it is
difficult to produce excess returns by using it because the improved
performance resulting from staying out of the market during bad
times can be more than offset by larger losses incurred when the
barometer incorrectly predicts a bull market.

RELATED TERMS:
- *Bull Market*
- *Index*
- *Standard & Poor's 500 Index—S&P 500*
- *Business Cycle*
- *New York Stock Exchange—NYSE*

JUMBO LOAN

What Does *Jumbo Loan* Mean?

A mortgage with a loan amount that exceeds the conforming loan limits set by the Office of Federal Housing Enterprise Oversight (OFHEO) and therefore is not eligible to be purchased, guaranteed, or securitized by Fannie Mae or Freddie Mac. OFHEO sets the conforming loan limit size on an annual basis. Also referred to as a jumbo mortgage.

Investopedia explains *Jumbo Loan*

Jumbo loans often are securitized by institutions other than Fannie Mae and Freddie Mac. These securities carry more credit risk than do those issued by Fannie Mae or Freddie Mac and therefore trade at a yield premium that translates into slightly higher interest rates. However, in recent years the spread in interest rates between jumbo and conventional mortgages has been reduced.

RELATED TERMS:
- Debt
- Debt Financing
- Interest Rate
- Mortgage
- Real Estate Investment Trust—REIT

JUNIOR SECURITY

What Does *Junior Security* Mean?

A security that ranks lower than other securities in regard to the owner's claims on assets and income if the issuer becomes insolvent.

Investopedia explains *Junior Security*

When bankruptcy occurs, holders of both preferred shares and debt securities have first claim on the remaining assets. Only after preferred shareholders have been paid back are the remaining assets (if any) divided among common shareholders.

RELATED TERMS:
- Bankruptcy
- Bond
- Common Stock
- Preferred Stock
- Subordinated Debt

JUNK BOND

What Does *Junk Bond* Mean?
A bond rated BB or lower because of its high risk of default. Also known as a high-yield bond or speculative bond. This type of bond is considered less than investment grade.

Investopedia explains *Junk Bond*
These bonds usually are purchased for speculative purposes. Junk bonds typically offer interest rates three to four percentage points higher than those on safer government issues. The higher interest rate is meant to compensate investors for the higher risks associated with the issuer.

RELATED TERMS:
- *Bond Rating*
- *Investment Grade*
- *Yield*
- *Credit Rating*
- *Risk*

copyright JackGuinan

"My portfolio is well balanced, it's my financial adviser who's unstable."

"The good news is, we started investing for college when you were just babies. The bad news, we had no idea what we were doing!"

KEOGH PLAN

What Does *Keogh Plan* Mean?

A tax-deferred pension plan available to self-employed individuals or unincorporated businesses for retirement purposes. A Keogh plan can be set up as either a defined-benefit or a defined-contribution plan, although most are defined-contribution plans. Contributions are generally tax-deductible. Keogh plan types include money-purchase plans (used by high-income earners), defined-benefit plans (which have high annual minimums), and profit-sharing plans (which offer annual flexibility based on profits). Also known as HR(10) plans, Keogh plans can invest in the same set of securities as 401(k)s and IRAs, including stocks, bonds, certificates of deposit, and annuities.

Investopedia explains *Keogh Plan*

Keogh plans were established through legislation by Congress in 1962 and were spearheaded by Eugene Keogh. As with other qualified retirement accounts, funds can be accessed as early as age 59.5 and withdrawals must begin by age 70.5. Keoghs are known to have more administrative burdens and higher upkeep costs than Simplified Employee Pension (SEP) plans, but the contribution limits are higher, making Keoghs a popular option for many business owners and proprietors.

RELATED TERMS:
- *401(k) Plan*
- *Defined-Contribution Plan*
- *Individual Retirement Account—IRA*
- *Defined-Benefit Plan*
- *Qualified Retirement Plan*

KNOCK-IN OPTION

What Does *Knock-In Option* Mean?
A latent option contract that begins to function as a normal option ("knocks in") only after a certain price level is reached before expiration.

Investopedia explains *Knock-In Option*
Technically, this type of contract is not an option until a certain price is met, and so if the price is never reached, it is as if the contract never existed. Knock-ins are a type of barrier option that may be either a down-and-in option or an up-and-in option.

RELATED TERMS:
- *Derivative*
- *Plain Vanilla*
- *Triple Witching*
- *Expiration Date*
- *Stock Option*

"Your broker may have research, low fees and experience, but does he have one of these?!"

LARGE CAP (BIG CAP)

What Does *Large Cap (Big Cap)* Mean?

A term used by the investment community to describe companies with a market capitalization value more than $10 billion. Large cap is an abbreviation of the term "large market capitalization." Market capitalization is calculated by multiplying the number of a company's shares outstanding by its stock price per share.

Investopedia explains *Large Cap (Big Cap)*

Large cap companies are the big Kahunas of the financial world. Examples include Walmart, Microsoft, and Exxon. One should keep in mind that the dollar amounts used for the classifications large cap, mid cap, and small cap are only approximations that change over time. Among market participants, their exact definitions can vary.

RELATED TERMS:
- Asset Allocation
- Mid Cap
- Standard & Poor's 500 Index—S&P 500
- Small Cap
- Market Capitalization

LAW OF DEMAND

What Does *Law of Demand* Mean?

A microeconomic law that states that all things being equal, as the price of a good or service increases, consumer demand for that good or service will decrease and vice versa.

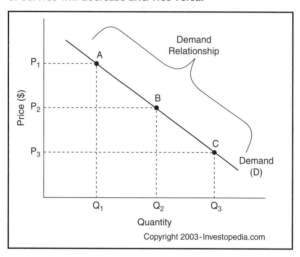

Copyright 2003-Investopedia.com

Investopedia explains *Law of Demand*

This law summarizes the effect price changes have on consumer behavior. For example, a consumer will purchase more pizzas if the price of pizza falls. The opposite is true if the price of pizza rises.

RELATED TERMS:
- Consumer Price Index—CPI
- Law of Supply
- Market Economy
- Demand
- Macroeconomics

LAW OF DIMINISHING MARGINAL UTILITY

What Does *Law of Diminishing Marginal Utility* Mean?

A law of economics that states that as a person increases consumption of a product while keeping consumption of other products constant, there is a decline in the marginal utility that person derives from consuming each additional unit of that product.

Investopedia explains *Law of Diminishing Marginal Utility*
This is the premise on which buffet-style restaurants operate. They entice customers with "all you can eat," knowing full well that each additional plate of food provides less utility than did the one before it. Despite the hook, most people will eat only until the utility they derive from additional food is slightly lower than the original utility. For example, you go to a buffet, and the first plate of food you eat is very good. On a scale of 10, you would give it a 10. Now your hunger has been tamed somewhat, but you get another full plate of food. Since you are not as hungry, your enjoyment rates at a 7 at best. Most people will stop before their utility drops even more, but say you go back to eat a third full plate of food and your utility drops to 3. If you kept eating, you eventually will reach a point at which eating makes you sick, providing dissatisfaction, or disutility.

RELATED TERMS:
- *Efficiency Ratio*
- *Market Economy*
- *Technical Analysis*
- *Fundamental Analysis*
- *Quantitative Analysis*

LAW OF SUPPLY

 What Does *Law of Supply* **Mean?**
A microeconomic law that states that all things being equal, as the price of a good or service increases, the quantity of that good or service offered by suppliers increases and vice versa.

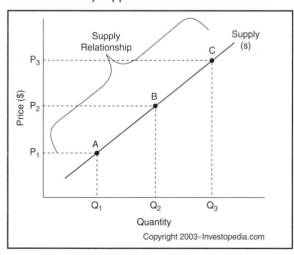

Copyright 2003-Investopedia.com

Investopedia explains *Law of Supply*
As the price of a good increases, suppliers will attempt to maximize profits by increasing the quantity of the product sold.

RELATED TERMS:
- *Economies of Scale*
- *Macroeconomics*
- *Technical Analysis*
- *Law of Demand*
- *Quantitative Analysis*

LEHMAN AGGREGATE BOND INDEX

 What Does *Lehman Aggregate Bond Index* **Mean?**
An index used by bond funds as a benchmark to measure their relative performance. The index includes government securities, mortgage-backed securities, asset-backed securities, and corporate securities. The maturities of the bonds in the index are more than one year.

 Investopedia explains *Lehman Aggregate Bond Index*
The index, which is constructed by Lehman Brothers, is considered by investors to be the best total market bond tracking index. Along with the aggregate index, Lehman has bond indexes tailored to European and Asian investors. This index cannot be purchased, but it is tracked by bond index funds; there are also exchange-traded funds (ETFs) that track the index. The Lehman Aggregate Bond Index trades on an exchange just like a stock.

RELATED TERMS:
- *Bond*
- *Index*
- *Mortgage-Backed Securities—MBS*
- *Corporate Bond*
- *Index Fund*

LETTER OF CREDIT

 What Does *Letter of Credit* **Mean?**
A letter from a bank guaranteeing that a buyer's payment to a seller will be received on time and for the correct amount. If the buyer is unable to make a payment on the purchase, the bank will be required to cover the full or remaining amount of the purchase.

 Investopedia explains *Letter of Credit*
Letters of credit often are used in international transactions to ensure that payment will be received. Because of the nature of

international dealings, including factors such as distance, differing laws in different countries, and the difficulty of knowing each party personally, the use of letters of credit has become a very important aspect of international trade. The bank also acts on behalf of the buyer (holder of a letter of credit) by ensuring that the supplier will not be paid until the bank receives a confirmation that the goods have been shipped.

RELATED TERMS:
- *Accounts Receivable—AR*
- *Accounts Payable—AP*
- *Cash and Cash Equivalents—CCE*
- *Debt*
- *Money Market*

LEVERAGE

What Does *Leverage* Mean?
(1) The use of various financial instruments or borrowed capital, such as margin, to increase the potential return of an investment. (2) The amount of debt used to finance a firm's assets. A firm with significantly more debt than equity is considered highly leveraged.

Investopedia explains *Leverage*
(1) Leverage can be created through options, futures, margin, and other financial instruments. For example, say you have $1,000 to invest. This amount could be invested in 10 shares of Microsoft stock, or you could increase your leverage by buying five option contracts worth $1,000. You then would control 500 shares instead of 10. (2) Most companies use debt to finance operations. By doing so, a company increases its leverage because it can invest in business operations without increasing its equity. For example, a company started with an investment of $5 million from investors has equity of $5 million; this is the money the company uses to operate. If the company uses debt financing by borrowing $20 million, the company now has $25 million to invest in business operations and more opportunity to increase value for shareholders. Leverage helps both the investor and the firm invest and operate. However, it comes with greater risk. If an investor uses leverage to make an investment and the investment moves against the investor, his or her loss is much greater than it would have been if the investment had been made with cash; leverage magnifies both gains and losses. In the business world, a company can use leverage to try to generate shareholder

wealth, but if it fails to do so, the interest expense and credit risk of default can destroy shareholder value.

RELATED TERMS:
- Debt Ratio
- Leveraged Buyout—LBO
- Operating Leverage
- Deleverage
- Margin

LEVERAGE RATIO

What Does *Leverage Ratio* Mean?
(1) Any ratio used to calculate the financial leverage of a company to get an idea of that company's methods of financing or measure its ability to meet its financial obligations. There are several ratios, but the main factors evaluated by a ratio include debt, equity, assets, and interest expenses. (2) A ratio used to measure a company's mix of operating costs that yields an approximation of how changes in output will affect operating income. Fixed costs and variable costs are the two types of operating costs; depending on the company and the industry, the mix will differ.

Investopedia explains *Leverage Ratio*
(1) The best-known financial leverage ratio is the debt-to-equity ratio. For example, if a company has $10 million in debt and $20 million in equity, it has a debt-to-equity ratio of 0.5 ($10 million/$20 million). (2) Companies with high fixed costs, after reaching the breakeven point, see a greater increase in operating revenue when output is increased compared with companies with high variable costs. The reason for this is that the costs already have been incurred, and so every sale above breakeven transfers to the operating income. In contrast, a company with high variable costs sees little increase in operating income with additional output, because costs continue to rise as outputs rise. The degree of operating leverage is the ratio used to calculate this mix and its effects on operating income.

RELATED TERMS:
- Debt Financing
- Deleverage
- Operating Leverage
- Debt Ratio
- Leverage

LEVERAGED BUYOUT (LBO)

What Does *Leveraged Buyout (LBO)* Mean?
The acquisition of another company by using a significant amount of debt (bonds or loans) to meet the cost of the acquisition. Often, the assets of the company being acquired are used as collateral for the loans in addition to the assets of the acquiring company. The purpose of leveraged buyouts is to allow companies to make large acquisitions without having to commit a lot of capital.

Investopedia explains *Leveraged Buyout (LBO)*
In an LBO, there is usually a ratio of 90% debt to 10% equity. Because of this high debt/equity ratio, the bonds usually are not investment grade and are referred to as junk bonds. Leveraged buyouts have had a notorious history, especially in the 1980s, when several prominent buyouts led to the eventual bankruptcy of the acquired companies. This was due mainly to the fact that the leverage ratio was nearly 100% and the interest payments were so large that the company's operating cash flows were unable to meet the obligation. Sometimes a company's success (in the form of assets on the balance sheet) can be used against it as collateral by a hostile company that acquires it. For this reason, some regard LBOs as an especially ruthless, predatory tactic.

RELATED TERMS:
- *Debt Financing*
- *Leveraged Loan*
- *Takeover*
- *Leverage*
- *Merger*

LEVERAGED LOAN

What Does *Leveraged Loan* Mean?
Leveraged loans are loans extended to companies or individuals that already have considerable amounts of debt. Lenders consider that these loans carry a higher risk of default, and as a result, a leveraged loan is more costly to the borrower in the form of the need to pay higher interest rates.

Investopedia explains *Leveraged Loan*
Leveraged loans for companies or individuals with debt tend to have higher interest rates than do typical loans. These rates reflect the higher level of risk involved in issuing the loan. In business, leveraged loans often are used in leveraged buyouts (LBOs) of other companies.

RELATED TERMS:
- Debt
- Leverage
- Margin
- Debt Financing
- Leveraged Buyout—LBO

LIABILITY

What Does *Liability* Mean?
A company's legal debts or obligations that arise during the course of business operations. Liabilities are settled over time through the transfer of economic benefits, including money, goods, and services.

Investopedia explains *Liability*
Recorded on the balance sheet (right side), liabilities include loans, accounts payable, mortgages, deferred revenues, and accrued expenses. Liabilities are a vital aspect of a company's operations because they are used to finance operations and pay for large expansions. They also can make transactions between businesses more efficient. For example, the outstanding money that a company owes to its suppliers would be considered a liability. Outside of accounting and finance, this term refers to any money or service that is currently owed to another party. One form of liability, for example, would be the property taxes that a homeowner owes to the municipal government. Current liabilities are debts payable within one year, and long-term liabilities are debts payable over a longer period.

RELATED TERMS:
- Asset
- Balance Sheet
- Debt
- Accounts Payable—AP
- Current Liabilities

LIAR LOAN

What Does *Liar Loan* Mean?
Slang for any mortgage that is based on low documentation or no documentation. On certain low-documentation loan programs, such as stated income/stated asset (SISA) loans, income and assets are stated on the loan application. With other types, such as no income/no asset (NINA) loans, no income or assets are listed on the loan application form. These loan programs open the door for unethical behavior by unscrupulous borrowers and lenders. Also called predatory loans.

Investopedia explains *Liar Loan*
These loan programs are designed for borrowers who cannot produce income- or asset-verifying documents such as prior tax returns
or who have untraditional sources of income, such as tips, food
stamps, and welfare. These loans are called liar loans because the
SISA or NINA features open the door for abuse when borrowers or
their mortgage brokers overstate income and/or assets to qualify the
borrower for a larger mortgage. Liar loans fall into the Alt-A category
of mortgage lending. Alt-A lending depends heavily on a borrower's
credit score (FICO score) and the mortgage's loan-to-value ratio
(LTV) to determine the borrower's ability to repay the mortgage.

RELATED TERMS:
- Debt
- Mortgage
- Subprime Meltdown
- Interest Rate
- Subprime

LIMIT ORDER

 What Does *Limit Order* Mean?
A type of order placed with a broker specifying the intention to buy
or sell a stated number of shares at a specified price or better. Limit
orders also enable investors to limit the length of time an order can
be outstanding before being canceled. Limit orders are sometimes
referred to specifically as a buy limit order, or a sell limit order. A
limit order is the opposite of a market order.

 Investopedia explains *Limit Order*
Limit orders are beneficial because when the trade is executed, investors get the specified purchase or sell price or better. Limit orders
are suitable for low-volume or highly volatile stocks.

RELATED TERMS:
- Ask
- Market Order
- Stop-Limit Order
- Bid
- Stop Order

LIQUIDITY

 What Does *Liquidity* Mean?
(1) The degree to which an asset or security can be bought or sold in
the market without affecting its price. Liquidity is characterized by a

high level of trading activity. (2) The ability to convert an asset into cash quickly. Also known as marketability.

Investopedia explains *Liquidity*
(1) Sometimes it is safer to invest in liquid assets than in illiquid ones because liquid assets make it easier for an investor to get his or her money out of the investment more quickly. (2) Examples of assets that are easily converted into cash include blue-chip stocks and money market securities.

RELATED TERMS:
- *Illiquid*
- *Cash and Cash Equivalents—CCE*
- *Liquidity Ratios*
- *Volume*
- *Short Squeeze*

LIQUIDITY RATIOS

What Does *Liquidity Ratios* **Mean?**
A class of financial metrics used to help determine a company's ability to pay off its short-term debt obligations. Generally, the higher the value of the ratio is, the larger the margin of safety that the company possesses to cover short-term debts.

Investopedia explains *Liquidity Ratios*
Common liquidity ratios include the current ratio, the quick ratio, and the operating cash flow ratio. Different analysts consider different assets to be relevant in calculating liquidity. Some analysts calculate only the sum of cash and equivalents divided by current liabilities because they feel that they are the most liquid assets and therefore are the most likely to be used to cover short-term debts in an emergency. A company's ability to turn short-term assets into cash is of the utmost importance when creditors are seeking payment. Bankruptcy analysts and mortgage originators frequently use the liquidity ratios to determine whether a company will be able to continue as a going concern.

RELATED TERMS:
- *Acid-Test Ratio*
- *Cash and Cash Equivalents—CCE*
- *Current Ratio*
- *Operating Cash Flow Ratio*
- *Liquidity*

LISTED

What Does *Listed* Mean?

Securities that are included and traded on a particular exchange; exchanges have specific listing requirements that companies must meet to be listed and stay listed.

Investopedia explains *Listed*

Exchanges add listed securities on an ongoing basis. Occasionally companies that have not fulfilled all the necessary listing requirements become delisted for a period of time until they again meet the exchange's listing requirements. Generally, companies prefer to be listed on the major exchanges, such as the NYSE and Nasdaq, since these exchanges provide liquidity and visibility for a company's stock.

RELATED TERMS:
- Common Stock
- Nasdaq
- New York Stock Exchange—NYSE
- Stock Market
- Marketable Security

LOAD FUND

What Does *Load Fund* Mean?

A mutual fund that charges a sales commission. The fund investor pays the load, which goes toward compensating a sales intermediary (broker, financial planner, investment advisor, etc.) for his or her time and expertise in selecting an appropriate fund for the investor.

Investopedia explains *Load Fund*

The load is paid up front at the time of purchase (front-end load), when the shares are sold (back-end load), or as long as the fund is held by the investor (level-load). If a fund limits its load to no more than 0.25% (the maximum is 1%), it can call itself a no-load fund in its marketing literature. Front-end and back-end loads are not part of a mutual fund's operating expenses, but level-loads, called 12b-1 fees, are included. Data shows that the performance of load and no-load funds is similar.

RELATED TERMS:
- Breakpoint
- Mutual Fund
- No-Load Fund
- Front-End Load
- Net Asset Value—NAV

LONDON INTERBANK OFFERED RATE (LIBOR)

What Does *London Interbank Offered Rate (LIBOR)* Mean?
An interest rate at which banks borrow funds from other banks in the London interbank market; the LIBOR is fixed on a daily basis by the British Bankers' Association and derived from a filtered average of the world's most creditworthy banks' interbank deposit rates for larger loans with maturities between overnight and a full year.

Investopedia explains *London Interbank Offered Rate (LIBOR)*
The LIBOR is the world's most widely used benchmark for short-term interest rates. It is important because it is the rate at which the world's most preferred borrowers are able to borrow money. It is also the rate on which rates for less preferred borrowers are based. For example, a multinational corporation with a very good credit rating may be able to borrow money for one year at LIBOR plus four or five points. Countries that rely on the LIBOR for a reference rate include the United States, Canada, Switzerland, and the United Kingdom.

RELATED TERMS:
- Euro LIBOR
- Interbank Rate
- Singapore Interbank Offered Rate—SIBOR
- Swap
- Interest Rate

LONG (OR LONG POSITION)

What Does *Long (or Long Position)* Mean?
(1) The buying of a security such as a stock, commodity, or currency, with the expectation that the asset will rise in value. (2) In the context of options, the buying of an options contract. The term "long" is the opposite of "short" (or short position).

Investopedia explains *Long (or Long Position)*
(1) As an example, if an investor owns shares in McDonald's Corp., that investor is said to be "long McDonald's" or "have a long position in McDonald's." (2) For options, buying a call (or put) options contract from an options writer gives the investor the right, not the obligation, to buy (or sell) a specific commodity or asset for a specified amount at a specified date. Buying the contract makes the investor "long" the contract.

RELATED TERMS:

- Call Option
- Futures
- Short (or Short Position)

- Commodity
- Put Option

LONG SQUEEZE

What Does *Long Squeeze* Mean?

A long squeeze, which involves a single stock, occurs when a sudden drop in the price of that stock leads to further selling, which pressures stockholders to sell their shares to protect themselves against a dramatic loss. Long squeezes are most likely to be found in smaller, more illiquid stocks; a few determined or panicked sellers can create unwarranted price volatility in a short period.

Investopedia explains *Long Squeeze*

Short sellers can monopolize the trading in a stock for a brief period, creating a sudden drop in price. The main reason long squeezes are so rare is that value buyers will step in once the price falls to a point that is deemed too low and bid the shares back up. A rapidly falling stock that is still fundamentally sound usually is seen as a "value" play, but a rapidly rising stock will be seen as increasingly risky with every upward tick.

RELATED TERMS:

- Demand
- Long (or Long Position)
- Short Squeeze

- Fundamental Analysis
- Short (or Short Position)

LONG-TERM DEBT

What Does *Long-Term Debt* Mean?

Loans and financial obligations with maturities lasting over a year; in the United Kingdom, long-term debts are known as long-term loans.

Investopedia explains *Long-Term Debt*

As an example, debt obligations such as bonds and notes that have maturities greater than one year are considered long-term debt. Loans such as T-bills and commercial paper are not considered long-term debt because their maturities are typically less than one year.

RELATED TERMS:
- Bond
- Commercial Paper
- Long-Term Debt to Capitalization Ratio
- Treasury Bond
- Yield to Maturity

LONG-TERM DEBT TO CAPITALIZATION RATIO

What Does *Long-Term Debt to Capitalization Ratio* Mean?
A ratio that shows the financial leverage of a firm; it is calculated by dividing long-term debt by the amount of capital available:

$$= \frac{\text{Long-Term Debt}}{\text{Long-Term Debt} + \text{Preferred Stock} + \text{Common Stock}}$$

Investopedia explains *Long-Term Debt to Capitalization Ratio*
A variation of the traditional debt-to-equity ratio, this ratio computes the proportion of a company's long-term debt relative to its available capital. By using this ratio, investors can identify the amount of leverage utilized by a specific company and compare it with others to help analyze the company's risk exposure. Generally, companies that finance a greater portion of their capital through debt are considered riskier than those with lower leverage ratios.

RELATED TERMS:
- Capital Structure
- Leverage
- Long-Term Debt
- Preferred Stock
- Shareholders' Equity

copyright JackGuinan

"The dollar may be out of favor overseas, but it sure is popular here at home."

MACROECONOMICS

What Does *Macroeconomics* Mean?

The field of economics that studies the behavior of the aggregate economy. Macroeconomics examines economywide phenomena such as changes in unemployment, national income, rate of growth, gross domestic product, inflation, and price levels.

Investopedia explains *Macroeconomics*

Macroeconomics is focused on the overall movements and trends in the economy, whereas its counterpart—microeconomics—focuses on factors that affect the decisions made by firms and individuals. Macro and micro factors often influence each other; for example, the current level of unemployment in the economy as a whole will affect the supply of available workers from which a company can select.

RELATED TERMS:
- *Gross Domestic Product—GDP*
- *Microeconomics*
- *Unsystematic Risk*
- *Market Economy*
- *Systematic Risk*

MAINTENANCE MARGIN

What Does *Maintenance Margin* Mean?

The minimum amount of equity that must be maintained in a margin account. According to the NYSE and NASD, once an investor buys securities on margin, the minimum required level of margin is 25% of the total market value of the securities in the margin account. One should keep in mind that this level is a minimum, and many brokerages have higher "house" maintenance requirements of 30 to 40%. Also referred to as minimum maintenance or maintenance requirement.

Investopedia explains *Maintenance Margin*

As governed by the Federal Reserve's Regulation T, when a trader buys on margin, key minimum margin requirements must be maintained throughout the life of the trade. First, a broker cannot extend any credit to accounts with less than $2,000 in cash (or securities). Second, the initial margin of 50% is required for each initial margin trade. Third, the maintenance margin states that an equity level of at least 25% must be maintained. The investor will receive a margin call if the value of securities falls below the maintenance margin.

RELATED TERMS:
- Leverage
- Margin Account
- Regulation T—Reg T
- Margin
- Margin Call

MANAGERIAL ACCOUNTING

What Does *Managerial Accounting* Mean?

The process of identifying, measuring, analyzing, interpreting, and communicating information in the pursuit of a company's business goals. Also known as cost accounting.

Investopedia explains *Managerial Accounting*

The key difference between managerial accounting and financial accounting is that managerial accounting is intended to help managers within the organization make decisions. In contrast, financial accounting is intended to provide information to parties outside the organization.

RELATED TERMS:
- Accrual Accounting
- Earnings
- Generally Accepted Accounting Principles—GAAP
- Off-Balance-Sheet Financing
- Operating Leverage

MARGIN

What Does *Margin* Mean?

(1) Borrowed money that is used to purchase securities. This practice is referred to as buying on margin. (2) The amount of equity contributed by a customer as a percentage of the current market value of the securities held in a margin account. (3) In a general business context, the difference between a product's (or service's) selling price and the cost of production. (4) The portion of the interest rate on an adjustable-rate mortgage that is over and above the adjustment-index rate. This portion is retained as profit by the lender.

Investopedia explains *Margin*

(1) Buying with borrowed money can be extremely risky because both gains and losses are magnified. That is, although the potential for greater profit exists, it comes with the potential for greater losses. Margin also subjects the investor to a number of unique risks, such as interest payments for the use of the borrowed money. (2) For example, if an investor holds futures contracts in a margin account, that investor has to maintain a certain level of margin, depending on how the market value of the contracts changes. (3) Gross profit margin (which is the difference between revenue and expenses) is one measure of a company's performance. (4) The formula for calculating the interest rate on an adjustable-rate mortgage is the adjustment-index rate (e.g., Treasury Index) plus the percentage of the margin. For example, if the Treasury Index is 6% and the interest rate on the mortgage is 8%, the margin is 2%.

RELATED TERMS:
- Leverage
- Maintenance Margin
- Margin Account
- Margin Call
- New York Stock Exchange—NYSE

MARGIN ACCOUNT

What Does *Margin Account* Mean?

A brokerage account in which the broker lends the customer cash to purchase securities. The loan in the account is collateralized by securities and cash. As the value of the stock drops, the account holder may be required to deposit more cash or sell a portion of the stock to bring the account back up to the proper margin levels.

Investopedia explains *Margin Account*

In a margin account, the investor is borrowing money from the broker to buy a security. By using leverage in this way, the investor magnifies his or her potential gains and losses.

RELATED TERMS:
- Debt
- Leverage
- Margin Call
- Interest Rate
- Maintenance Margin

MARGIN CALL

What Does *Margin Call* Mean?

A broker's demand for an investor to deposit additional money or securities to bring a margin account up to the minimum maintenance margin requirements; sometimes referred to as a fed call, maintenance call, or house call.

Investopedia explains *Margin Call*

An investor would receive a margin call from his or her broker if one or more of the securities purchased on margin (with borrowed money) decreased in value below a certain point. When this happens, the investor is forced to either deposit more money in the account or to sell off some of his or her assets.

RELATED TERMS:
- Leverage
- Margin
- Minimum Margin
- Liquidity
- Market Value

MARK TO MARKET (MTM)

What Does *Mark to Market (MTM)* Mean?
(1) The act of recording and/or updating the price or value of a security, portfolio, or account to reflect its current market value rather than its book value. (2) In mutual funds, an MTM is when the net asset value (NAV) of the fund is based on the most current market values.

Investopedia explains *Mark to Market (MTM)*
(1) This often is done in the future's market to help ensure that margin requirements are met. If the current market value causes the margin account to fall below its required level, the trader will be faced with a margin call. (2) Mutual funds are marked to market on a daily basis at the market close so that investors have an idea of a fund's NAV.

RELATED TERMS:
- Book Value
- Margin Call
- Net Asset Value—NAV
- Maintenance Margin
- Market Value

MARKET CAPITALIZATION

What Does *Market Capitalization* Mean?
The total dollar market value of a company's outstanding shares, calculated by multiplying the company's outstanding shares by the current market share price; the investment community uses this figure to determine a company's size (worth), as opposed to sales or total asset figures. Frequently referred to as market cap.

Investopedia explains *Market Capitalization*
If a company has 35 million shares outstanding with a current share price of $100, the company's market capitalization is $3.5 billion (35,000,000 × $100 per share). Company size is a basic determinant of asset allocation and risk-return parameters for stocks and stock mutual funds. The term should not be confused with a company's "capitalization," which is a financial accounting term that refers to the sum of a company's shareholders' equity plus its long-term debt. The stocks of large, medium, and small companies are referred to as large-cap, mid-cap, and small-cap, respectively. In general, market

cap breakdowns look like this: large cap: $10 billion or more, mid cap: $2 billion to $10 billion, small cap: less than $2 billion.

RELATED TERMS:
- Asset Allocation
- Large Cap—Big Cap
- Small Cap
- Index
- Mid Cap

MARKET ECONOMY

What Does *Market Economy* Mean?
An economy in which economic decisions and the pricing of goods and services are guided solely by the aggregate interactions of a country's citizens and businesses, with little government intervention or central planning. This is the opposite of a centrally planned economy, in which government decisions drive most aspects of a country's economic activity.

Investopedia explains *Market Economy*
Market economies work on the assumption that market forces such as supply and demand are the best determinants of what is right for a nation's well-being. These economies rarely engage in government interventions such as price fixing, license quotas, and industry subsidization. Although most developed nations today have mixed economies, they are referred to as market economies because they allow market forces to drive most of their activities, with government intervening only to provide stability. Although the market economy is clearly the system of choice in today's global marketplace, discussions persist about the proper balance of free market principles and government intervention.

RELATED TERMS:
- Common Stock
- Gross Domestic Product—GDP
- Law of Demand
- Corporate Bonds
- Inflation

MARKET MAKER

What Does *Market Maker* Mean?
A broker-dealer firm that accepts the risk of holding a certain number of shares of a particular security to facilitate trading in that

security. Each market maker competes for investor order flow by displaying buy (bid) and sell (ask) quotations for a specific number of shares (size). Once an order is received, the market maker immediately sells from its own inventory or seeks an offsetting order. This process takes place in seconds. Market makers buy and sell for their own accounts to make a profit.

Investopedia explains *Market Maker*
The Nasdaq is the prime example of an operation that uses market makers. There are over 500 member firms that act as Nasdaq market makers. These broker-dealer firms add liquidity and keep the financial markets running efficiently because they are willing to quote both bid and ask prices for an asset.

RELATED TERMS:
- *Ask*
- *Bid*
- *Broker-Dealer*
- *Electronic Communication Network—ECN*
- *Over the Counter*

MARKET ORDER

What Does *Market Order* **Mean?**
An order to buy or sell a stock immediately at the best available price at the time the order is presented in the market. Sometimes referred to as an unrestricted order.

Investopedia explains *Market Order*
A market order guarantees execution and often has lower commissions because a broker does not need to do much work. One should be wary of using market orders on stocks with a low average daily volume: In such market conditions the ask price can be a lot higher than the current market price (resulting in a large spread). In other words, the investor may end up paying a lot more than he or she originally anticipated. It is much safer to use a market order on high-volume stocks.

RELATED TERMS:
- *Bid-Ask Spread*
- *Limit Order*
- *Stock*
- *Stop Order*
- *Stop-Loss Order*

MARKET RISK PREMIUM

What Does *Market Risk Premium* Mean?

The difference between the expected return on an investment and the risk-free rate of return.

Investopedia explains *Market Risk Premium*

It is equal to the slope of the security market line (SML).

RELATED TERMS:

- Beta
- Risk
- Unsystematic Risk
- Relative Strength Index
- Systematic Risk

MARKET VALUE

What Does *Market Value* Mean?

(1) The current price at which investors buy or sell a share of common stock or a bond at a specific time. Also known as market price. (2) The market capitalization plus the market value of debt. Sometimes referred to as total market value.

Investopedia explains *Market Value*

(1) In the context of securities, market value is often different from book value because the market value reflects future expectations. Most investors who pick stocks by using fundamental analysis look at a company's market value and then determine whether the market value is adequate or is undervalued in comparison to its book value, net assets, or another measure.

RELATED TERMS:

- Book Value
- Fair Value
- Market Capitalization
- Face Value
- Intrinsic Value

MARKETABLE SECURITIES

What Does *Marketable Securities* Mean?

Securities that can be converted into cash quickly at a reasonable price; marketable securities are liquid because they exhibit high trading volumes and tend to have short-term maturities of less than one year. Furthermore, the rate at which these securities can be bought or sold has little effect on their prices.

Investopedia explains *Marketable Securities*
Examples of marketable securities are commercial paper, banker's acceptances, Treasury bills, and other money market instruments.

RELATED TERMS:
- *Common Stock*
- *Liquidity*
- *Nonmarginal Securities*
- *Illiquid*
- *Listed*

MATURITY

What Does *Maturity* Mean?
(1) The length of time until the principal amount of a bond must be repaid. (2) The end of the life of a security.

Investopedia explains *Maturity*
In other words, the maturity is the date on which the borrower must pay back the money he or she borrowed through the issuance of a bond.

RELATED TERMS:
- *Bond*
- *Long-Term Debt*
- *Yield to Maturity*
- *Interest Rate*
- *Par Value*

MERGER

What Does *Merger* Mean?
When two or more companies combine their businesses into one business entity, generally by offering the stockholders of one company securities in the acquiring company in exchange for the surrender of their stock.

Investopedia explains *Merger*
Basically, when two companies become one. This decision is usually mutual between both firms, unlike a forced merger, which is known as a hostile takeover.

RELATED TERMS:
- *Dilution*
- *Leveraged Buyout*
- *Mergers and Acquisitions—M&A*
- *Takeover*
- *Leverage*

MERGERS AND ACQUISITIONS (M&A)

What Does *Mergers and Acquisitions (M&A)* Mean?

A term used to refer to the consolidation or merging of two companies into one. A merger is a combination of two companies to form a new company, whereas an acquisition is the purchase of one company by another in which no new company is formed.

Investopedia explains *Mergers and Acquisitions (M&A)*

An example of a major merger is the merging of JDS Fitel Inc. and Uniphase Corp. in 1999 to form JDS Uniphase. An example of a major acquisition is Manulife Financial Corporation's 2004 acquisition of John Hancock Financial Services Inc. The term "M&A" also refers to the department at financial institutions that deals with mergers and acquisitions.

RELATED TERMS:

- Dilution
- Mezzanine Financing
- Poison Pill
- Leverage
- Merger

MEZZANINE FINANCING

What Does *Mezzanine Financing* Mean?

A hybrid of debt and equity financing that typically is used to finance a company's expansion. Mezzanine financing is basically debt capital that gives the lender the right to convert to an ownership or equity interest in the company if the loan is not paid back in time and in full. It generally is subordinated to debt provided by senior lenders such as banks and venture capital companies. Since mezzanine financing usually is provided to the borrower very quickly with little due diligence on the part of the lender and little or no collateral on the part of the borrower, this type of financing is priced aggressively, with the lender seeking a return in the range of 20 to 30%.

Investopedia explains *Mezzanine Financing*

Mezzanine financing is advantageous for financing because it is treated like equity on a company's balance sheet and may make it easier to obtain standard bank financing. To attract mezzanine financing, a company usually must demonstrate a track record in the industry with an established reputation and product, a history of profitability, and a viable expansion plan for the business (e.g., expansions, acquisitions, an IPO).

RELATED TERMS:
- Capital Structure
- Due Diligence—DD
- Subordinated Debt
- Coefficient of Variation
- Initial Public Offering—IPO
- Venture Capital

MICROECONOMICS

What Does *Microeconomics* Mean?

The branch of economic study that analyzes the market behavior of individual consumers and firms in an attempt to understand their decision-making processes; it focuses on the interaction between individual buyers and sellers and the factors that influence the choices they make, particularly the trends of supply and demand and the determination of price and output in individual markets.

Investopedia explains *Microeconomics*

Economics can be separated into two fields of study: microeconomics and macroeconomics. Microeconomics looks at the smaller picture and focuses more on basic theories of supply and demand and how businesses make production and pricing decisions. People who are starting their own businesses or who want to learn the rationale behind the pricing of particular products and services would find this approach helpful. Macroeconomics, in contrast, looks at the big picture (hence the prefix "macro"). It focuses on the national economy as a whole and provides a basic knowledge of how things work in the business world. For example, macroeconomists analyze and interpret Gross Domestic Product or unemployment figures. This perspective provides an overall view of the entire economy. Together, microeconomics and macroeconomics are powerful tools.

RELATED TERMS:
- Fundamental Analysis
- Gross Domestic Product—GDP
- Quantitative Analysis
- Macroeconomics
- Technical Analysis

MID CAP

What Does *Mid Cap* Mean?

Refers to a company with a market capitalization between $2 and $10 billion, calculated by multiplying the number of company shares outstanding by the company's current stock price. Mid cap is an abbreviation for the term "middle capitalization."

Investopedia explains *Mid Cap*

As the name implies, a mid cap company is in the middle of the pack between large cap and small cap companies. One should keep in mind that classifications such as large cap, mid cap, and small cap are only approximations, and sometimes their guidelines can vary slightly among investors.

RELATED TERMS:
- *Asset Allocation*
- *Large Cap—Big Cap*
- *Small Cap*
- *Growth Stock*
- *Market Capitalization*

MINIMUM MARGIN

What Does *Minimum Margin* Mean?

The initial margin amount required to be deposited in a margin account before buying or selling short on margin. For example, the NYSE and the NASD require investors to deposit a minimum of $2,000 in cash or securities to open a margin account. One should keep in mind that this amount is only a minimum; some brokerages may require deposits over $2,000.

Investopedia explains *Minimum Margin*

When an investor buys on margin, there are different minimums that are governed by the Federal Reserve Board's Regulation T and that must be met throughout the life of a margin trade. The minimum margin, which states that a broker cannot extend any credit to accounts with less than $2,000 in cash (or securities), is the first requirement. Second, an initial margin of 50% of the market value of the trade is required for the trade. Third, the maintenance margin says that an investor must maintain equity of at least 25% or be hit with a margin call.

RELATED TERMS:
- *Leverage*
- *Margin Account*
- *Regulation T—Reg T*
- *Maintenance Margin*
- *Margin Call*

MINORITY INTEREST

What Does *Minority Interest* Mean?
(1) A significant but noncontrolling ownership of less than 50% of a company's voting shares by either an investor or another company. (2) A noncurrent liability that can be found on a parent company's balance sheet, representing the fractional proportions of its subsidiaries owned by minority shareholders.

Investopedia explains *Minority Interest*
(1) In accounting terms, if a company owns a minority interest in another company but has only a minority passive position (i.e., it is unable to exert influence), the only thing that is recorded from this investment are the dividends received from the minority interest. If the company has a minority active position (i.e., it is able to exert influence), both dividends and a percentage of income are recorded on the company's books. (2) If ABC Corp. owns 90% of XYZ Inc., which is a $100 million company, ABC Corp.'s balance sheet will show a $10 million liability in the minority interest account, representing the 10% of XYZ Inc. that ABC Corp. does not own.

RELATED TERMS:
- Balance Sheet
- Long-Term Debt
- Shareholders' Equity
- Dividend
- Net Operating Income—NOI

MODERN PORTFOLIO THEORY (MPT)

What Does *Modern Portfolio Theory (MPT)* Mean?
An investment theory that demonstrates how risk-averse investors can construct portfolios that best maximize expected returns on the basis of a specific level of market risk while emphasizing that risk is inevitable when one is seeking higher returns; also called portfolio theory or portfolio management theory.

Investopedia explains *Modern Portfolio Theory (MPT)*
According to the theory, it is possible to construct an efficient frontier of optimal portfolios that offers the maximum possible expected return for a specific level of risk. This theory was pioneered by Harry Markowitz in his paper "Portfolio Selection," which was published in 1952 in the *Journal of Finance*. The four basic steps involved

in portfolio construction are (1) security valuation, (2) asset alloca-tion, (3) portfolio optimization, and (4) performance measurement.

RELATED TERMS:
- Asset Allocation
- Efficient Market Hypothesis—EMH
- Risk
- Correlation
- Mutual Fund

MODIFIED DURATION

What Does *Modified Duration* Mean?
A formula that expresses the measurable change in the value of a security in response to a change in interest rates. It is calculated as follows:

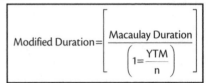

$$\text{Modified Duration} = \left[\frac{\text{Macaulay Duration}}{\left(1 = \frac{\text{YTM}}{n} \right)} \right]$$

Where n = number of coupon periods per year, YTM = the bond's yield to maturity.

Investopedia explains *Modified Duration*
Modified duration adheres to the principle that interest rates and bond prices move in opposite directions. This formula is used to determine the effect that a 100-basis-point (1%) change in interest rates will have on the price of a bond.

RELATED TERMS:
- Basis Point
- Coupon
- Interest Rates
- Bond
- Duration

MODIFIED INTERNAL RATE OF RETURN (MIRR)

What Does *Modified Internal Rate of Return (MIRR)* Mean?
Whereas the internal rate of return (IRR) assumes that the cash flows from a project are reinvested at the IRR, the modified MIRR assumes that all cash flows are reinvested at the firm's cost of capital. There-fore, MIRR more accurately reflects the profitability of a project.

Investopedia explains *Modified Internal Rate of Return (MIRR)*
As an example, if a two-year project with an initial outlay of $195 and a cost of capital of 12% returns $121 in the first year and $131

in the second year, one finds the IRR of the project so that the net present value (NPV) = 0 as follows: NPV = 0 = −195 + 121/(1+ IRR) + 131/(1 + IRR)^2; NPV = 0 when IRR = 18.66% . However, using the MIRR method, the investor would substitute IRR with MIRR = cost of capital of 12%: NPV = −195 + 121/(1+ .12) + 131/(1 + .12)^2; NPV = 17.47 when MIRR = 12%. Thus, using the IRR could result in a positive NPV (good project), but it could turn out to be a bad project (NPV is negative) as revealed by the MIRR method. Therefore, using MIRR versus IRR reflects the value of a project more comprehensively.

RELATED TERMS:
- Discounted Cash Flow—DCF
- Net Present Value—NPV
- Internal Rate of Return—IRR
- Payback Period

MOMENTUM

What Does *Momentum* Mean?
The rate of acceleration of the price or volume of a security.

Investopedia explains *Momentum*
Once a momentum trader sees acceleration in a stock's price, earnings, or revenues, that trader often will take a long or short position in the stock with the hope that its momentum will continue in the current direction. This strategy relies more on short-term movements in price than on a company's fundamentals; it is not recommended for novice investors.

RELATED TERMS:
- Downtrend
- Moving Average Convergence Divergence
- Swing Trading
- Uptrend
- Trend Analysis

MONETARY POLICY

What Does *Monetary Policy* Mean?
The actions of a central bank, a currency board, or another regulatory committee that determine the size and rate of growth of the money supply, which in turn affects interest rates.

Investopedia explains *Monetary Policy*
In the United States, the Federal Reserve is in charge of monetary policy.

RELATED TERMS:
- Discount Rate
- Federal Open Market Committee—FOMC
- Interest Rate
- Federal Funds Rate
- Required Rate of Return

MONEY MARKET

 What Does *Money Market* Mean?
The segment of the financial markets in which highly liquid short-term assets trade; the money market is used by participants as a means to borrow and lend on a short-term basis from several days to just under a year. Money market securities consist of negotiable certificates of deposit (CDs), banker's acceptances, U.S. Treasury bills, commercial paper, municipal notes, federal funds, and repurchase agreements (repos).

 Investopedia explains *Money Market*
The money market is used by a wide array of participants, from a company raising money by selling commercial paper to an individual investor buying CDs at a bank. The money market typically is seen as a safe place to put money as a result of the highly liquid nature of the securities and short maturities, but there are risks, including the risk of default on securities such as commercial paper.

RELATED TERMS:
- Banker's Acceptance—BA
- Commercial Paper
- Money Market Account
- Certificate of Deposit—CD
- Liquidity

MONEY MARKET ACCOUNT

 What Does *Money Market Account* Mean?
A savings account that pays interest on deposited monies. Also known by the acronym MMDA, which stands for "money market demand account" or "money market deposit account."

Investopedia explains *Money Market Account*
Many money market accounts place restrictions on the amount of transactions an investor can make in a month (e.g., five or less). Furthermore, the investor usually has to maintain a certain balance in the account to receive a higher rate of interest. Some banks require minimum initial deposits, and others require minimum account balances. Money markets are similar to savings accounts except that they frequently pay higher interest rates in return for adhering to minimum account requirements.

RELATED TERMS:
- *Annual Percentage Yield—APY*
- *Cash and Cash Equivalents—CCE*
- *Interest*
- *Money Market*
- *Liquidity*

MONEY SUPPLY

What Does *Money Supply* Mean?
The entire quantity of bills, coins, loans, credit, and other liquid instruments circulating in a country's economy.

Investopedia explains *Money Supply*
The money supply is divided into multiple categories—M0, M1, M2, and M3—in accordance with the type and size of account in which the instrument is kept. The money supply is important to economists who try to understand how policies (monetary policies) will affect interest rates and growth.

RELATED TERMS:
- *Cash and Cash Equivalents—CCE*
- *Fiscal Policy*
- *Monetary Policy*
- *Discount Rate*
- *Inflation*

MONOPOLY

What Does *Monopoly* Mean?
A situation in which a single company or group owns all or nearly all of the market share for a specific type of product or service. By definition, monopoly is characterized by an absence of competition, which often results in high prices and inferior products. According to a strict academic definition, a monopoly is a market containing a single firm.

Investopedia explains *Monopoly*

Monopoly is the extreme case in capitalism. Most believe that with few exceptions, the free market system does not work when there is only one provider of a good or service because there is no incentive to improve it to meet the demands of consumers. Governments attempt to prevent monopolies from arising through the use of antitrust laws. Of course, there are gray areas; for example, the granting of patents on new inventions in effect permits monopolies for a set period. The reasoning behind patents is to give innovators time to recoup what are often large research and development costs. In theory, they are a way of using monopolies to promote innovation. Another example of legal monopolies involves public monopolies set up by governments to provide essential services such as clean water and electricity.

RELATED TERMS:
- *Efficient Market Hypothesis—EMH*
- *Law of Supply*
- *Oligopoly*
- *Law of Demand*
- *Market Economy*

MORTGAGE

 What Does *Mortgage* **Mean?**

A debt instrument that is collateralized by real estate property; the borrower (mortgage owner) is obliged to pay back both the principal and the interest with periodic payments over the course of the loan. Mortgages are used by individuals and businesses to make large purchases of real estate without paying the entire value of the purchase up front. Mortgages also are known as liens against property and claims on property.

 Investopedia explains *Mortgage*

In a residential mortgage, a home buyer pledges his or her house to the bank. The bank has a claim on the house if the home buyer defaults on paying the mortgage. In the case of a foreclosure, the bank may evict the home's tenants and sell the house, using the income from the sale to pay off the mortgage debt.

RELATED TERMS:
- *Debt*
- *Fannie Mae—Federal National Mortgage Association (FNMA)*
- *Interest*
- *Liability*
- *Mortgage-Backed Security*

MORTGAGE FORBEARANCE AGREEMENT

What Does *Mortgage Forbearance Agreement* Mean?
An agreement made between a mortgage lender and a delinquent borrower by which the lender agrees not to exercise its legal right to foreclose on a mortgage and the borrower agrees to a mortgage plan that will, over a specified period, bring the borrower current on his or her payments. A forbearance agreement is not a long-term solution for delinquent borrowers; it is designed for borrowers who have temporary financial problems caused by unforeseen problems such as temporary unemployment or health problems.

Investopedia explains *Mortgage Forbearance Agreement*
Borrowers who are faced with mortgage financial problems such as having chosen an adjustable-rate mortgage on which the interest rate has reset to a level that makes the monthly payments unaffordable usually must seek remedies other than a forbearance agreement.

RELATED TERMS:
- *Bankruptcy*
- *Liability*
- *Subprime Meltdown*
- *Credit Crunch*
- *Mortgage*

MORTGAGE-BACKED SECURITIES (MBSs)

What Does *Mortgage-Backed Securities (MBSs)* Mean?
Refers to a type of asset-backed security secured by a mortgage or a collection of mortgages and grouped in one of the top two ratings as determined by a credit rating agency such as Moody's; usually make periodic payments that are similar to coupon payments. Furthermore, the mortgages must have originated from a regulated and authorized financial institution. Also known as a mortgage-related security or a mortgage pass-through. MBSs shift the loan risk from the originator to the agencies that bundle the mortgages into securities rather than to the investors who ultimately purchase the MBSs.

Investopedia explains *Mortgage-Backed Securities (MBSs)*
When one invests in a mortgage-backed security, one essentially is lending money to a home buyer or business. An MBS is a way for a smaller regional bank to lend mortgages to its customers without having to worry about whether the customers have the assets to cover the loans. Instead, the bank acts as a middleman between the

home buyer and the investment markets. This type of security also is used commonly to redirect the interest and principal payments from the pool of mortgages to shareholders. These payments can be broken down further into different classes of securities, depending on the riskiness of different mortgages as they are classified under the MBS.

RELATED TERMS:
- Collateralized Mortgage Obligation—CMO
- Credit Crunch   • Securitization
- Subprime Loan   • Subprime Meltdown

MOVING AVERAGE (MA)

What Does _Moving Average (MA)_ Mean?
An indicator used in technical analysis that shows the average value of the price of a security over a set period. Moving averages generally are used to measure momentum and define areas of possible support and resistance.

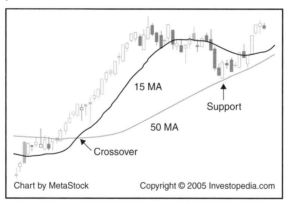

Chart by MetaStock   Copyright © 2005 Investopedia.com

Investopedia explains _Moving Average (MA)_
Moving averages are used to emphasize the direction of a trend and smooth out price and volume fluctuations, or "noise," that can cloud the analysis of a stock's price movement. Typically, upward momentum is confirmed when a short-term average (e.g., 15-day) crosses above a longer-term average (e.g., 50-day). Downward momentum is confirmed when a short-term average crosses below a long-term average.

RELATED TERMS:

- Moving Average Convergence Divergence—MACD
- Resistance
- Simple Moving Average—SMA
- Support   • Technical Analysis

MOVING AVERAGE CONVERGENCE DIVERGENCE (MACD)

What Does *Moving Average Convergence Divergence (MACD)* Mean?

A momentum indicator that shows the relationship between two moving price averages; the MACD is calculated by subtracting the 26-day exponential moving average (EMA) from the 12-day EMA. A nine-day EMA of the MACD, called the "signal line," then is plotted on top of the MACD, functioning as a trigger for buy and sell signals.

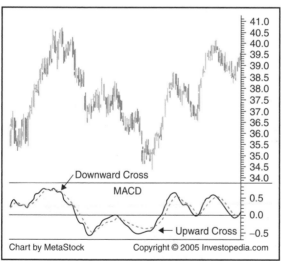

Investopedia explains *Moving Average Convergence Divergence (MACD)*

There are three common ways to interpret the MACD: (1) Cross-overs. As shown in the accompanying chart, when the MACD falls below the signal line, it is a bearish signal indicating that it may be time to sell. Conversely, when the MACD rises above the signal line, the indicator is bullish, which suggests that the price of the asset is likely to experience upward momentum. Many traders wait for a confirmed cross above the signal line before entering into a position so that they do not get "faked out" or enter into a position too early, as shown by the first arrow in the chart. (2) Divergence. When the security price diverges from the MACD, it signals the end of the current trend. (3) Dramatic rise. When the MACD rises dramatically—that is, the shorter moving average pulls away from the longer-term moving average—this is a signal that the security is overbought and soon will return to normal levels. In addition, traders generally watch for a move above or below the zero line because this signals the position of the short-term average relative to the long-term average. When the MACD is above zero, the short-term average is above the long-term average, which signals upward momentum. The opposite is true when the MACD is below zero. As the accompanying chart shows, the zero line often acts as an area of support and resistance for the indicator.

RELATED TERMS:
- Fundamental Analysis
- Quantitative Analysis
- Technical Analysis
- Moving Average
- Relative Strength Index

MSCI EMERGING MARKETS INDEX

What Does *MSCI Emerging Markets Index* Mean?
An index created by Morgan Stanley Capital International (MSCI) that is designed to measure equity market performance in global emerging markets. The Emerging Markets Index is a float-adjusted market capitalization index. Some of the emerging economies in the index are Argentina, Brazil, Chile, China, Colombia, Czech Republic, Egypt, Hungary, India, Indonesia, Israel, Jordan, Korea, Malaysia, Mexico, Morocco, Pakistan, Peru, Philippines, Poland, Russia, South Africa, Taiwan, Thailand, Turkey, and Venezuela.

Investopedia explains *MSCI Emerging Markets Index*
Emerging markets are considered relatively risky because they carry additional political, economic, and currency risks. They certainly are not for those who value safety and security above all else. An investor in emerging markets should be willing to accept greater risks for potentially greater returns. An upside to emerging markets is that their performance generally is correlated less with that of developed

markets. Thus, they can play a role in diversifying a portfolio (and thus reducing overall risk).

RELATED TERMS:
- *American Depositary Receipt—ADR*
- *Correlation*
- *Exchange-Traded Fund—ETF*
- *Global Depositary Receipt—GDR*
- *Index*

MULTIPLE

What Does *Multiple* Mean?
A term that measures a particular aspect of a company's financial well-being, determined by dividing one metric by another metric. The metric in the numerator is typically larger than the one in the denominator, because the top metric usually is supposed to be many times larger than the bottom metric. It is calculated as follows:

$$\text{Multiple} = \frac{\text{Performance Metric "A"}}{\text{Performance Metric "B"}}$$

Investopedia explains *Multiple*
As an example, the term "multiple" can be used to show how much investors are willing to pay per dollar of earnings, as computed by the P/E ratio. Suppose one is analyzing a stock with $2 of earnings per share (EPS) that is trading at $20; this stock has a P/E of 10. This means that investors are willing to pay a multiple of 10 times earnings for the stock.

RELATED TERMS:
- *Earnings*
- *Earnings per Share—EPS*
- *Forward Price to Earnings—Forward P/E*
- *Price-Earnings Ratio—P/E Ratio*
- *Price/Earnings to Growth Ratio—PEG Ratio*

MUNICIPAL BOND

What Does *Municipal Bond* Mean?
A debt security issued by a state, municipality, or county to finance its capital expenditures. Municipal bonds are exempt from federal taxes and most state and local taxes, especially if the investor lives in the state in which a bond is issued. Also known as a muni-bond.

Investopedia explains *Municipal Bond*
Municipal bonds may be used to fund expenditures such as the construction of highways, bridges, and schools. Muni-bonds, or "Munies," tend to offer low interest rates, but they do get favorable tax treatment (tax-free interest) and are thus popular with people in high income tax brackets.

RELATED TERMS:
- *Government Security*
- *Yield*
- *Tax Deferred*

- *Interest*
- *Yield to Maturity—YTM*

MUTUAL FUND

 ### What Does *Mutual Fund* Mean?
An investment instrument that is made up of a pool of funds collected from many investors for the purpose of investing in securities such as stocks, bonds, money market instruments, and similar assets. Mutual funds are operated by money managers, who actively manage a fund's assets in an attempt to produce positive returns for the fund's investors. A mutual fund's portfolio strategy is structured and maintained to match the investment objectives stated in its prospectus.

 Investopedia explains *Mutual Fund*
Mutual funds are popular because they give small investors access to professionally managed, diversified portfolios of stocks, bonds, and other securities that would be quite difficult (if not impossible) for investors to replicate on their own with a small amount of money. Each shareholder participates proportionally in the gain or loss of the fund. Mutual fund units, or shares, are issued and typically can be purchased or redeemed as needed at the fund's current net asset value (NAV) per share, which sometimes is expressed as NAVPS.

RELATED TERMS:
- *Closed-End Fund*
- *Net Asset Value—NAV*
- *Style*

- *Diversification*
- *Open-End Fund*

copyright JackGuinan

"Honey, I think it's time we raised our debt ceiling."

NAKED SHORTING

What Does *Naked Shorting* Mean?

The practice of short selling shares that have not been confirmed to exist. Ordinarily, traders must borrow a stock or determine that it can be borrowed before they sell it short. However, as a result of various loopholes in the rules and discrepancies between paper and electronic trading systems, naked shorting continues to happen. Although no exact system of measurement exists, most point to the level of trades that fail to deliver from the seller to the buyer within the mandatory three-day stock settlement period as evidence of naked shorting. Naked shorts may represent a major portion of these failed trades.

Investopedia explains *Naked Shorting*

Naked shorting is a form of price manipulation forcing stock prices down without regard for normal stock supply-demand patterns. In 2007, the Securities and Exchange Commission (SEC) amended Regulation SHO to limit possibilities for naked shorting further by removing the loopholes that existed for some broker-dealers. This regulation requires that lists be published that track stocks with un-usually high trends in "fail to deliver" shares. Some analysts point to the fact that naked shorting, albeit inadvertently, may help markets stay in balance by allowing negative sentiment to be reflected in certain stocks' prices.

RELATED TERMS:
- Margin
- Regulation T—Reg T
- Short Squeeze
- Option
- Stock Option

NASDAQ

What Does *Nasdaq* Mean?

A computerized market or exchange that facilitates trading by providing price quotations on more than 5,000 actively traded over-the-counter stocks. Created in 1971, the Nasdaq was the world's first electronic stock market. Stocks on the Nasdaq traditionally are listed by using four or five letters as their ticker symbols. If a company is a transfer from the New York Stock Exchange, the symbol may consist of three letters. Some companies are listed on two exchanges and are called dually listed stocks.

Investopedia explains *Nasdaq*

The term "Nasdaq" used to be capitalized "NASDAQ" as an acronym for National Association of Securities Dealers Automated Quotation. The acronym no longer is used, and Nasdaq is now a proper noun. The Nasdaq is traditionally home to many high-tech stocks, such as Microsoft, Intel, Dell, and Cisco.

RELATED TERMS:
- Electronic Communication Network—ECN
- Financial Industry Regulatory Authority—FINRA
- National Association of Securities Dealers—NASD
- Over the Counter—OTC
- Over-the-Counter Bulletin Board—OTCBB

NATIONAL ASSOCIATION OF SECURITIES DEALERS (NASD)

What Does *National Association of Securities Dealers (NASD)* Mean?

The self-regulatory organization (SRO) of the securities industry responsible for the operation and regulation of the Nasdaq stock market and over-the-counter markets. It also administers the licensing examinations for investment professionals, such as the Series 63, Series 6, and Series 7 examinations.

Investopedia explains *National Association of Securities Dealers (NASD)*
The NASD watches over the Nasdaq to make sure the market operates fairly and efficiently. In 2007, the NASD merged with the New York Stock Exchange's regulation committee to form the Financial Industry Regulatory Authority (FINRA).

RELATED TERMS:
- *Financial Industry Regulatory Authority—FINRA*
- *Nasdaq*   • *Over the Counter—OTC*
- *Over-the-Counter Bulletin Board—OTCBB*
- *Series 7*

NET ASSET VALUE (NAV)

What Does *Net Asset Value (NAV)* **Mean?**
A mutual fund's price per share or an exchange-traded fund's (ETF) price per share; in both cases, the per-share dollar amount of the fund is derived by dividing the total value of all the securities in its portfolio, minus any liabilities, by the number of fund shares outstanding. In terms of corporate valuations, the value of assets minus liabilities equals net asset value (NAV), or book value.

Investopedia explains *Net Asset Value (NAV)*
In the context of mutual funds, NAV per share is computed once a day, based on the closing market prices of the securities in a fund's portfolio. All mutual fund buy and sell orders are processed at the NAV of the trade date. However, investors must wait until the next day to get the trade price, which means that many mutual funds are priced just once a day, after the market closes. Mutual funds pay out virtually all of their income and capital gains. As a result, changes in NAV are just one measure of a mutual fund's performance; total return, which includes gains and distributions, is a more comprehensive measure. Because ETFs and closed-end funds trade like stocks, their shares trade at market value throughout the trading day, which means that at any particular time they can be trading at a premium (above NAV) or a discount (below NAV).

RELATED TERMS:
- Book Value
- Face Value
- Notional Value
- Exchange-Traded Fund—ETF
- Mutual Fund

NET INCOME (NI)

What Does *Net Income (NI)* Mean?

(1) A company's total earnings (or profit), calculated by taking revenues and adjusting for the cost of doing business, depreciation, interest, taxes, and other expenses. This number is found on a company's income statement and is an important measure of how profitable the company is over a period of time. The measure also is used in the calculation of earnings per share. NI often is referred to as the bottom line because net income is listed at the bottom of the income statement. In the United Kingdom, net income is known as profit attributable to shareholders. (2) An individual's income after deductions, credits, and taxes are factored into gross income. Deductions and credits are subtracted from gross income to arrive at taxable income, which is used to calculate income tax. Net income is income tax subtracted from taxable income.

Investopedia explains *Net Income (NI)*

(1) Net income is calculated by starting with a company's total revenue. From this, the cost of sales, along with any other expenses incurred during the period, is removed resulting in earnings before taxes. Tax then is deducted to reach NI. Like other accounting measures, NI is susceptible to accounting manipulation through practices such as aggressive revenue recognition or by hiding expenses. In basing an investment decision on net income numbers, it is important to review the quality of the numbers, not just the numbers. (2) Suppose, for example that a person's gross income is $50,000 and that person has $20,000 in deductions and credits. This leaves that person with a taxable income of $30,000. If another $5,000 of income tax is subtracted, the remaining $25,000 will be the person's net income.

RELATED TERMS:
- Cost of Goods Sold—COGS
- Gross Income
- Operating Income
- Economic Profit
- Income Statement

NET LONG

What Does *Net Long* Mean?

A condition in which an investor has more long positions than short positions in a specific asset class, market sector, portfolio, or trading strategy. Investors who are net long will benefit when the price of the asset increases.

Investopedia explains *Net Long*

Many mutual funds are restricted from short selling; this means the funds are usually net long. In fact, most individual investors do not hold large short positions, making the net long portfolio a common and usually expected investing situation. A position that is net long is the opposite of a position that is net short.

RELATED TERMS:
- Delta
- Long (or Long Position)
- Short (or Short Position)
- Hedge
- Overbought

NET OPERATING INCOME (NOI)

What Does *Net Operating Income (NOI)* Mean?

A company's operating income after operating expenses have been deducted but before income taxes and interest are deducted. If this is a positive value, it is referred to as net operating income; when it's negative, it is called a net operating loss (NOL).

Investopedia explains *Net Operating Income (NOI)*

NOI is a good gauge of a company's performance. Some believe that this figure is less susceptible to accounting manipulation by management than are other figures.

RELATED TERMS:
- *Minority Interest*
- *Nonoperating Income*
- *Net Income—NI*
- *Operating Income*

NET OPERATING PROFIT AFTER TAX (NOPAT)

What Does *Net Operating Profit after Tax (NOPAT)* Mean?
A company's potential cash earnings if its capitalization were unleveraged (that is, if it had no debt). NOPAT is used frequently in economic value added (EVA) calculations. It is calculated as follows:

NOPAT = Operating Income × (1 − Tax Rate)

Investopedia explains *Net Operating Profit after Tax (NOPAT)*
NOPAT constitutes a more accurate look at operating efficiency for leveraged companies. It does not include the tax savings many companies get because they have existing debt.

RELATED TERMS:
- *Accrual Accounting*
- *Diluted Earnings per Share*
- *Profit*
- *Balance Sheet*
- *Operating Expense*
- *Profitability Ratios*

NET PRESENT VALUE (NPV)

What Does *Net Present Value (NPV)* Mean?
The difference between the present value of cash inflows and the present value of cash outflows. NPV is used in capital budgeting to analyze the profitability of an investment or project. NPV analysis is sensitive to the reliability of future cash inflows that an investment or project may yield. It is calculated as shown here:

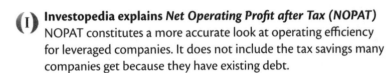

$$NPV = \sum_{t-1}^{T} \frac{C_t}{(1-r)^t} - C_o$$

Investopedia explains *Net Present Value (NPV)*
NPV compares the value of a dollar today to the value of that dollar at a future point, taking inflation and returns into account. If the NPV of a prospective project is positive, the project should be accepted. However, if NPV is negative, the project probably should be rejected because cash flows will be negative. For example, if a retail clothing business wants to purchase an existing store, it will estimate the future cash flows of the store and then discount those cash flows into one lump-sum present value amount, say, $565,000.

If the owner of the store is willing to sell the business for less than $565,000, the purchasing company probably will accept the offer because it is a positive NPV investment. Conversely, if the owner will not sell for less than $565,000, the purchaser will not buy the store, as the investment presents a negative NPV and therefore will reduce the overall value of the clothing company.

RELATED TERMS:
- Discounted Cash Flow—DCF
- Payback Period
- Time Value of Money
- Discount Rate
- Present Value—PV

NET SALES

What Does *Net Sales* Mean?

The amount of sales generated by a company after deducting returns, allowances for damaged or missing goods, and any discounts allowed. The sales number reported on a company's financial statements is a net sales number, reflecting these deductions.

Investopedia explains *Net Sales*

Deductions from the gross sales are represented in the net sales figure. Therefore, net sales provides a more accurate picture of the actual sales generated by the company, or the money that it expects to receive some time in the future. A company will book its revenue once the good or service is delivered or performed. However, even after a good has been sold, it often can be returned under a company's return policy. If the good is returned by the customer, it is not considered a sale, as the customer will receive a credit or money back, and so it has to be deducted from the gross sales. The allowances for damaged or missing goods reflect situations in which the goods are damaged in transit or are not what the customer expected. Many companies also offer discounts, especially on credit sales in which the customer pays off the amount early. This discount is deducted from gross sales, reducing overall revenue.

RELATED TERMS:
- Accounts Receivable—AR
- Cost of Goods Sold—COGS
- Operating Margin
- Asset Turnover
- Operating Income

NET TANGIBLE ASSETS

What Does *Net Tangible Assets* Mean?
Calculated as the total assets of a company, minus any intangible assets such as goodwill, patents, and trademarks, minus all liabilities and the par value of preferred stock. Also called net asset value and book value.

Investopedia explains *Net Tangible Assets*
To calculate a company's net asset value on a per bond or per share of preferred or common stock, divide the net tangible assets figure by the number of bonds, shares of preferred stock, or shares of common stock.

RELATED TERMS:
- Asset
- Price to Tangible Book Value—PTBV
- Tangible Asset
- Book Value
- Tangible Net Worth

NET WORTH

What Does *Net Worth* Mean?
The dollar amount by which assets exceed liabilities. This term can be applied to companies and individuals.

Investopedia explains *Net Worth*
For a company, this is known as shareholders' (or owners') equity and is determined by subtracting liabilities on the balance sheet from assets. For example, if a company has $45 million worth of liabilities and $65 million in assets, the company's net worth (shareholders' equity) is $20 million ($65 million − $45 million). Alternatively, say an individual has three assets—$100,000 of common stock, $30,000 worth of bonds, and title to a $190,000 house—and only one liability—$150,000 in mortgage debt. This individual's net worth would be $170,000 ([$100,000 + $30,000 + $190,000] − $150,000).

RELATED TERMS:
- Asset
- Debt
- Mortgage
- Balance Sheet
- Liabilities
- Shareholders' Equity

NEW YORK STOCK EXCHANGE (NYSE)

What Does *New York Stock Exchange (NYSE)* Mean?

Located in New York City, it is considered the largest equities-based exchange in the world, based on the total market capitalization of its listed securities. Formerly run as a private organization, the NYSE became a public entity in 2005 after the acquisition of the electronic trading exchange Archipelago. The parent company of the New York Stock Exchange is now called NYSE Euronext after a merger with the European exchange in 2007. Also known as the Big Board, the NYSE relied for many years on floor trading by "specialists" only, using the open outcry system. Today, more than half of all NYSE trades are conducted electronically, although floor traders still are used to facilitate liquidity and execute high-volume institutional trading.

Investopedia explains *New York Stock Exchange (NYSE)*

The origins of the exchange date back to 1792. Because of its long operating history, the NYSE is home to the majority of the world's largest and best-known companies. Foreign-based corporations can list their shares on the NYSE if they adhere to certain Securities and Exchange Commission (SEC) rules known as listing standards. The NYSE is open for trading Monday through Friday from 9:30 a.m. to 4:00 p.m. (ET), closing early on rare occasions. The market also shuts down during nine holidays throughout the year.

RELATED TERMS:
- American Stock Exchange—AMEX
- Benchmark   • Listed
- Nasdaq
- Securities and Exchange Commission—SEC

NO-LOAD FUND

What Does *No-Load Fund* Mean?

A mutual fund sold without a sales charge or commission. This is the opposite of a load fund, which charges an up-front commission, usually levied as a percentage, for example, a 3% front-end load, or as a level-load for as long as the investor holds the fund.

Investopedia explains *No-Load Fund*

Because there is no transaction cost to purchase a no-load fund, all the money is invested in the fund. For example, if an investor purchases $10,000 worth of a no-load mutual fund, the whole $10,000 will be invested in the fund. In contrast, if an investor buys a load fund that charges a front-end load (sales commission) of 5%, the amount actually invested in the fund is only $9,500. If the load is back-ended, when shares of the fund are sold, $500 is charged at the time of the sale. If the level-load (12b-1 fee) is 1%, the investor's fund balance will be charged $100 annually for as long as the investor owns the fund. The justification for a load fund is that investors are paying for professional management of the fund. Some research indicates that load funds do not outperform no-load funds.

RELATED TERMS:
- Expense Ratio
- Load Fund
- Net Asset Value—NAV
- Front-End Load
- Mutual Fund

NOMINAL GDP

What Does *Nominal GDP* Mean?
A gross domestic product (GDP) figure that has not been adjusted for inflation. Also known as current dollar GDP or chained dollar GDP.

Investopedia explains *Nominal GDP*
Any GDP figure that does not account for inflation can be misleading because GDP will appear higher than it actually is. The same concept that applies to return on investment (ROI) applies here. If a person has a 10% ROI and inflation for the year has been 3%, that person's real rate of return will be 7%. Similarly, if the nominal GDP figure has shot up 8% but inflation has been 4%, the real GDP has increased only 4%.

RELATED TERMS:
- Consumer Price Index—CPI
- Gross Domestic Product—GDP
- Market Economy
- Inflation
- Real Gross Domestic Product

NONMARGINABLE SECURITIES

What Does *Nonmarginable Securities* Mean?
Securities that cannot be purchased on margin. Some classes of securities, such as recent initial public offerings (IPOs),

over-the-counter bulletin board stocks, and penny stocks, are non-marginable by decree of the Federal Reserve Board. Other securities, such as stocks with share prices under $5 or with extremely high betas, may be excluded at the discretion of the broker. Nonmarginable securities must be paid for 100% with the investor's own cash, and holdings in nonmarginable securities do not add to the investor's margin buying power.

 Investopedia explains *Nonmarginable Securities*
Most brokerage firms have their own internal lists of nonmarginable securities, which investors can find online or by contacting their institutions. These lists will be adjusted over time to reflect changes in share prices and volatility. The main goal of keeping some securities nonmarginable is to mitigate investor risk and control the administrative costs of excessive margin calls.

RELATED TERMS:
- *Margin*
- *Margin Call*
- *Over-the-Counter Bulletin Board—OTCBB*
- *Penny Stock*
- *Margin Account*

NOTIONAL VALUE

 What Does *Notional Value* **Mean?**
The total value of a leveraged position's assets. This term is used commonly in the options, futures, and currency markets to describe how a very small amount of invested money can control a large position (and have a large consequence for the trader).

 Investopedia explains *Notional Value*
As an example, one S&P 500 Index futures contract obligates the buyer for 250 units of the S&P 500 Index. If the index is trading at $1,000, the futures contract is the equivalent to investing $250,000 (250 × $1,000). Therefore, $250,000 is the notional value underlying the futures contract.

RELATED TERMS:
- *Derivative*
- *Hedge*
- *Open Interest*
- *Futures*
- *Leverage*

What's wrong this time?

My stock was delisted. It's now trading on EBAY.

copyright JackGuinan

OCTOBER EFFECT

What Does *October Effect* Mean?
A theory that postulates that stocks tend to decline during the month of October.

Investopedia explains *October Effect*
Some investors may be nervous during October because some large historical market crashes occurred during that month. Black Monday, Tuesday, and Thursday all occurred in October 1929, after which came the Great Depression. In addition, the great crash of 1987 occurred on October 19 and saw the Dow plummet 22.6% in a single day. Today the October effect is considered a psychological expectation rather than an actual phenomenon. Most statistics go against the theory.

RELATED TERMS:
- Bear Market
- Behavioral Finance
- Swing Trading
- Bull Market
- January Effect

OFF-BALANCE-SHEET FINANCING

What Does *Off-Balance-Sheet Financing* Mean?
A form of financing in which large capital expenditures are kept off a company's balance sheet through various classification methods.

Companies often use off-balance-sheet financing to keep their debt-to-equity (D/E) and leverage ratios low, especially if the inclusion of a large expenditure would break negative debt covenants.

 Investopedia explains *Off-Balance-Sheet Financing*
Examples of off-balance-sheet financing include joint ventures, research and development partnerships, and operating leases (rather than purchases of capital equipment). Operating leases are one of the most common forms of off-balance-sheet financing. In these cases, the asset is kept on the lessor's balance sheet, and the lessee reports only the required rental expense for use of the asset. Generally accepted accounting principles (GAAP) in the United States set numerous rules regarding whether a lease should be capitalized (included on the balance sheet) or expensed. This term came into popular use during the Enron bankruptcy. Many energy traders' problems stemmed from setting up inappropriate off-balance-sheet entities.

RELATED TERMS:
- Balance Sheet
- Debt/Equity Ratio
- Generally Accepted Accounting Principles—GAAP
- Capital Structure
- Float

OLIGOPOLY

 What Does *Oligopoly* **Mean?**
A market condition in which a particular segment of the market is controlled by a small group of firms. An oligopoly is much like a monopoly, in which only one company exerts control over most of a market. In an oligopoly, there are at least two firms controlling the market.

 Investopedia explains *Oligopoly*
The retail gas market is a good example of an oligopoly because a small number of firms control a large majority of the market.

RELATED TERMS:
- Behavioral Finance
- Law of Supply
- Monopoly
- Law of Demand
- Market Economy

OPEN INTEREST

What Does *Open Interest* Mean?
(1) The total number of options and/or futures contracts that are not closed or delivered on a particular day. (2) The number of buy market orders entered before the stock market's open.

Investopedia explains *Open Interest*
(1) A common misconception is that open interest is the same thing as the volume of options and futures trades. This is not correct, as is shown in the following example:

Time	Trading Activity	Open Interest
Jan 1	**A** buys 1 option and **B** sells 1 option contract	1
Jan 2	**C** buys 5 options and **D** sells 5 options contracts	6
Jan 3	**A** sells his 1 option and **D** buys 1 options contract	5
Jan 4	**E** buys 5 options from **C** who sells 5 options contracts	5

On January 1, A buys an option, which leaves an open interest and also creates trading volume of 1. On January 2, C and D create a trading volume of 5, and there are also five more options left open. On January 3, A takes an offsetting position, open interest is reduced by 1, and trading volume is 1. On January 4, E simply replaces C, open interest does not change, and trading volume increases by 5.

RELATED TERMS:
- Futures
- Options
- Volume

- Index Futures
- Stock Option

OPEN-END FUND

What Does *Open-End Fund* Mean?
A type of mutual fund that does not have restrictions on the amount of shares the fund issues. If demand is high enough, the fund will continue to issue shares no matter how many investors there are. Open-end funds also buy back shares when investors want to sell them. These sales are called redemptions.

Investopedia explains *Open-End Fund*
The majority of mutual funds are open-end. Continuously selling and buying back fund shares provides investors with a useful
and convenient investing vehicle. Sometimes a fund's investment
manager(s) may determine that a fund's total assets have become
too large to manage effectively for a desired total return. When this
happens, the fund may close to new investors and in extreme cases
may stop any new investments by existing fund investors.

RELATED TERMS:
- *Closed-End Fund*
- *Index Fund*
- *Net Asset Value—NAV*
- *Exchange-Traded Fund—ETF*
- *Mutual Fund*

OPERATING CASH FLOW (OCF)

 What Does *Operating Cash Flow (OCF)* Mean?
The cash generated from the operations of a company; generally
defined as revenues minus all operating expenses but calculated
through a series of adjustments to net income. The OCF can be
found on the statement of cash flows. Also known as cash flow
provided by operations or cash flow
from operating activities. One method
of calculating OCF is shown here:

$$OCF = EBIT + Depreciation - Taxes$$

 Investopedia explains *Operating Cash Flow (OCF)*
Operating cash flow is the cash that a company generates as a result
of normal business operations. It is arguably a better measure of a
business's profits than is earnings because a company can show positive net earnings (on the income statement) and not be able to pay
its debts. It is cash flow that pays the bills: OCF also can be used to
check on the quality of a company's earnings. If a firm reports record
earnings but negative cash, it may be using aggressive accounting
techniques.

RELATED TERMS:
- *Cash Flow*
- *Operating Expenses*
- *Operating Margin*
- *Cash Flow Statement*
- *Operating Income*

OPERATING CASH FLOW (OCF) RATIO

What Does *Operating Cash Flow (OCF) Ratio* Mean?

A measure of how well current liabilities are covered by the cash flow generated from a company's operations. It is calculated as shown here:

$$\text{OCF Ratio} = \frac{\text{Cash Flow from Operations}}{\text{Current Liabilities}}$$

Investopedia explains *Operating Cash Flow (OCF) Ratio*

The operating cash flow ratio helps gauge a company's liquidity in the short term. Using cash flow as opposed to income is sometimes a better indication of liquidity, because cash is how bills are normally paid off.

RELATED TERMS:

- Current Liabilities
- Liquidity Ratios
- Quick Ratio
- Income Statement
- Operating Cash Flow—OCF

OPERATING EXPENSE

What Does *Operating Expense* Mean?

An expenditure that a business incurs as a result of normal business operations; a challenge faced by a company's management is to determine how much operating expenses can be reduced without significantly affecting the firm's ability to compete with its competitors. Also known as OPEX.

Investopedia explains *Operating Expense*

As an example, the payment of employee wages and the allocation of funds for research and development are operating expenses. In the absence of raising prices or finding new markets or product channels to increase sales and raise profits, some businesses attempt to increase the bottom line solely by cutting expenses. Although laying off employees and reducing product quality initially can boost earnings and may even be necessary when a company has lost its competitiveness, operating expenses can be cut only so much before the quality of business operations is damaged.

RELATED TERMS:

- Expense Ratio
- Operating Income
- Operating Profit
- Operating Cash Flow—OCF
- Operating Margin

OPERATING INCOME

What Does *Operating Income* Mean?
The amount of profit realized from a business's own operations, excluding operating expenses (such as cost of goods sold) and depreciation from gross income. Also referred to as operating profit and recurring profit. It is calculated as shown here:

Operating Income = Gross Income − Operating Expenses − Depreciation

Investopedia explains *Operating Income*
Operating income does not include items such as investments in other firms, taxes, and interest expenses. In addition, nonrecurring items such as cash paid for a lawsuit settlement often are not included. Operating income is necessary to calculate operating margin, which describes a company's operating efficiency.

RELATED TERMS:
- Cash Conversion Cycle
- Gross Income
- Operating Expenses
- Cost of Goods Sold—COGS
- Net Operating Income—NOI

OPERATING LEVERAGE

What Does *Operating Leverage* Mean?
A measurement of the degree to which a firm or project incurs a combination of fixed and variable costs. (1) A business that has limited sales, with each sale providing a very high gross margin, is said to be highly leveraged. A business that makes many sales, with each sale contributing a very low margin, is said to be less leveraged. As the volume of sales in a business increases, each new sale contributes less to fixed costs and more to profitability. (2) A business that has a higher proportion of fixed costs and a lower proportion of variable costs is said to use more operating leverage. Conversely, businesses with lower fixed costs and higher variable costs are said to employ less operating leverage.

Investopedia explains *Operating Leverage*
The higher the degree of operating leverage, the greater the potential danger for inaccurately forecasting risk. That is, if a relatively small error is made in forecasting sales, it can be magnified into large errors in projections of cash flow. The opposite is true for businesses that

are less leveraged. A business that sells millions of products a year, with each contributing slightly to paying for fixed costs, is not as dependent on each individual sale. For example, convenience stores are significantly less leveraged than are high-end car dealerships.

RELATED TERMS:
- Cash Flow
- Gross Margin
- Volume
- Debt
- Leverage

OPERATING MARGIN

What Does *Operating Margin* Mean?
A ratio used to measure a company's pricing strategy and operating efficiency. It is calculated as shown here:

$$\text{Operating Margin} = \frac{\text{Operating Income}}{\text{Net Sales}}$$

Operating margin is a measurement of the proportion of a company's revenue that is left over after variable costs of production such as wages, and raw materials have been paid. A healthy operating margin is required for a company to be able to pay for its fixed costs, such as interest on debt. Also known as operating profit margin and net profit margin.

Investopedia explains *Operating Margin*
The operating margin gives analysts an idea of how much a company makes (before interest and taxes) on each dollar of sales. In evaluating the quality of a company, it is best to look at the change in operating margin over time and compare the company's yearly or quarterly figures with those of its competitors. If a company's margin is increasing, it is earning more per dollar of sales. The higher the margin, the better. For example, if a company has an operating margin of 12%, that means that it makes $0.12 (before interest and taxes) for every dollar of sales. Often, nonrecurring cash flows such as cash paid out in a lawsuit settlement are excluded from the calculation of operating margin because they do not represent a company's true operating performance.

RELATED TERMS:
- Contribution Margin
- Operating Income
- Revenue
- Net Sales
- Operating Leverage

OPERATING PROFIT

What Does *Operating Profit* Mean?

The profit earned from a firm's core business operations. It does not include profit earned from the firm's investments (such as earnings from firms in which the company has a partial interest) and the effects of interest and taxes. Also known as earnings before interest and taxes (EBIT). It is calculated as shown here:

Operating Profit = Operating Revenue − Operating Expenses

Investopedia explains *Operating Profit*

As an example, suppose ABC Printing Company earns $50 million from its core printing-related operations, $10 million from its 40% stake in XYZ Corp., and $3.5 million from interest earned in its money market and bank accounts. In addition, the company spends $10 million in production-related costs. Overall, the company's operating profit is $40 million. This is calculated by subtracting the $10 million in production costs from the $50 million in operating revenue. The other $10 million and $3.5 million in earnings are not included in operating income because they are investment income.

RELATED TERMS:
- *Inventory Turnover*
- *Operating Income*
- *Revenue*
- *Operating Expense*
- *Operating Margin*

OPPORTUNITY COST

What Does *Opportunity Cost* Mean?

(1) The cost of an alternative action that must be forgone to pursue a certain action. Put another way, the benefits an investor could have received by taking an alternative action. (2) The difference in return between an investment that was undertaken and one that was passed up. For example, say a person invests in a stock and it returns a paltry 2% over the year. In placing his or her money in the stock, the investor gave up the opportunity of another investment, say, a risk-free government bond yielding 6%. In this situation, the opportunity costs are 4% (6% − 2%).

Investopedia explains *Opportunity Cost*
(1) The opportunity cost of going to college is the money the student would have earned by working instead. On the one hand, the student loses four years of salary while getting a degree; on the other hand, the student hopes to earn more during his or her career, thanks to education, to offset the lost wages. Put another way, if a gardener decides to grow carrots, his or her opportunity cost is the alternative crop that might have been grown instead (potatoes, tomatoes, pumpkins, etc.). In both cases, a choice between two options must be made. It would be an easy decision if one knew the outcome; however, the risk that one could receive greater "benefits" (monetary or otherwise) with another option is the opportunity cost.

RELATED TERMS:
- *Capital Structure*
- *Gross Profit Margin*
- *Profit and Loss Statement*
- *Earnings*
- *Net Sales*

OPTIMIZATION

 What Does *Optimization* Mean?
In the context of technical analysis, the process of adjusting one's trading system in an attempt to make it more effective. These adjustments include changing the number of periods used in moving averages, changing the number of indicators used, and simply taking away what does not work.

 Investopedia explains *Optimization*
As an example, if an investor has a simple trading system that is composed of a crossover of the closing price and a moving average, by changing the periods of the moving average, the trader will get different profits, risk, capital drawdowns, and so on. Thus, optimization helps investors select the optimal parameters to trade.

RELATED TERMS:
- *Modern Portfolio Theory—MPT*
- *Simple Moving Average*
- *Trend Analysis*
- *Moving Average*
- *Technical Analysis*

OPTION

What Does *Option* Mean?

A financial derivative that represents a contract sold by one party (option writer) to another party (option holder). The contract offers the buyer the right, but not the obligation, to buy (call) or sell (put) a security or another financial asset at an agreed-on price (the strike price) during a certain period or on a specific date (excercise date).

Investopedia explains *Option*

Options are extremely versatile securities that can be used in many different ways. Traders use options to speculate, which is a relatively risky practice, whereas hedgers use options to reduce the risk of holding an asset. In terms of speculation, option buyers and writers have opposite views on the direction of the underlying security. For example, because the option writer will need to provide the underlying shares if the stock's market price will exceed the strike price, an option writer that sells a call option believes that the underlying stock's price will drop relative to the option's strike price during the life of the option, as that is how he or she will reap maximum profit. This is exactly the opposite to the outlook of the option buyer. The buyer believes that the underlying stock will rise, because if this happens, the buyer will be able to acquire the stock for a lower price and then sell it for a profit.

RELATED TERMS:
- *Call*
- *Intrinsic Value*
- *Put*
- *Derivative*
- *Maturity*

OUT OF THE MONEY (OTM)

What Does *Out of the Money (OTM)* Mean?

(1) For a call option, when an option's strike price is higher than the market price of the underlying asset. (2) For a put option, when the strike price is below the market price of the underlying asset.

Investopedia explains *Out of the Money (OTM)*

Basically, an option that would be worthless if it expired today.

RELATED TERMS:
- Call Option
- Put Option
- Strike Price

- In the Money
- Stock Option

OUTSTANDING SHARES

What Does *Outstanding Shares* Mean?
Stock currently held by investors, including restricted shares owned by the company's officers and insiders, as well as those held by the public. Shares that have been repurchased by the company are not considered outstanding stock. Also referred to as issued and outstanding if all repurchased shares have been retired.

Investopedia explains *Outstanding Shares*
Outstanding shares are shown on a company's balance sheet under the heading "Capital Stock" and are more important figures than the authorized shares or float numbers. Outstanding shares are used to calculate several metrics, including market capitalization and earnings per share (EPS).

RELATED TERMS:
- Capital Structure
- Float
- Market Capitalization

- Diluted Earnings per Share—Diluted EPS
- Fully Diluted Shares

OVERBOUGHT

What Does *Overbought* Mean?
(1) A situation in which the demand for a certain asset unjustifiably pushes the price of an underlying asset to levels that do not support the fundamentals. (2) In technical analysis, this term describes a situation in which the price of a security has risen to such a degree—usually on high volume—that an oscillator has reached its upper bound. This generally is interpreted as a sign that the asset is becoming overvalued and may experience a pullback.

Investopedia explains *Overbought*
(1) An asset that has experienced sharp upward movements over a very short period often is deemed to be overbought. Determining the degree in which an asset is overbought is very subjective and

can differ between investors. (2) Technicians use indicators such as the relative strength index, the stochastic oscillator, and the money flow index to identify securities that are becoming overbought. An overbought security is the opposite of one that is oversold.

RELATED TERMS:
- *Law of Demand*
- *Relative Strength Index—RSI*
- *Technical Analysis*
- *Oversold*
- *Stochastic Oscillator*

OVERNIGHT INDEX SWAP

What Does *Overnight Index Swap* Mean?
An interest rate swap in which the overnight rate is exchanged for another fixed interest rate.

Investopedia explains *Overnight Index Swap*
Generally short-term, the interest of the overnight rate portion of the swap is compounded and paid at maturity.

RELATED TERMS:
- *Arbitrage*
- *Interest Rate*
- *Swap*
- *Index*
- *Interest Rate Swap*

OVERSOLD

What Does *Oversold* Mean?
(1) A condition in which the price of an underlying asset has fallen sharply to a level below its fundamental value. This condition is usually a result of market overreaction or panic selling. (2) A situation in technical analysis in which the price of an asset has fallen to such a degree—usually on high volume—that an oscillator has reached a lower bound. This generally is interpreted as a sign that the price of the asset is becoming undervalued and may represent a buying opportunity for investors.

Investopedia explains *Oversold*
(1) Assets that have experienced sharp declines over a brief period often are deemed to be oversold. Determining the degree to which an asset is oversold is very subjective and can differ between investors.

(2) Identifying areas where the price of an underlying asset has been pushed unjustifiably to extremely low levels is the main goal of technical indicators such as the relative strength index, the stochastic oscillator, the moving average convergence divergence, and the money flow index. Oversold is the opposite of overbought.

RELATED TERMS:
- *Moving Average*
- *Moving Average Convergence Divergence—MACD*
- *Overbought*   • *Relative Strength Index—RSI*
- *Stochastic Oscillator*

OVER THE COUNTER (OTC)

 What Does *Over the Counter (OTC)* Mean?
A security traded off exchanges such as the NYSE, TSX, and AMEX. The phrase "over the counter" can be used to refer to stocks that trade via a dealer network as opposed to on a centralized exchange. It also refers to debt securities and other financial instruments, such as derivatives, which are traded through a dealer network.

 Investopedia explains *Over the Counter (OTC)*
In general, the reason a stock is traded over the counter is usually that the company is small, making it unable to meet the rigorous listing requirements of more traditional stock exchanges such as the New York Stock Exchange. Also known as unlisted stock, OTC securities are traded by broker-dealers who negotiate directly with one another over computer networks and by phone. Although Nasdaq operates as a dealer network, Nasdaq stocks generally are not classified as OTC because the Nasdaq is considered a stock exchange. As such, OTC stocks are generally unlisted stocks that trade on the Over-the-Counter Bulletin Board (OTCBB) or on the pink sheets. One must be very wary of some OTC stocks; OTCBB stocks either are penny stocks or are offered by companies with bad credit records. Instruments such as bonds do not trade on a formal exchange and therefore also are considered OTC securities. Most debt instruments are traded by investment banks that make markets for specific issues. If an investor wants to buy or sell a bond, he or she must call the bank that makes the market in that bond and ask for quotes.

RELATED TERMS:
- *Electronic Communications Network*
- *Nasdaq*
- *New York Stock Exchange—NYSE*
- *Over-the-Counter Bulletin Board—OTCBB*
- *Pink Sheets*

OVER-THE-COUNTER BULLETIN BOARD (OTCBB)

What Does *Over-the-Counter Bulletin Board (OTCBB)* Mean?
A regulated electronic trading service offered by the National Association of Securities Dealers (NASD) that shows real-time quotes, last-sale prices, and volume information for over-the-counter (OTC) equity securities. Companies listed on this exchange are required to file current financial statements with the SEC or a banking or insurance regulator. There are no listing requirements such as those found on the Nasdaq and the New York Stock Exchange. Stocks that trade on the OTCBB have the suffix "OB."

Investopedia explains *Over-the-Counter Bulletin Board (OTCBB)*
It is important to note that companies listed on the OTCBB are not a part of the Nasdaq exchange. OTCBB stocks are not especially large or stable and are considered very risky. As a result, very few OTCBB stocks are successful in making the jump from this market to the Nasdaq or any other major exchange because they are unable to meet the listing requirements. Furthermore, because OTCBB stocks tend to trade infrequently, they are less liquid, and consequently, the bid-ask spread is larger.

RELATED TERMS:
- *Nasdaq*
- *National Association of Securities Dealers—NASD*
- *Nonmarginable Security*
- *Over the Counter—OTC*
- *Pink Sheets*

"Our children haven't a clue about finances. They think the economic cycle starts when they buy something and ends when we pay for it!"

copyright JackGuinan

PAID-UP CAPITAL

What Does *Paid-Up Capital* Mean?
The total amount of shareholder capital that has been paid in full by shareholders.

Investopedia explains *Paid-Up Capital*
Paid-up capital is essentially the portion of authorized stock that the company has issued and received payment for.

RELATED TERMS:
- *Capital*
- *Float*
- *Shareholders' Equity*
- *Common Stock*
- *Outstanding Shares*

PAR VALUE

What Does *Par Value* Mean?
(1) The face value of a bond. (2) A dollar amount that is assigned to a security in the process of representing the value contributed for each share in cash or goods.

Investopedia explains *Par Value*
(1) The par values for different fixed-income products vary. Bonds generally have a par value of $1,000, whereas most money market

instruments have higher par values. (2) Stocks will have a par value of $0.01 or no par value.

RELATED TERMS:
- Face Value
- Fair Value
- Yield to Maturity—YTM
- Corporate Bond
- Market Value

PARI-PASSU

What Does *Pari-Passu* Mean?
Two securities or obligations that have equal rights to payment.

Investopedia explains *Pari-Passu*
The term is Latin and translates to "without partiality." For example, a secondary issue of shares that carry equal rights with existing shares are said to rank pari-passu.

RELATED TERMS:
- Bond
- Parity
- Subordinated Debt
- Debt
- Stock

PARITY

What Does *Parity* Mean?
(1) In general, a situation of equality. Parity can occur in many different contexts, but it always means that two things are equal. (2) The official value. (3) In an exchange market, the situation that occurs when all brokers bidding for the same security have equal standing as a result of identical bids.

Investopedia explains *Parity*
(1) For example, in the foreign exchange market, currencies are at parity when their exchange rate is exactly one to one. (2) In other words, the par value. (3) When parity occurs, the market must determine which bidding broker will obtain the security. This winning bid typically is awarded by means of a random drawing.

RELATED TERMS:
- Bond
- Market Maker
- Stock Market
- Broker-Dealer
- Par Value

PASSIVE INVESTING

What Does *Passive Investing* Mean?
An investment strategy that does not include active buying and selling of securities. Passive investors purchase investments with the intention of long-term appreciation and thus have limited portfolio turnover. Index fund investing, in which shares in the fund simply mirror an index, is a form of passive investing.

Investopedia explains *Passive Investing*
Also known as a buy-and-hold or couch potato strategy, passive investing requires good initial research, patience, and a well-diversified portfolio. Unlike active investors, passive investors buy a security and typically do not actively attempt to profit from short-term price fluctuations. Passive investors instead rely on their belief that in the long term the investment will be profitable.

RELATED TERMS:
- *Diversification*
- *Index*
- *Mutual Fund*
- *Exchange-Traded Fund*
- *Index Fund*

PAYBACK PERIOD

What Does *Payback Period* Mean?
The length of time it takes to recover the cost of an investment. It is calculated as shown here:

$$= \frac{\text{Cost of Project}}{\text{Annual Cash Inflows}}$$

Investopedia explains *Payback Period*
All other things being equal, the better investment is the one with the shorter payback period. For example, if a project costs $100,000 and is expected to return $20,000 annually, the payback period will be $100,000/$20,000, or five years. There are two main deficiencies with the payback period method: (1) It ignores any benefits that occur after the payback period and therefore does not measure profitability. (2) It ignores the time value of money. Because of these factors, other methods of capital budgeting, such as net present value, internal rate of return, and discounted cash flow, generally are preferred.

RELATED TERMS:
- *Cost of Capital*
- *Internal Rate of Return—IRR*
- *Return on Investment*
- *Discounted Cash Flow—DCF*
- *Opportunity Cost*

PENNY STOCK

What Does *Penny Stock* Mean?

A stock that trades at a very low share price and market capitalization; usually it trades off a major market exchange. These types of stocks generally are considered highly speculative and risky because they lack liquidity, have large bid-ask spreads, are small capitalization, and have limited analyst coverage and disclosure. They often trade on the OTCBB and pink sheets.

Investopedia explains *Penny Stock*

The term is a misnomer, because there are no standard criteria for defining a penny stock. Some consider one to be any stock that trades for pennies or under $5, whereas others consider it to be any stock that trades off a major market exchange. However, there are some very large companies, based on market capitalization, that trade below $5 per share, and there are many very small companies that trade for $5 per share or more. The typical penny stock is a very small company with highly illiquid and speculative shares. The company also generally is subject to limited listing requirements along with fewer filing and regulatory standards. The bottom line is that penny stocks can be risky investments.

RELATED TERMS:
- *Illiquid*
- *Over-the-Counter Bulletin Board—OTCBB*
- *Nonmarginable Security*
- *Over the Counter—OTC*
- *Pink Sheets*

PINK SHEETS

What Does *Pink Sheets* Mean?

A daily publication compiled by the National Quotation Bureau that quotes bid and ask prices of over-the-counter (OTC) stocks along with all the market makers that trade them. Unlike companies on a stock exchange, companies quoted on the pink sheets are not required to meet listing minimums or file with the SEC. The term also refers to OTC trading.

Investopedia explains *Pink Sheets*

Pink sheets got their name because they were printed on pink paper. One can tell whether a company trades on the pink sheets because the stock symbol will end in "PK."

RELATED TERMS:
- *Illiquid*
- *Over-the-Counter Bulletin Board—OTCBB*
- *Market Risk Premium*
- *Penny Stock*
- *Securities and Exchange Commission—SEC*

PIP

What Does *Pip* Mean?
The smallest price change that a particular exchange rate can process. Because most major currency pairs are priced to four decimal places, the smallest change is that of the last decimal point; for most pairs this is the equivalent of 1/100 of 1 percent, or one basis point.

Investopedia explains *Pip*
As an example, the smallest move the USD/CAD currency pair can make is $0.0001, or one basis point. The smallest move in a currency does not always have to be equal to one basis point, but this is the case with most currency pairs.

RELATED TERMS:
- *Bid-Ask Spread*
- *Currency Forward*
- *Money Market*
- *Basis Point—BPS*
- *Currency Swap*

PIVOT POINT

What Does *Pivot Point* Mean?
A technical indicator derived by calculating the numerical average of a particular stock's high, low, and closing prices.

Investopedia explains *Pivot Point*
The pivot point is used as a predictive indicator. If the following day's market price falls below the pivot point, it may signal a new resistance level. Conversely, if the market price rises above the pivot point, it may act as the new support level.

RELATED TERMS:
- *Bear Market*
- *Resistance*
- *Technical Analysis*
- *Bull Market*
- *Support*

PLAIN VANILLA

What Does *Plain Vanilla* Mean?

A term used to describe a standardized financial instrument: option, bond, future, and swap. Its opposite is an exotic instrument that alters the components of a traditional financial instrument, resulting in a more complex security.

Investopedia explains *Plain Vanilla*

As an example, a plain vanilla option is the standard type of option, one with a simple expiration date and strike price and no additional features. With an exotic option such as a knock-in option, an additional contingency is added so that the option becomes active only after the underlying stock hits a set price point.

RELATED TERMS:
- Convertible Bond
- Futures Contract
- Swap
- Derivative
- Knock-In Option

PLUS TICK

What Does *Plus Tick* Mean?

A price designation that refers to the trading of a security at a price higher than the previous sale price for that security. Also known as an uptick.

Investopedia explains *Plus Tick*

There are several rules regarding the tick status of a security that affect the type of trade orders that are permissible for that security at a specific moment in time. For example, some orders can be executed only on a plus tick or a zero plus tick (a transaction at the same price as the preceding trade but at a higher price than the last different trade).

RELATED TERMS:
- Ask
- Downtrend
- Uptrend
- Bid
- Uptick

POISON PILL

What Does *Poison Pill* Mean?

A defensive strategy used by a corporation to discourage a hostile takeover by another company. Poison pills are used to make the target company less attractive to the acquirer. There are two types of poison pills: (1) A flip-in allows existing shareholders (except the acquirer) to buy more shares at a discount. (2) A flip-over allows stockholders to buy the acquirer's shares at a discounted price after the merger.

Investopedia explains *Poison Pill*

(1) When more shares are purchased cheaply (flip-in), they dilute the shares held by the acquiring company. As a result, the competitor's takeover attempt is made more difficult and expensive. (2) An example of a flip-over occurs when shareholders have the right to purchase stock of the acquirer on a 2-for-1 basis in any subsequent merger. This is similar to the macaroni defense except that it uses equity rather than bonds.

RELATED TERMS:
- Common Stock
- Mergers and Acquisitions—M&A
- Shareholders' Equity
- Merger
- Takeover

PORTFOLIO

What Does *Portfolio* Mean?

A group of investments such as stocks, bonds and cash equivalents, mutual funds, exchange-traded funds, and closed-end funds that are selected on the basis of an investor's short-term or long-term investment goals. Portfolios are held directly by investors and/or managed by financial professionals.

Investopedia explains *Portfolio*

Prudence suggests that investors construct an investment portfolio in accordance with their risk tolerance and investment objectives. One should think of an investment portfolio as a pie that is divided into pieces of varying sizes that represent a variety of asset classes and/or types of investments to accomplish an appropriate risk-adjusted return. For example, a conservative investor may favor a portfolio with large-cap value stocks, broad-based market index funds, investment-grade bonds, and cash. In contrast, a risk-loving investor may hold small-cap growth stocks, aggressive large-cap growth stocks, some high-yield bonds, international investments, and maybe some alternative investments.

RELATED TERMS:
- Alpha
- Diversification
- Modern Portfolio Theory—MPT
- Asset Allocation
- Style Drift

PREFERRED STOCK

What Does *Preferred Stock* Mean?

A class of stock that has a priority claim on a company's assets and earnings over common stock. Preferred stockholders are paid dividends before common stockholders are, but preferred shares do not normally have voting rights. The characteristics of preferred stock are unique to each corporation. One way to think of preferred stock is as a financial instrument that has characteristics of both debt (fixed dividends) and equity (potential appreciation). Also known as preferred shares.

Investopedia explains *Preferred Stock*

There are pros and cons with preferred shares. Preferred shareholders have priority over common stockholders on earnings and assets in the event of liquidation and may have a fixed dividend (paid before common stockholders), but investors must weigh these positives against the drawback of having no voting rights as a shareholder.

RELATED TERMS:
- Common Stock
- Dividend Yield
- Yield
- Dividend
- Ex-Dividend

PREMIUM

What Does *Premium* Mean?

(1) The market price of an option contract. (2) The difference between the higher price paid for a fixed-income security and the security's face amount at issue (par value). (3) The specified amount

of payment required periodically by an insurer to provide coverage under a specific insurance plan for a defined period. The premium is paid by the insured party to the insurer and primarily compensates the insurer for bearing the risk of a payout if the insurance agreement's coverage is required.

Investopedia explains *Premium*
(1) The premium of an option is basically the sum of that option's intrinsic value and time value. It is important to note that volatility also affects the premium. (2) If a fixed-income security (bond) is purchased at a premium, existing interest rates are lower than the coupon rate. Investors pay a premium for an investment that will return an amount greater than existing interest rates. (3) A common example of an insurance premium is auto insurance. A vehicle owner can insure the value of his or her vehicle against loss resulting from an accident, theft, and other potential problems. The owner usually pays a fixed premium amount in exchange for the insurance company's guarantee to cover any economic losses incurred under the scope of the agreement.

RELATED TERMS:
- Coupon
- Market Risk Premium
- Time Value of Money
- Intrinsic Value
- Option

PRESENT VALUE (PV)

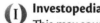

What Does *Present Value (PV)* Mean?
The current worth of a future sum of money or stream of cash flows when there is a specified rate of return. Future cash flows are discounted at the discount rate, and the higher the discount rate, the lower the present value of the future cash flows. Determining the appropriate discount rate is the key to valuing future cash flows properly, whether they are earnings or obligations. Also referred to as discounted value.

Investopedia explains *Present Value (PV)*
This may sound confusing, but it really is not. The basic idea is that receiving $1,000 now is worth more than receiving $1,000 five years from now, because a person who has money today can invest it and receive an additional return over the five years. The calculation

of discounted value or present value is extremely important in many financial calculations. For example, net present value, bond yields, spot rates, and pension obligations all rely on the principle of discounted value or present value. Learning how to use a financial calculator to make present value calculations can help an investor decide whether to accept a cash rebate, 0% financing on the purchase of a car, or to pay points on a mortgage. Investopedia recommends that investors get a calculator that computes PV.

RELATED TERMS:
- *Discount Rate*
- *Internal Rate of Return—IRR*
- *Time Value of Money*
- *Future Value*
- *Net Present Value—NPV*

PRESENT VALUE INTEREST FACTOR (PVIF)

What Does *Present Value Interest Factor (PVIF)* Mean?
A factor that can simplify the calculation for finding the present value of a series of values; PVIFs can be presented in the form of a table with PVIF values separated by respective period and interest rate combinations, as is shown here.

$$PVIF = \frac{1}{(1+r)^t}$$

The "r" represents the discount interest rate, and the "t" represents the number of periods.

Investopedia explains *Present Value Interest Factor (PVIF)*
PVIF works best when one is attempting to discount one value in the future. For example, assume an investor is going to receive $5,000 in four years and the current discount interest rate is 8%. Using the standard present value formula, the calculation would be $5,000/(1 + .08 ^ 4). This would result in a present value of approximately $3,675.15. Using a PVIF table, an individual finds that the factor for this calculation is 0.73503 (calculated 1/(1.08 ^ 4)). Then, that individual multiplies the $5,000 by 0.73503, giving the same result—$3,675.15. This is another way to express the standard present value but is more helpful when one is faced with a large number of values.

RELATED TERMS:
- *Discounted Cash Flow—DCF*
- *Net Present Value—NPV*
- *Time Value of Money*
- *Internal Rate of Return—IRR*
- *Present Value—PV*

PRICE TO TANGIBLE BOOK VALUE (PTBV)

What Does *Price to Tangible Book Value (PTBV)* Mean?

A valuation ratio that expresses the price of a security compared with its hard, or tangible, book value as reported in the company's balance sheet. The tangible book value number is equal to the company's total book value minus the value of any intangible assets. Intangible assets are usually assets such as patents, intellectual property, and goodwill. The ratio is calculated as shown here:

$$PTBV = \frac{\text{Share Price}}{\text{Tangible Book Value per Share}}$$

Investopedia explains *Price to Tangible Book Value (PTBV)*

In theory, a stock's tangible book value per share represents the amount of money an investor would receive for each share if the company went out of business and liquidated all of its assets at book value. As a rule of thumb, stocks that trade at higher price to tangible book value ratios have the potential to leave investors with greater share price losses compared with those which trade at lower ratios, since the tangible book value per share can be viewed as about the lowest price a stock realistically could be expected to trade at.

RELATED TERMS:
- Book Value
- Net Tangible Assets
- Price-to-Book Ratio—P/B Ratio
- Intangible Asset
- Tangible Asset

PRICE-WEIGHTED INDEX

What Does *Price-Weighted Index* Mean?

A stock index in which each stock influences the index in proportion to its price per share. The value of the index is generated by adding the prices of each of the stocks in the index and dividing them by the total number of stocks. Stocks with a higher price will be given more weight and therefore will have a greater influence on the performance of the index.

Investopedia explains *Price-Weighted Index*

As an example, assume that an index contains only two stocks: one priced at $1 and one priced at $10. The $10 stock is weighted nine times higher than is the $1 stock. Overall, this means that this index is composed of 90% of the $10 stock and 10% of the $1 stock. In this case, a change in the value of the $1 stock will not affect the index's value by a large amount, because that stock makes up such a small percentage of the index. A popular price-weighted stock market index is the Dow Jones Industrial Average. It includes a price-weighted average of 30 actively traded blue-chip stocks.

RELATED TERMS:
- *Dow Jones Industrial Average—DJIA*
- *New York Stock Exchange—NYSE*
- *Stock Market*
- *Standard & Poor's 500 Index—S&P 500*
- *Volume Weighted Average Price*

PRICE/EARNINGS TO GROWTH RATIO (PEG RATIO)

What Does *Price/Earnings to Growth Ratio (PEG Ratio)* Mean?

A ratio used to determine a stock's value while taking into account a company's earnings growth. The calculation is as shown here:

$$PEG\ Ratio = \frac{Price/Earnings\ Ratio}{Annual\ EPS\ Growth}$$

Investopedia explains *Price/Earnings to Growth Ratio (PEG Ratio)*

PEG is a widely used indicator of a stock's potential value. It is favored by many over the price-earnings ratio because it also accounts for growth. It is similar to the P/E ratio in that a lower PEG means that the stock is more undervalued. One should keep in mind that the numbers used in the calculation are projected and therefore are only estimates. Also, there are many variations using earnings from different time periods (e.g., one year versus five years). An investor should know the exact method the source is using.

RELATED TERMS:
- *Accounts Receivable—AR*
- *Earnings*
- *Price-Earnings Ratio—P/E Ratio*
- *Balance Sheet*
- *Earnings per Share—EPS*

PRICE-EARNINGS RATIO (P/E RATIO)

What Does *Price-Earnings Ratio (P/E Ratio)* Mean?

A popular valuation ratio of a company's current share price compared with its per-share earnings. It is calculated as shown here:

$$= \frac{Market\ Value\ per\ Share}{Earnings\ per\ Share\ (EPS)}$$

For example, if a company currently is trading at $43 a share and earnings over the last 12 months were $1.95 per share, the P/E ratio for the stock will be 22.05 ($43/$1.95). EPS usually is calculated from data from the previous four quarters (trailing P/E), but sometimes future earnings estimates are used (projected or forward P/E). A third variation uses the sum of the last two actual quarters and the estimates for the next two quarters. P/E sometimes is called the price multiple or earnings multiple.

Investopedia explains *Price-Earnings Ratio (P/E Ratio)*

In general, a high P/E suggests that investors are expecting higher earnings growth in the future compared with companies with a lower P/E. However, the P/E ratio does not tell the whole story. It is more helpful to compare the P/E ratios of companies in the same industry, the overall market, or the company's own historical P/E. It would not be useful for investors to compare the P/E of a technology company (high P/E) to that of an electric utility company (low P/E) as each industry has a much different growth potential. The P/E sometimes is referred to as the multiple, because it shows how much investors are willing to pay per dollar of earnings. If a company trades at a multiple (P/E) of 20, this means that investors are willing to pay $20 for $1 of current earnings. Note: The earnings number in the denominator (earnings) is susceptible to manipulation, making the quality of the P/E only as good as the quality of the underlying earnings number.

RELATED TERMS:
- *Earnings*
- *Forward Price to Earnings—Forward P/E*
- *Multiple*
- *Price-to-Book Ratio—P/B Ratio*
- *Price/Earnings to Growth Ratio—PEG Ratio*

PRICE-TO-BOOK RATIO (P/B RATIO)

What Does *Price-to-Book Ratio (P/B Ratio)* mean?

A ratio used to compare a stock's market value with its book value. It is calculated by dividing the current closing price of the stock by the latest quarter's book value per share. Also known as the price-equity ratio. It is calculated as shown here:

$$\text{P/B Ratio} = \frac{\text{Stock Price}}{\text{Total Assets} - \text{Intangible Assets and Liabilities}}$$

Investopedia explains *Price-to-Book Ratio (P/B Ratio)*
A lower P/B ratio could mean that the stock is undervalued. However, it also could mean that something is fundamentally wrong with the company. As with most ratios, one must be aware that this varies by industry. This ratio also can provide some idea of whether one is paying too much for what would be left if the company went bankrupt immediately.

Related Terms:
- Book Value
- Market Value
- Price-Earnings Ratio—P/E Ratio
- Gearing Ratio
- Value Investing

PRICE-TO-CASH-FLOW RATIO

 What Does *Price-to-Cash-Flow Ratio* Mean?
A measure of the market's expectations of a firm's future financial health. Because this measure deals with cash flow, the effects of depreciation and other noncash factors are removed. As with the price-earnings ratio, this measure provides an indication of relative value. It is calculated as shown here:

$$\text{Free Cash Flow} = \frac{\text{Share Price}}{\text{Cash Flow per Share}}$$

 Investopedia explains *Price-to-Cash-Flow Ratio*
Because accounting policies covering depreciation vary across jurisdictions, the price-to-cash-flow ratio helps investors assess foreign companies from the same industry (e.g., the mining industry) with a bit more ease.

Related Terms:
- Cash Flow
- Cash and Cash Equivalents—CCE
- Price-Earnings Ratio—P/E Ratio
- Cash Flow Statement

PRICE-TO-SALES RATIO (PRICE/SALES)

 What Does *Price-to-Sales Ratio (Price/Sales)* Mean?
A ratio that values a stock relative to its past performance, other companies, or the overall market; it is calculated by dividing a stock's

current price by its revenue per share for the trailing 12 months, as shown here:

$$PSR = \frac{Share\ Price}{Revenue\ per\ Share}$$

The ratio also is referred to as a stock's PSR.

 Investopedia explains *Price-to-Sales Ratio (Price/Sales)*
The price-to-sales ratio varies substantially across industries. Therefore, it is used mainly to compare like companies in the same industry. Also, because the ratio does not take any expenses or debt into account, it is somewhat limited in the story it tells.

RELATED TERMS:
- *Accounts Receivables—AR*
- *Price-Earnings Ratio—P/E Ratio*
- *Price/Earnings to Growth Ratio—PEG Ratio*
- *Revenue*
- *Cash Conversion Cycle—CCC*

PRIME RATE

 What Does *Prime Rate* Mean?
The interest rate charged by commercial banks to their most credit-worthy customers. Generally, a bank's best customers consist of large corporations.

 Investopedia explains *Prime Rate*
Default risk is a major consideration in setting interest rates. Because a bank's best customers have little chance of defaulting, the bank can charge them a rate that is lower than the rate charged to a customer with a higher likelihood of defaulting on a loan.

RELATED TERMS:
- *Basis Point*
- *Federal Funds Rate*
- *Working Capital*
- *Discount Rate*
- *Interest Rate*

PRIVATE EQUITY

 What Does *Private Equity* Mean?
Equity capital that is not quoted on a public exchange. Private equity consists of investors and funds that invest directly in private companies or conduct buyouts of public companies that result in a delisting of public equity. Capital for private equity is raised from

very wealthy individuals and institutional investors and is used to fund new technologies, expand working capital, make acquisitions, or strengthen a company's balance sheet. The majority of private equity consists of institutional investors and accredited investors (rich people) who commit large sums of money for long periods. Private equity investments are often long-term in cases of company turnarounds or a liquidity event such as an IPO or a sale to a public company.

 Investopedia explains *Private Equity*
The size of the private equity market has grown steadily since the 1970s. Private equity firms sometimes pool their funds to take very large public companies private. Private equity deals can rise into the range of billions of dollars. Many private equity firms conduct what are known as leveraged buyouts (LBOs), in which large amounts of debt are issued to fund a large purchase. Private equity firms then try to improve the company's financials in the hopes of reselling the company to another firm or cashing out by taking the company public in an IPO.

RELATED TERMS:
- *Equity*
- *Mezzanine Financing*
- *Shareholders' Equity*
- *Leveraged Buyout—LBO*
- *Private Placement*

PRIVATE PLACEMENT

 What Does *Private Placement* **Mean?**
Raising capital through a private rather than a public placement; the result is the sale of securities to a relatively small number of investors, such as large banks, mutual funds, insurance companies, and pension funds.

 Investopedia explains *Private Placement*
Because a private placement is offered to a few select individuals, the placement does not have to be registered with the Securities and Exchange Commission. In many cases, detailed financial information is not disclosed and the prospectus requirements are waived. The average investor usually is not aware of a private placement until after it happens, if ever.

Related Terms:
- Capital Structure
- Private Equity
- Venture Capital

- Initial Public Offering—IPO
- Prospectus

PRO FORMA

What Does *Pro Forma* Mean?
A Latin term meaning "for the sake of form." In the investing world, it is used to describe a method of calculating financial results to emphasize either current or projected figures.

Investopedia explains *Pro Forma*
Pro forma financial statements could be designed to reflect a proposed change, such as a merger or acquisition, or to emphasize certain figures when a company issues an earnings announcement to the public. Investors should be careful when reading a company's pro forma financial statements, as the figures may not comply with generally accepted accounting principles (GAAP). In some cases, the pro forma figures may differ greatly from those derived from GAAP.

Related Terms:
- Balance Sheet
- Generally Accepted Accounting Principles—GAAP
- Income Statement

- Earnings

- Retained Earnings

PROFIT AND LOSS STATEMENT (P&L)

What Does *Profit and Loss Statement (P&L)* Mean?
A financial statement that summarizes the revenues, costs, and expenses incurred during a specific period, usually a fiscal quarter or a year. P&L statements provide information that shows the ability of a company to generate profit by increasing revenue and reducing costs; it also is known as a statement of profit and loss, an income statement, or an income and expense statement.

Investopedia explains *Profit and Loss Statement (P&L)*
A P&L statement follows a general format, beginning with a revenue figure and then subtracting the costs of running the business, including the cost of goods sold, operating expenses, tax expense, and interest expense. The bottom line (literally and figuratively) is

net income (profit). The balance sheet, the income statement, and the statement of cash flows are the most important financial statements produced by a company and should be analyzed when one is making an investment decision.

RELATED TERMS:
- Cost of Goods Sold—COGS
- Income Statement
- Revenue
- Expense Ratio
- Profit Margin

PROFIT MARGIN

What Does *Profit Margin* Mean?
A ratio of profitability calculated as net income divided by revenues or net profits divided by sales. It measures the dollar amount of the sales that a company actually retains in earnings. Profit margin is very useful in comparing companies in similar industries. A higher profit margin indicates a more profitable company. Profit margin is displayed as a percentage; a 20% profit margin, for example, means that the company has a net income of $0.20 for each dollar of sales.

Investopedia explains *Profit Margin*
A company's earnings do not always tell the entire story. Increased earnings are good, but an increase does not mean that the profit margin of a company is improving. For instance, if a company's costs are rising at a faster pace than are sales, this will lead to a lower profit margin, indicating that the company should rein in its costs. Consider a company that has net income of $10 million from sales of $100 million, giving it a profit margin of 10% ($10 million/$100 million). If in the next year net income rises to $15 million on sales of $200 million, the company's profit margin will fall to 7.5%. Although the company has increased its net income, it has done so with diminishing profit margins.

RELATED TERMS:
- Gross Margin
- Operating Margin
- Revenue
- Net Income—NI
- Profitability Ratios

PROFITABILITY RATIOS

What Does *Profitability Ratios* Mean?

A class of financial metrics that help investors assess a business's ability to generate earnings compared with its expenses and other relevant costs incurred during a specific period. When these ratios are higher than a competitor's ratio or than the company's ratio from a previous period, this is a sign that the company is doing well.

Investopedia explains *Profitability Ratios*

Some examples of profitability ratios are profit margin, return on assets, and return on equity. It is important to note that one should understand the company and its business before making decisions that are based solely on ratios. For instance, some industries are seasonal, such as retailers, which typically experience higher revenues and earnings during the holiday season. Therefore, it would not be helpful to compare a retailer's fourth-quarter profit margin with its first-quarter profit margin. In contrast, comparing a retailer's fourth-quarter profit margin with the profit margin from the same period a year before would be far more helpful.

RELATED TERMS:
- *Operating Profit*
- *Return on Assets—ROA*
- *Return on Investment Capital—ROIC*
- *Profit Margin*
- *Return on Equity—ROE*

PROSPECTUS

What Does *Prospectus* Mean?

A legal document required by and filed with the Securities and Exchange Commission; provides details about an investment offering that is for sale to the public. A prospectus should contain all the material facts of the offering so that an investor can make an informed investment decision. Also known as an offer document.

Investopedia explains *Prospectus*

There are two types of prospectuses for stocks and bonds: preliminary and final. The preliminary prospectus is the first offering document provided by a securities issuer and includes most of the details of the business and transaction in question. Some lettering on the front cover is printed in red, which results in the use of the nickname "red herring" for this document. The final prospectus is printed after the deal has been made effective and can be offered for sale and supersedes the preliminary prospectus. It contains finalized background information, including details such as the exact number of shares/certificates issued and the precise offering price. In the case of mutual funds, which, apart from their initial share offering, continuously offer shares for sale to the public, the prospectus used is a final prospectus. A fund prospectus contains details on the fund's objectives, investment strategies, risks, performance, distribution policy, fees and expenses, and management.

Related Terms:
- *Common Stock*
- *Initial Public Offering—IPO*
- *Securities and Exchange Commission—SEC*
- *Due Diligence*
- *Mutual Fund*

PUT

What Does *Put* Mean?
An option contract that gives the owner the right, but not the obligation, to sell a specified amount of an underlying asset at a set price within a specified period. The buyer of a put option hopes that the underlying asset will drop below the exercise price before the expiration date. The possible payoff for a holder of a put option contract is illustrated by the accompanying diagram.

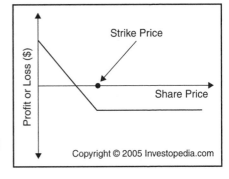

Investopedia explains *Put*

When an individual purchases a put, that person expects that the underlying asset will decline in price. The investor then will profit by selling the put option at a profit or by exercising the option, in other words, "putting the stock" to the option seller. If an individual writes a put contract, he or she expects the stock price to stay above the exercise price. Say an investor purchases one put contract for 100 shares of ABC Co. at $1 (total of $100 ($1 × 100)). The exercise price of the shares is $10, and the current ABC share price is $12. This contract has given the investor the right, but not the obligation, to sell shares of ABC at $10. When ABC shares drop to $8, the investor's put option is in the money and can be closed by selling the option contract on the open market. Alternatively, the investor could go into the market and buy 100 shares of ABC at the market price of $8 and then exercise the put by selling (putting) the shares to the option writer for $10. Excluding commissions, the investor's total profit for this position would be $100 [100 × ($10 – $8 – $1)]. If the investor already owned 100 shares of ABC, this is called a married put position and serves as a hedge against a decline in share price.

RELATED TERMS:
- Call
- In the Money
- Short (or Short Position)
- Derivative
- Option

PUT OPTION

What Does *Put Option* mean?
An option contract that gives the owner the right, but not the obligation, to sell (put) a specified amount of an underlying security at a specified price within a specified period. This is the opposite of a call option, which gives the holder the right to buy shares.

Investopedia explains *Put Option*
A put becomes more valuable as the price of the underlying stock depreciates below the option's strike price. For example, if an investor has one Mar 08 Taser 10 put, he or she has the right to sell 100 shares of Taser at $10 until March 2008 (usually the third Friday of the month). If shares of Taser fall to $5 and the investor exercises the option, he or she can purchase 100 shares of Taser for $5 in the market and sell the shares to the option's writer for $10 each; this means the investor makes $500 (100 × ($10 – $5)) on the put option. Note that in determining the profit, one must consider commissions and the actual cost of buying the put in the first place.

RELATED TERMS:
- Call Option
- Put-Call Ratio
- Stock Option
- Option
- Short (or Short Position)

PUT-CALL RATIO

What Does *Put-Call Ratio* Mean?
A ratio of the trading volume of put options to call options. It is used to gauge investor sentiment.

Investopedia explains *Put-Call Ratio*
As an example, a high volume of puts compared with calls indicates bearish sentiment in the market.

RELATED TERMS:
- Call Option
- Option
- Volume
- Open Interest
- Put Option

"Two years filling this up and not a word about my purchasing power being eroded by inflation."

QUALIFIED RETIREMENT PLAN (QUALIFIED PLAN)

What Does *Qualified Retirement Plan (Qualified Plan)* Mean?
A plan that meets the requirements of the Internal Revenue Code and as a result is eligible to receive certain tax benefits. These plans must be for the exclusive benefit of retirees or employees or their beneficiaries.

Investopedia explains *Qualified Retirement Plan (Qualified Plan)*
Two types of qualified plans are defined—benefit and defined—contribution plans. Some examples of defined-contribution plans are 401(k) plans, money-purchase pension plans, and profit-sharing plans.

RELATED TERMS:
- *Defined-Benefit Plan*
- *Defined-Contribution Plan*
- *Individual Retirement Account—IRA*
- *Roth IRA*
- *Tax Deferred*

QUANTITATIVE ANALYSIS

What Does *Quantitative Analysis* Mean?

A business or financial analysis technique that is used to understand market behavior by employing complex mathematical and statistical modeling, measurement, and research. By assigning a numerical value to variables, quantitative analysts try to replicate reality in mathematical terms. Quantitative analysis helps measure performance evaluation or valuation of a financial instrument. It also can be used to predict real-world events such as changes in a share's price.

Investopedia explains *Quantitative Analysis*

In broad terms, quantitative analysis is a way of measuring things. Examples of quantitative analysis include everything from simple financial ratio calculations such as earnings per share to more complicated analyses such as discounted cash flow or option pricing. Although quantitative analysis is a powerful tool for evaluating investments, it only tells half the story; the other half is qualitative analysis. In financial circles, quantitative analysts are referred to as quants, quant jockeys, and rocket scientists.

RELATED TERMS:
- *Fundamental Analysis*
- *Head and Shoulders Pattern*
- *Trend Analysis*
- *Gordon Growth Model*
- *Technical Analysis*

QUICK RATIO

What Does *Quick Ratio* Mean?

Also known as the "acid-test ratio" or the quick assets ratio, this is an indicator of a company's short-term liquidity. The quick ratio measures a company's ability to meet its short-term obligations with its most liquid assets. The higher the quick ratio, the better the position of the company. The quick ratio is calculated as shown here:

$$\text{Quick Ratio} = \frac{\text{Current Assets} - \text{Inventories}}{\text{Current Liabilities}}$$

Investopedia explains *Quick Ratio*

The quick ratio is more conservative than the current ratio, a better-known liquidity measure, because it excludes inventory from current assets. Inventory is excluded because some companies have difficulty turning their inventory into cash. If short-term obligations have to be paid off immediately, there are circumstances in which the current ratio could overestimate a company's short-term financial strength.

RELATED TERMS:
- Acid-Test Ratio
- Current Liabilities
- Liquidity
- Current Assets
- Current Ratio

QUOTE

What Does *Quote* Mean?
(1) The last price at which a security or commodity traded, meaning the most recent price on which a buyer and a seller agreed and at which some amount of the asset was transacted. (2) The bid or ask quotes are the most current prices and quantities at which the shares can be bought or sold. The bid quote shows the price and quantity at which a current buyer is willing to purchase the shares, and the ask quote shows what a current participant is willing to sell the shares for. This also is known as an asset's quoted price.

Investopedia explains *Quote*
(1) Price quotes for stocks and bonds change throughout the trading day as new transactions occur one after another in a continual stream of trades. When one looks up a stock quote for a particular company, one is looking at the most recent price at which a trade was executed successfully for that particular security. (2) Potential investors or sellers are more concerned about the bid and ask quotes because they reflect the prices at which the stock can be bought or sold, whereas the price quote as described in the first definition shows the price at which the stock traded most recently.

RELATED TERMS:
- Ask
- Bid-Ask Spread
- Volume
- Bid
- Security

REAL ESTATE INVESTMENT TRUST (REIT)

What Does *Real Estate Investment Trust (REIT)* Mean?
A security that trades like a stock on an exchange; REITs invest directly in real estate through either properties or mortgages. REITs receive special tax considerations and typically offer investors high yields as well as opportunities to invest in the real estate market without buying properties. REITs include equity REITs, in which one invests in and owns properties and thus is responsible for the equity or value of the real estate assets; the revenues come principally from the properties' rents. Mortgage REITs involve investment in and ownership of property mortgages; these REITs loan money for mortgages to owners of real estate or purchase existing mortgages or mortgage-backed securities. The revenues are generated primarily by the interest earned on the mortgage loans. Hybrid REITs combine the investment strategies of equity REITs and mortgage REITs by investing in both properties and mortgages.

Investopedia explains *Real Estate Investment Trust (REIT)*
Individuals can invest in REITs by purchasing their shares directly on an exchange or by investing in a mutual fund that invests in real estate. An additional benefit to investing in REITs is the fact that many are accompanied by dividend reinvestment plans (DRIPs). Among other things, REITs invest in shopping malls, office buildings, apartments, warehouses, and hotels. Some REITs invest specifically in one

area of real estate—shopping malls, for example—or in a specific region, state, or country. Investing in REITs is a liquid, dividend-paying means of participating in the real estate market.

RELATED TERMS:
- Asset
- Dividend
- Mortgage-Backed Securities—MBSs
- Stock
- Derivative

REAL GROSS DOMESTIC PRODUCT (GDP)

What Does *Real Gross Domestic Product (GDP)* Mean?
This inflation-adjusted measure reflects the value of all the goods and services produced in a particular year, expressed in base-year prices. Often referred to as constant-price GDP, inflation-corrected GDP, or constant dollar GDP.

Investopedia explains *Real Gross Domestic Product (GDP)*
Unlike nominal GDP, real GDP can account for changes in the price level and thus provide a more accurate figure. It is important to understand that a rise in GDP does not necessarily indicate growth unless inflation is factored in. Real GDP figures are normally lower than nominal GDP figures.

RELATED TERMS:
- Consumer Price Index—CPI
- Gross Domestic Product—GDP
- Nominal GDP
- Deflation
- Inflation

REAL RATE OF RETURN

What Does *Real Rate of Return* Mean?
The annual percentage return realized on an investment, adjusted for changes in prices that result from inflation or other external factors. This method expresses the nominal rate (not adjusted for inflation) of return in real terms, which keeps the purchasing power of a specific level of capital constant over time.

Investopedia explains *Real Rate of Return*
Adjusting the nominal rate of return to compensate for factors such as inflation allows investors to determine how much of their nominal

return is real return. Let's say a bank pays 5% interest per year in an investor's savings account. If the inflation rate is currently 3% per year, the real return on the investor's savings today is 2%. In other words, even though the nominal rate of return on the savings is 5%, the real rate of return is only 2%, which means that the real value of the investor's savings increases only 2% during a one-year period.

RELATED TERMS:
- Earnings
- Inflation
- Total Return
- Equity Risk Premium
- Return on Investment—ROI

RECEIVABLES TURNOVER RATIO

What Does *Receivables Turnover Ratio* Mean?
An accounting measure used to quantify a firm's effectiveness in extending credit and collecting debts. The receivables turnover ratio is an activity ratio, measuring how efficiently a firm uses its assets. It is calculated as shown here:

$$\text{Accounts Receivable Turnover} = \frac{\text{Net Credit Sales}}{\text{Average Accounts Receivable}}$$

Some companies' reports will only show sales—this can affect the ratio depending on the size of cash sales.

Investopedia explains *Receivables Turnover Ratio*
By holding accounts receivable on their books, companies are indirectly extending interest-free loans to their clients who haven't paid for their goods yet. A high ratio implies either that a company operates on a cash basis or that its extension of credit and collection of accounts receivable are efficient. A low ratio implies that the company should reassess its credit policies to ensure the timely collection of accounts receivable.

RELATED TERMS:
- Accounts Payable—AP
- Balance Sheet
- Net Sales
- Accounts Receivable—AR
- Income Statement

RECESSION

What Does *Recession* Mean?

A prolonged decline in activity across the economy that lasts longer than a few months; recessions have a negative impact on industrial production, employment, real income, and wholesale-retail trade. Technically, a recession is said to have occurred when there have been two consecutive quarters of negative economic growth as measured by a country's gross domestic product (GDP).

Investopedia explains *Recession*

Recession is a normal (albeit unpleasant) part of the business cycle; however, one-time crisis events can often trigger the onset of a recession. A recession generally lasts from 6 to 18 months. Interest rates usually fall are lowered in recessionary times to stimulate the economy by offering cheap rates at which to borrow money.

RELATED TERMS:
- Bear Market
- Consumer Price Index—CPI
- Gross Domestic Product—GDP
- Business Cycle
- Market Economy

RECORD DATE

What Does *Record Date* Mean?

The date established by an issuer of a security for the purpose of determining the holders who are entitled to receive a dividend or distribution.

Investopedia explains *Record Date*

On the record date, a company checks its records to see who its shareholders or "holders of record" are. Essentially, a date of record ensures that the dividend checks are sent to the right people.

RELATED TERMS:
- Dividend
- Ex-Dividend
- Stock Split
- Ex-Date
- Settlement Date

REGULATION T (REG T)

What Does *Regulation T (Reg T)* Mean?
The Federal Reserve Board regulation that governs customer cash accounts and the amount of credit that brokerage firms and dealers can extend to customers for the purchase of securities on margin.

Investopedia explains *Regulation T (Reg T)*
According to Regulation T, a person may borrow up to 50% of the initial purchase price of a marginable security; this is known as buying on margin. Reg T refers to the initial margin requirement. After the purchase, the margin account must meet minimum maintenance requirements.

RELATED TERMS:
- *Margin*
- *Margin Account*
- *Nonmarginable Security*
- *Maintenance Margin*
- *Minimum Margin*

RELATIVE STRENGTH INDEX (RSI)

What Does *Relative Strength Index (RSI)* Mean?
A technical momentum indicator that compares the magnitude of recent gains to that of recent losses in an attempt to determine overbought and oversold conditions of an asset. It is calculated by using this formula:

$$RSI = 100 - \frac{100}{1+RS}$$

RS = Average of x days' up closes/Average of x days' down closes

As can be seen in the following chart, the RSI ranges from 0 to 100. An asset is deemed to be overbought once the RSI approaches a level of 70, meaning that the asset may be getting overvalued and is a good candidate for a pullback. Similarly, if the RSI approaches 30, it is an indication that the asset may be getting oversold and therefore is likely to become undervalued.

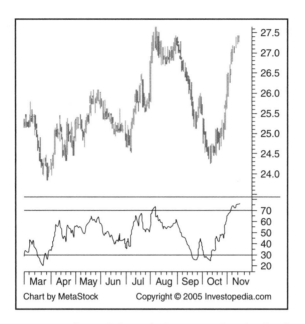

Chart by MetaStock   Copyright © 2005 Investopedia.com

 Investopedia explains *Relative Strength Index (RSI)*
A trader using RSI should be aware that large surges and drops in the price of an asset will affect the RSI by creating false buy and sell signals. The RSI is best used as a valuable complement to other stock-picking tools.

RELATED TERMS:
- Bear Market
- Momentum
- Trend Analysis
- Downtrend
- Oversold

REPURCHASE AGREEMENT (REPO)

 What Does *Repurchase Agreement (Repo)* Mean?
A short-term borrowing instrument for dealers in government securities. The dealer sells the government securities to investors, usually on an overnight basis, and buys them back the next day. For the sellers, who agree to repurchase the securities in the future, it is a repo; for the party on the other end of the transaction (buying the securities and agreeing to sell them in the future), it is a reverse repurchase agreement.

Investopedia explains *Repurchase Agreement (Repo)*
Repos are classified as money market instruments. They are used to
raise short-term capital.

RELATED TERMS:
- *Commercial Paper*
- *Liquidity*
- *U.S. Treasuries*
- *Debt*
- *Money Market*

REQUIRED MINIMUM DISTRIBUTION (RMD)

 What Does *Required Minimum Distribution (RMD)* **Mean?**
The amount that Traditional, SEP, and SIMPLE IRA owners and qualified plan participants must begin distributing from their qualified
retirement accounts by April 1 after the year they reach age 70.5
years. RMD amounts must be distributed each subsequent year.

 Investopedia explains *Required Minimum Distribution (RMD)*
These required minimum distributions are calculated by dividing
the retirement account's prior year-end fair market value by the
applicable distribution period or life expectancy. Some qualified
plans allow certain participants to put off their RMDs until they
retire even if they are older than age 70.5. Qualified plan participants
should check with their employers about the rules governing RMD
requirements.

RELATED TERMS:
- *401(k) Plan*
- *Individual Retirement Account—IRA*
- *Qualified Retirement Plan*
- *Tax Deferred*
- *Roth IRA*

REQUIRED RATE OF RETURN

 What Does *Required Rate of Return* **Mean?**
The minimum rate of return needed to induce investors or companies to invest in something.

 Investopedia explains *Required Rate of Return*
For example, if a person buys a stock, that person may desire a required rate of return of 10% per year. The investor's reasoning is that
if he or she does not receive 10% return, he or she would be better

off paying down an outstanding mortgage on which he or she is paying 10% interest.

RELATED TERMS:
- Capital Asset Pricing Model—CAPM
- Discount Rate
- Expected Return
- Return on Assets—ROA
- Return on Investment—ROI

RESIDUAL INCOME

What Does *Residual Income* Mean?
In personal finance, the amount of income remaining after all personal debts, including mortgage obligations, have been factored in; this calculation usually is done on a monthly basis, after the monthly bills and debts have been paid. Also, once a mortgage is paid off, the income that had been put toward the mortgage payments becomes residual income.

Investopedia explains *Residual Income*
Residual income is often an important component of securing a loan. The loan institution usually assesses an individual's residual income before granting the loan. If the individual requesting the loan has sufficient residual income to take on another loan, the lending institution is more likely to grant the loan once it affirms that the borrower will have sufficient funds to make the monthly loan payments.

RELATED TERMS:
- Debt
- Debt Financing
- Income Statement
- Mortgage
- Net Income

RESISTANCE

What Does *Resistance* Mean?
A price level at which a stock or a market index trades up to, but usually does not exceed during a certain period of time. Often referred to as the "resistance level." The following chart shows the resistance level for a hypothetical stock.

Notice how the price has a difficult time
breaking above the resistance of $50.50.

54
53
52
51
50
49
48
47
46
45
44
43

May Jun Jul Aug Sep Oct Nov Dec 2006 Feb

Chart by MetaStock

Investopedia explains *Resistance*

If a stock trades above resistance, it could be a sign that the stock
will reach and sustain new highs.

RELATED TERMS:
- *Moving Average*
- *Technical Analysis*
- *Uptrend*
- *Support*
- *Trend Analysis*

RETAINED EARNINGS

What Does *Retained Earnings* Mean?

Also called retention ratio or retained surplus, it is the percentage of
net earnings not paid out as dividends but retained by the company
to be reinvested in its core business or to pay debt. It is recorded
under shareholders' equity on the balance sheet. It is calculated by
adding net income to or subtracting any net losses from beginning
retained earnings and subtracting any dividends paid to shareholders, as shown here:

Retained Earnings (RE) = Beginning RE + Net Income − Dividends

Investopedia explains *Retained Earnings*
In most cases, companies retain their earnings to invest them in areas where the company can create growth opportunities, such as buying new machinery or spending the money on research and development. If a net loss is greater than beginning retained earnings, retained earnings can become negative, creating a deficit.

RELATED TERMS:
- *Balance Sheet*
- *Income Statement*
- *Shareholders' Equity*
- *Cost of Capital*
- *Net Income—NI*

RETURN ON ASSETS (ROA)

What Does *Return on Assets (ROA)* Mean?
An indicator of how profitable a company is relative to its total assets. ROA provides an idea of how efficient management is at using its assets to generate earnings. It is calculated, as shown here, by dividing a company's annual earnings by its total assets, with ROA displayed as a percentage. Sometimes this is referred to as return on investment.

$$= \frac{\text{Net Income}}{\text{Total Assets}}$$

Note: Some investors add interest expense back into net income when performing this calculation because they would like to use operating returns before the cost of borrowing.

Investopedia explains *Return on Assets (ROA)*
ROA shows earnings that are generated from invested capital (assets). ROA for public companies can vary substantially and is industry-specific. Thus, when one is using ROA as a comparative measure, it is best to compare it with a company's previous ROA numbers or the ROA of a similar company. A company's assets consist of both debt and equity, which are used to fund the operations of the company. ROA gives investors some idea of how effectively the company is converting the money it has into net income. The higher the ROA, the more a company earns on a smaller investment. For example, if one company has a net income of $1 million and total assets of $5 million, its ROA is 20%. If another company earns the same amount but has total assets of $10 million, it has an ROA of 10%. In this scenario, the first company is doing a better job of converting its investments into profit. When one thinks about it,

this is management's ultimate job: to make wise choices in allocating company resources. Anybody can make a profit by throwing a ton of money at a problem, but very few managers excel at making large profits with a small investment.

RELATED TERMS:

- *Assets*
- *Profitability Ratios*
- *Return on Net Assets—RONA*

- *Earnings*
- *Return on Equity—ROE*

RETURN ON EQUITY (ROE)

What Does *Return on Equity (ROE)* Mean?

A measure of a corporation's profitability; ROE reveals how much profit a company generates with the money shareholders have invested. Also known as return on net worth (RONW). It is calculated as shown here:

$$= \frac{\text{Net Income}}{\text{Shareholders' Equity}}$$

Investopedia explains *Return on Equity (ROE)*

ROE is useful for comparing the profitability of a company with that of other firms in the same industry. There are several ways for investors to use ROE: (1) Investors want to see the return on common equity so they may modify the formula shown here by subtracting preferred dividends from net income and subtracting preferred equity from shareholders' equity, giving the following: return on common equity (ROCE) = net income − preferred dividends/common equity. (2) Return on equity also may be calculated by dividing net income by average shareholders' equity. Average shareholders' equity is calculated by adding shareholders' equity at the beginning of a period to shareholders' equity at the end of the period and dividing the result by 2. (3) Investors also can calculate the change in ROE for a period by using the shareholders' equity figure from the beginning of a period as a denominator to calculate the beginning ROE. Then the end-of-period shareholders' equity can be used as the denominator to calculate the ending ROE. Calculating both helps investors determine the change in profitability over the period.

RELATED TERMS:

- *Equity*
- *Profitability Ratios*
- *Shareholders' Equity*

- *Gross Margin*
- *Return on Assets—ROA*

RETURN ON INVESTMENT (ROI)

What Does *Return on Investment* Mean?

A performance measure used to evaluate the efficiency of an investment or compare the efficiency of a number of different investments. To calculate ROI, the return on an investment is divided by the cost of the investment, as shown here; the result is expressed as a percentage or a ratio.

Return on investment is a popular metric be-

$$ROI = \frac{(\text{Gain from Investment} - \text{Cost of Investment})}{\text{Cost of Investment}}$$

cause it is versatile and simple to use. If an investment does not have a positive ROI or if there are alternative investment opportunities with a higher ROI, the investment should not be undertaken.

Investopedia explains *Return on Investment*

One should keep in mind that the ROI calculation can be modified to suit the situation, depending on how an investment's returns and costs are calculated. In the broader sense, ROI is used to measure the profitability of an investment and there really is no "right" calculation. For example, a marketer may compare two different products by dividing the revenue that each product has generated by its costs. A financial analyst, however, may compare the same two products by using an entirely different ROI calculation, perhaps by dividing the net income of an investment by the total value of all resources that have been employed to make and sell the product. As can be seen, this can cause problems as ROI calculations can be manipulated to suit the user's purposes. In using ROI, one must be sure to know the inputs that are being applied.

RELATED TERMS:
- Compounding
- Return on Investment Capital—ROIC
- Return on Net Assets—RONA
- Return on Equity—ROE
- Total Return

RETURN ON NET ASSETS (RONA)

What Does *Return on Net Assets* Mean?

A measure of financial performance. It is calculated as shown here:

$$= \frac{\text{Net Income}}{\text{Fixed Assets} + \text{Net Working Capital}}$$

Investopedia explains *Return on Net Assets*
The higher the RONA is, the better a company's profit performance is.

RELATED TERMS:
- *Asset*
- *Profitability Ratios*
- *Working Capital*
- *Net Income—NI*
- *Return on Assets—ROA*

RETURN ON SALES (ROS)

 What Does *Return on Sales* Mean?
A widely used ratio that is used to evaluate a company's operational efficiency; also known as operating profit margin. It is calculated by using this formula:

$$= \frac{\text{Net Income (Before Interest and Tax)}}{\text{Sales}}$$

 Investopedia explains *Return on Sales*
This measure provides management with insights into how much profit is being produced per dollar of sales. As with many ratios, it is best to compare a company's ROS over time to look for trends and compare it with that of other companies in the industry. When ROS is increasing, this indicates that the company is growing efficiently, whereas a decreasing ROS could signal looming financial troubles.

RELATED TERMS:
- *Asset Turnover*
- *Net Income—NI*
- *Revenue*
- *Gross Margin*
- *Profit Margin*

REVENUE

 What Does *Revenue* Mean?
The amount of money a company actually receives over a specific period; it accounts for sales discounts and deductions for returned merchandise. It is the "top line" or "gross income" figure from which costs are subtracted to determine net income. Revenue is calculated by multiplying the price at which goods or services are sold by the number of units or amount sold. Also known as REV.

 Investopedia explains *Revenue*
Revenue is the amount of money a company receives as a result of its business activities. In the case of government, revenue is the

money received from taxation, fees, fines, intergovernmental grants or transfers, securities sales, mineral rights, and resource rights as well as any sales that are made. For companies, it comes from selling goods and services.

RELATED TERMS:
- Accounts Receivable—AR
- Contribution Margin
- Profit Margin
- Cash Conversion Cycle
- Cost of Goods Sold—COGS

REVERSE STOCK SPLIT

What Does *Reverse Stock Split* Mean?
A reduction in the number of company shares outstanding, which results in an increase in the par value of its stock or its earnings per share; the market value of the total number of shares (market capitalization) remains the same.

Investopedia explains *Reverse Stock Split*
For example, a 1-for-2 reverse split means that a shareholder will get half as many shares but at twice the price. A company that is forced into a reverse split may be in trouble because firms sometimes do it to artificially inflate their stock's price. A company also may do a reverse split to meet exchange listing requirements and avoid being delisted.

RELATED TERMS:
- Dilution
- Outstanding Shares
- Stock Split
- Market Capitalization
- Record Date

RIGHTS OFFERING (ISSUE)

What Does *Rights Offering (Issue)* Mean?
An offer extended to existing shareholders that gives them an opportunity to buy a proportional number of additional shares at a specific price (usually at a discount) within a fixed period.

Investopedia explains *Rights Offering (Issue)*
Rights are often transferable, allowing the holder to sell them on the open market.

RELATED TERMS:
- *Common Stock*
- *Premium*
- *Warrant*
- *Float*
- *Stock*

RISK

What Does *Risk* Mean?

The chance that an investment's actual return will be different from the expected return, including the ultimate risk of losing all of one's original investment. Risk usually is measured by calculating the standard deviation of the historical returns or average returns of a specific investment.

Investopedia explains *Risk*

A fundamental premise of investing is the risk-reward trade-off. The greater the amount of risk an investor is willing to take on, the greater the potential return. The reason for this is that investors need to be compensated for taking on additional risk. For example, a U.S. Treasury bond is considered to be one of the safest investments and therefore provides low potential returns. Stocks are riskier; they offer no guarantee and thus can yield higher returns. After all, the U.S. government is unlikely to go out of business, whereas many companies fail every day. In the end, investors should expect to be rewarded for taking on additional risk.

RELATED TERMS:
- *Beta*
- *Risk-Return Trade-Off*
- *Unsystematic Risk*
- *Correlation*
- *Systematic Risk*

RISK-FREE RATE OF RETURN

What Does *Risk-Free Rate of Return* Mean?

The theoretical rate of return for an investment that has zero risk. The risk-free rate represents the expected return from an absolutely risk-free investment over a specified period.

Investopedia explains *Risk-Free Rate of Return*

In theory, the risk-free rate of return is the minimum return an investor expects for any investment because he or she will not accept additional risk unless the potential rate of return is greater than the risk-free rate. In practice, however, the risk-free rate does not exist because even the safest investments carry a very small amount of risk. The interest rate on a three-month U.S. Treasury bill often is used as the risk-free rate.

RELATED TERMS:
- Modified Internal Rate of Return
- Risk-Return Trade-Off
- U.S. Treasury
- Return on Investment—ROI
- Treasury Bill—T-Bill

RISK-RETURN TRADE-OFF

What Does *Risk-Return Trade-Off* Mean?
The principle that potential return rises with an increase in risk. Low levels of uncertainty (low risk) are associated with low potential returns, whereas high levels of uncertainty (high risk) are associated with high potential returns. According to the risk-return trade-off, invested money can render higher profits only if it is subject to the possibility of being lost.

Investopedia explains *Risk-Return Trade-Off*
Because of the risk-return trade-off, investors must recognize their personal risk tolerance when choosing investments. Taking on additional risk is the price of achieving potentially higher returns; therefore, if an investor wants to make money, he or she cannot cut out all risk. The goal instead is to find an appropriate balance that generates some profit but allows the investor to sleep at night.

RELATED TERMS:
- Modern Portfolio Theory—MPT
- Return
- Risk-Free Rate of Return
- Opportunity Cost
- Risk

RISK-WEIGHTED ASSETS

What Does *Risk-Weighted Assets* Mean?
The minimum amount of capital that is required within banks and other institutions, based on a percentage of the assets, weighted by risk.

Investopedia explains *Risk-Weighted Assets*
The idea behind risk-weighted assets is to move away from having a static requirement for capital. Instead, it is based on the riskiness of a bank's assets. For example, loans that are secured by a letter of

credit are considered riskier than a mortgage loan that is secured with collateral.

RELATED TERMS:
- *Asset*
- *Correlation*
- *Weighted Average*
- *Capital*
- *Risk*

ROTH IRA

What Does *Roth IRA* Mean?
An individual qualified retirement plan that is similar to a Traditional IRA except that contributions are not tax-deductible and qualified distributions are tax-free. As with other retirement plan accounts, nonqualified distributions from a Roth IRA may be subject to a penalty for early withdrawal, which is usually before age 59.5.

Investopedia explains *Roth IRA*
A qualified distribution is a distribution taken at least five years after the taxpayer establishes his or her first Roth IRA or when he or she reaches age 59.5 or older, is disabled, is using the withdrawal to purchase a first home (limit $10,000), or is deceased (in which case the beneficiary collects). Because qualified distributions from a Roth IRA are always tax-free, some argue that a Roth IRA may be more advantageous than a Traditional IRA.

RELATED TERMS:
- *401(k) Plan*
- *Individual Retirement Account—IRA*
- *Qualified Retirement Plan*
- *Required Minimum Distribution*
- *Tax Deferred*

R-SQUARED

What Does *R-Squared* Mean?
A statistical measure that represents the percentage of a mutual fund's or security's price movements that can be explained by price movements in a benchmark index; for fixed-income securities, the benchmark is the T-bill. For equities, the benchmark is the S&P 500.

Investopedia explains *R-Squared*
R-squared values range from 0 to 100. An R-squared of 100 means that all the movements of a security are explained completely by movements in the index. A high R-squared (between 85 and 100) indicates that the fund's performance patterns have been in line with the index. A fund with a low R-squared (70 or less) does not move in lockstep with an index. A higher R-squared value indicates a more useful beta figure. For example, if a fund has an R-squared value close to 100 but has a beta below 1, it most likely is offering higher risk-adjusted returns. A low R-squared means that an investor should ignore the beta.

RELATED TERMS:
- Alpha
- Mutual Fund
- Treasury Bill—T-Bill
- Benchmark
- Risk

RUN RATE

 ### What Does *Run Rate* Mean?
(1) How the financial performance of a company would look if one extrapolated current results out over a certain period. (2) The average annual dilution from company stock option grants over the most recent three-year period recorded in the annual report.

 Investopedia explains *Run Rate*
In the context of extrapolating future performance, the run rate helps put a company's latest results in perspective. For example, if a company has revenues of $100 million in its latest quarter, the CEO may say: "Our latest quarter puts us at a $400 million run rate." All this is saying is that if the company performed at the same level the next year, it would have annual revenues of $400 million. The run rate can be a very deceiving metric, especially in seasonal industries. A good example of this is a retailer after the holiday season. Almost all retailers experience higher sales during this time of year. It is very unlikely that the coming quarters will have sales as strong as those in the fourth quarter, and so the run rate probably will overstate the next year's revenue.

RELATED TERMS:
- Annual Percentage Yield—APY
- Fundamental Analysis
- Trend Analysis
- Cash Flow Statement
- Pro Forma

copyright JackGuinan

"Diversification can help reduce your exposure to many risks, but fire isn't one of them."

SECONDARY MARKET

What Does *Secondary Market* Mean?

A market in which investors purchase securities or assets from other investors rather than directly from the issuing companies; exchanges such as the New York Stock Exchange and the Nasdaq are secondary markets. Secondary markets also are used by mutual funds, investment banks, and entities such as Fannie Mae to purchase mortgages from issuing lenders. In any secondary market trade, the cash proceeds go to an investor rather than to the underlying company or entity directly.

Investopedia explains *Secondary Market*

A newly issued IPO is considered a primary market trade when the shares first are purchased by investors directly from the underwriting investment bank; after that, any shares traded on an exchange will be on the secondary market. In the primary market, prices are often set beforehand, whereas in the secondary market, prices are determined by supply and demand. In the case of assets such as mortgages, several secondary markets may exist, as bundles of mortgages often are repackaged into securities such as GNMA pools and resold to investors.

RELATED TERMS:
- *Initial Public Offering—IPO*
- *New York Stock Exchange—NYSE*
- *Over the Counter—OTC*   • *Private Placement*
- *Stock Market*

SECONDARY OFFERING

What Does *Secondary Offering* Mean?

(1) The issuance of new stock for public sale from a company that already has made its initial public offering (IPO). Usually, this type of offering is made by companies that want to refinance or raise additional capital for growth. The money raised often goes to the company via the investment bank that underwrites the offering. Investment banks are given an allotment of the offering and possibly an overallotment that they can choose to exercise if they think they can make money on the spread between the allotment price and the selling price of the securities. (2) A sale of securities in which one or more major stockholders in a company sell all or a large portion of their holdings. The proceeds from this sale are paid to the selling stockholders. Often, the company that issued the shares holds a large percentage of the stocks it issues.

Investopedia explains *Secondary Offering*

(1) This sort of secondary public offering is a way for a company to increase outstanding stock and spread market capitalization (the company's value) over a greater number of shares. Secondary offerings in which new shares are underwritten and sold dilute the ownership position of existing stockholders. (2) Typically, this type of offering occurs when the founders of a business (and perhaps some of the original financial backers) determine that they would like to decrease their positions in the company. This kind of secondary offering is common after the initial offering (IPO) and after the termination of the lock-up period. Owners of closely held companies sell shares gradually so that the company's share price does not plummet as a result of high selling volume. This kind of offering does not increase the number of shares of stock on the market, and it is undertaken most commonly in the case of a company whose stock is thinly traded. Secondary offerings of this sort do not dilute the owners' holdings, and no new shares are released. There is no "new" underwriting process in this kind of offering.

RELATED TERMS:
- *Capital Structure*
- *Dilution*
- *Shareholders' Equity*
- *Common Stock*
- *Initial Public Offering—IPO*

SECURITIES AND EXCHANGE COMMISSION (SEC)

What Does *Securities and Exchange Commission (SEC)* Mean?
A government commission created by Congress to regulate the securities markets and protect investors. In addition to regulation and protection, it monitors corporate takeovers in the United States. The SEC is composed of five commissioners appointed by the U.S. president and approved by the Senate. The statutes administered by the SEC are designed to promote full public disclosure and protect the investing public against fraudulent and manipulative practices in the securities markets. Generally, most issues of securities offered in interstate commerce, through the mail or on the Internet, must be registered with the SEC.

Investopedia explains *Securities and Exchange Commission (SEC)*
Here is an example of an activity that falls within the SEC's domain: If someone purchases more than 5% of a company's equity, he or she must report to the SEC within 10 days of the purchase because of the takeover threats that action may cause.

RELATED TERMS:
- *Initial Public Offering—IPO*
- *National Association of Securities Dealers—NASD*
- *Nasdaq*
- *Regulation T—Reg T*
- *Stock Market*

SECURITIZATION

What Does *Securitization* Mean?
The process by which an issuer creates a financial instrument by combining other financial assets into a security and then marketing different tiers of the repackaged instruments to investors. The process can encompass any type of financial asset and promotes liquidity in the marketplace.

Investopedia explains *Securitization*

Mortgage-backed securities are a perfect example of securitization. By combining mortgages into one large pool, the issuer can divide the large pool into smaller pieces on the basis of each individual mortgage's inherent risk of default and then sell the smaller pieces to investors. The process enables smaller investors to purchase shares in a larger asset pool. Using the mortgage-backed security example, individual retail investors are able to purchase portions of a mortgage as a type of bond. Without the securitization of mortgages, retail investors would not be able to afford to buy into a large pool of mortgages; considering the financial mortgage collapse of 2008, that might be a good thing.

RELATED TERMS:
- *Asset-Backed Security—ABS*
- *Mortgage-Backed Securities—MBS*
- *Subprime Meltdown*
- *Derivative*
- *Subprime Loan*

SECURITY

 What Does *Security* Mean?

An instrument representing ownership (stocks), a debt agreement (bonds), or the rights to ownership (derivatives) in a corporation or another entity.

 Investopedia explains *Security*

A security is essentially a contract that is assigned a value and traded. Examples of a security include a note, stock, preferred share, bond, debenture, option, future, swap, right, or warrant or virtually any other financial asset.

RELATED TERMS:
- *Earnings*
- *Penny Stock*
- *Stock*
- *Equity*
- *Shareholders' Equity*

SECURITY MARKET LINE (SML)

 What Does *Security Market Line (SML)* Mean?

A line that graphs the systematic or market risk versus the return of the whole market at a certain point in time. SML shows all risky marketable securities. Also referred to as the characteristic line.

Investopedia explains *Security Market Line (SML)*
The SML essentially graphs the results from the capital asset pricing model (CAPM) formula. The x-axis represents the risk (beta), and the y-axis represents the expected return. The market risk premium is determined from the slope of the SML. The security market line is a useful tool in determining whether an asset being considered for a portfolio offers a reasonable expected return for its risk. Individual securities are plotted on the SML graph. If a security's risk versus expected return is plotted above the SML, it is undervalued because the investor can expect a greater return for the inherent risk. A security plotted below the SML is overvalued because the investor would be accepting less return for the amount of risk assumed.

RELATED TERMS:
- *Beta*
- *Modern Portfolio Theory—MPT*
- *Unsystematic Risk*
- *Capital Market Line*
- *Systematic Risk*

SERIES 63

 What Does *Series 63* **Mean?**
A securities license administered by the Financial Industry Regulatory Authority (FINRA) that legally permits the holder to solicit orders for any type of security in a particular state. This license is required in addition to the Series 7 or Series 6.

 Investopedia explains *Series 63*
The Series 63 examination mainly covers state laws and regulations, often referred to as blue-sky laws.

RELATED TERMS:
- *Broker-Dealer*
- *Financial Industry Regulatory Authority—FINRA*
- *Mutual Fund*
- *National Association of Securities Dealers—NASD*
- *Series 7*

SERIES 7

 What Does *Series 7* **Mean?**
A general securities registered representative license administered by the Financial Industry Regulatory Authority (FINRA) that entitles

the holder to sell all types of securities products with the exception of commodities and futures. This is basically a broker's license.

 Investopedia explains *Series 7*
The bulk of the Series 7 exam focuses on investment risk, taxation, equity and debt instruments, packaged securities, options, retirement plans, and interactions with clients such as account management. To sit for the Series 7 exam, a candidate must be sponsored by a broker-dealer that is a member of FINRA or a self-regulatory organization (SRO). Successfully completing the Series 7 exam is a prerequisite for most of the FINRA principal examinations.

RELATED TERMS:
- *Broker-Dealer*
- *Financial Industry Regulatory Authority—FINRA*
- *National Association of Securities Dealers—NASD*
- *Securities and Exchange Commission—SEC*
- *Series 63*

SETTLEMENT DATE

 What Does *Settlement Date* Mean?
(1) The date on which a security trade must be settled, that is, the date when the buyer must pay for the securities delivered by the seller. (2) The payment date of benefits from a life insurance policy.

 Investopedia explains *Settlement Date*
The settlement date for stocks and bonds is usually three business days after a trade was executed. For government securities and options, the settlement date is usually the next business day.

RELATED TERMS:
- *Ex-Date*
- *Securities and Exchange Commission—SEC*
- *Record Date*
- *Margin Call*
- *Regulation T—Reg T*

SHAREHOLDERS' EQUITY

What Does *Shareholders' Equity* Mean?
A firm's total assets minus its total liabilities; also expressed as shareholder capital plus retained earnings minus Treasury shares. Shareholders' equity shows how much a company is financed through

common and preferred shares. Also known as share capital, net worth, and stockholders' equity. It is calculated as shown here:

> Shareholders' Equity = Total Assets − Total Liabilities
>
> OR
>
> Shareholders' Equity = Share Capital + Retained Earnings − Treasury Shares

 Investopedia explains *Shareholders' Equity*
Shareholders' equity comes from two main sources. The first is the money that originally was invested in the company, along with any additional investments made thereafter. The second is the retained earnings that the company is able to accumulate over time through its operations. In most cases, retained earnings are the larger of the two figures.

RELATED TERMS:
- *Capital Structure*
- *Equity*
- *Retained Earnings*
- *Common Stock*
- *Preferred Stock*

SHARPE RATIO

 What Does *Sharpe Ratio* Mean?
A ratio developed by Nobel laureate William F. Sharpe that is used to measure risk-adjusted performance. The Sharpe ratio is calculated by subtracting the risk-free rate, such as that of the 10-year U.S. Treasury bond, from the rate of return of a portfolio and then dividing the result by the standard deviation of the portfolio returns.

$$= \frac{\overline{r}_p - r_f}{\sigma_p}$$

Where:

$\overline{r}_p$ = Expected portfolio return

r_f = Risk free rate

σ_p = Portfolio standard deviation

 Investopedia explains *Sharpe Ratio*
The Sharpe ratio indicates whether a portfolio's returns are due to smart investment decisions or are a result of excess risk. This measurement is very useful because although one portfolio or fund can reap higher returns than its peers, it is a good investment only if those higher returns are not a result of taking on too much additional risk. The greater a portfolio's Sharpe ratio is, the better its risk-adjusted performance has been. A variation of the Sharpe ratio is the Sortino ratio, which removes the effects of upward price movements on standard deviation to measure only return against downward price volatility.

RELATED TERMS:
- *Portfolio*
- *Risk-Free Rate of Return*
- *Total Return*
- *Risk*
- *Standard Deviation*

SHORT (OR SHORT POSITION)

What Does *Short (or Short Position)* Mean?
(1) The sale of a borrowed security, commodity, or currency with the expectation that the asset will fall in value. (2) In the context of options, it is the sale (also known as "writing") of an options contract. The term "short" is the opposite of "long (or long position)."

Investopedia explains *Short (or Short Position)*
(1) As an example, an investor who borrows shares of stock from a broker and sells them on the open market is said to have a short position in the stock. The investor eventually must return the borrowed stock by buying it back on the open market. If the stock falls in price, the investor buys it for less than he or she sold it for, thus making a profit. Short sales are typically margin transactions. (2) Selling a call (or put) option contract to a buyer gives the buyer the right, not the obligation, to buy from (or sell to) the option seller a specific commodity or asset for a specified price and at a quantity by a specified date.

RELATED TERMS:
- *Bear Market*
- *Long (or Long Position)*
- *Short Squeeze*
- *Buy to Cover*
- *Short Interest*

SHORT COVERING

What Does *Short Covering* Mean?
Buying back a security to close an open short position. This is done by buying the same type and number of securities that were sold short. Most often, traders cover their short positions whenever they anticipate a rise in the price of the underlying security. To make a profit, a short seller must cover the short position by purchasing the security below the original short selling price. Also referred to as buy to cover or buyback.

Investopedia explains *Short Covering*
For example, suppose a trader sells short 50 shares of ABC stock at $10 per share, hoping that ABC's stock price will fall. However, if ABC rises, say, to $15 per share, the trader may decide to cover the short and buy it back at that price. In this case, the trader loses $5 per share ($10 – $15).

RELATED TERMS:
- *Buy to Cover*
- *Naked Shorting*
- *Short Squeeze*
- *Margin Call*
- *Short Interest*

SHORT INTEREST

 What Does *Short Interest* **Mean?**
The total number of shares (securities) in the market that have been sold short by customers and securities firms.

 Investopedia explains *Short Interest*
Short interest typically is expressed as a percentage. For example, 3% short interest means that 3% of the outstanding shares are held short. If there is a large short interest in a particular company, this signals that investors are pessimistic about that company's future and the direction of its stock price.

RELATED TERMS:
- *Long Squeeze*
- *Short Interest Ratio*
- *Volume*
- *Short Sale*
- *Short Squeeze*

SHORT INTEREST RATIO

 What Does *Short Interest Ratio* **Mean?**
A sentiment indicator that is derived by dividing the short interest by the average daily volume for a stock. This indicator is used by both fundamental and technical traders to identify the prevailing sentiment in the market for a specific stock. Also known as the short ratio. It is calculated as shown here:

$$\text{Short Interest Ratio} = \frac{\text{Short Interest}}{\text{Average Daily Trading Volume}}$$

Investopedia explains *Short Interest Ratio*
This ratio helps investors determine how long (in days) it will take short sellers to cover their entire short positions if the price of a stock begins to rise. The short interest ratio also can be applied to entire exchanges to determine the sentiment of the market as a whole. If an exchange has a high short interest ratio of around 5 or greater, this can be taken as a bearish signal.

RELATED TERMS:
- Short (or Short Position)
- Short Interest
- Volume
- Short Covering
- Short Squeeze

SHORT SALE

 What Does *Short Sale* Mean?
A market transaction in which an investor sells borrowed securities in the hope that the share price will fall some time in the future; short sellers are required to return (cover) an equal number of shares at some point in the future. The payoff for selling short is the opposite of that of a long position. A short seller makes money if the stock goes down in price, whereas a long buyer makes money when the stock goes up. The profit that the investor receives is equal to the value of the borrowed shares minus the cost of repurchasing the borrowed shares.

 Investopedia explains *Short Sale*
Suppose an investor sells short 1,000 shares at $25; the investor's account then is credited $25,000. Let's say the price falls to $20 and the investor closes out (buys back) the position. To close out the position, the investor will need to purchase 1,000 shares at $20 each ($20,000). The investor's gain/profit is the difference between the amount that he or she receives from the short sale and the amount that was paid to close the position, in this case a profit of $5,000. There are margin rule requirements for a short sale in which 150% of the value of the shares shorted must be on hand at the time of the transaction. Therefore, if the value is $25,000, the initial margin requirement is $37,500 (which includes the $25,000 of proceeds

from the short sale). Investors cannot use the proceeds from the sale to purchase other shares before the borrowed shares are returned. Short selling is an advanced trading strategy with inherent risks. Novice investors should avoid this strategy because its risks are unlimited. A stock price may fall to $0 but could rise to infinity.

RELATED TERMS:
- Buy to Cover
- Naked Shorting
- Short Covering
- Minimum Margin
- Short (or Short Position)

SHORT SQUEEZE

What Does *Short Squeeze* Mean?
A situation in which the price of a stock moves upward because of a lack of supply and an excess of demand.

Investopedia explains *Short Squeeze*
Short squeezes occur more often in smaller-cap stocks with small floats. If a stock starts to rise rapidly, the trend may continue because the short sellers probably will want to unwind their short positions (buy back to cover the short). For example, say a stock rises 15% in one day; those with short positions may be forced to liquidate and cover their position by purchasing the stock. As short sellers continue to buy back the stock, the price is pushed even higher.

RELATED TERMS:
- Buy to Cover
- Long Squeeze
- Short Interest
- Long (or Long Position)
- Short Covering

SIMPLE MOVING AVERAGE (SMA)

What Does *Simple Moving Average (SMA)* Mean?
A moving average that is calculated by simply adding the closing price of a security for a number of periods and dividing the total by the number of periods; short-term averages respond quickly to price

changes in the underlying securities, whereas long-term averages are slow to react.

Notice how momentum builds once the shorter-term average crosses above the longer-term average.

SMA (15)

SMA (50)

Crossover

16 | 23 | 30 | 7 | 13 | 20 | 27 | 4 | 11 | 18

Chart by MetaStock   Copyright © 2005 Investopedia.com

Investopedia explains *Simple Moving Average (SMA)*

Generally, this is the average stock price over a certain period. One should keep in mind that equal weighting is given to each daily price. As shown in the accompanying chart, many traders watch for short-term averages to cross above longer-term averages to signal the beginning of an uptrend. As shown by the arrows, short-term averages (e.g., 15-period SMA) act as levels of support when the price experiences a pullback. Support levels become stronger and more significant as the number of periods used in the calculations increases. The term "moving average" refers to a simple moving average. This is important, especially when one is comparing it with an exponential moving average (EMA).

RELATED TERMS:
- *Moving Average—MA*
- *Support*
- *Volume*
- *Resistance*
- *Technical Analysis*

SINGAPORE INTERBANK OFFERED RATE (SIBOR)

What Does *Singapore Interbank Offered Rate (SIBOR)* Mean?
The interest rate at which Asian banks can borrow funds from other banks in the region. In Asia, the SIBOR is used more commonly than is the LIBOR. It is set daily by the Association of Banks in Singapore (ABS). More than anything else, the SIBOR serves as a benchmark, or a reference rate for borrowers and lenders that are involved directly or indirectly in an Asian financial market.

Investopedia explains *Singapore Interbank Offered Rate (SIBOR)*
Because of its location, political stability, and strict legal and regulatory environment as well as the volume of business undertaken there, Singapore is regarded as a major hub of Asian finance. Large regional loans and interest rate swaps involving businesses participating in the Asian economy are quoted or denominated in SIBOR plus a number of basis points.

RELATED TERMS:
- *Cash and Cash Equivalents—CCE*
- *London Interbank Offered Rate—LIBOR*
- *Money Markets*
- *Euro LIBOR*
- *Swap*

SMALL CAP

What Does *Small Cap* Mean?
Stocks of companies that have a relatively small market capitalization; the criteria for small-cap stocks can vary among investors, but generally, stocks of companies with a market capitalization between $300 million and $2 billion are considered small cap.

Investopedia explains *Small Cap*
One advantage of investing in small-cap stocks is the opportunity to beat institutional investors. Because many mutual funds have restrictions that limit purchases of large portions of any one issuer's outstanding shares, some mutual funds would not be able to give a small cap a meaningful position in the fund. To overcome these limitations, the fund usually would have to file with the SEC; that would involve tipping its hand and potentially inflating the share price. One should keep in mind that classifications such as large cap

and small cap are only approximations that change over time. Also, the exact definition can vary between brokerage houses.

RELATED TERMS:
- Benchmark
- Large Cap—Big Cap
- Mutual Fund
- Growth Stock
- Mid Cap

SOLVENCY RATIO

What Does *Solvency Ratio* Mean?

One of many ratios used to measure a company's ability to meet its long-term obligations. The solvency ratio measures the size of a company's after-tax income, excluding noncash depreciation expenses, compared with the firm's total debt obligations. It provides a measurement of how likely it is a company can continue to meet its debt obligations. The measure is calculated as shown here:

$$\text{Solvency Ratio} = \frac{\text{After-Tax Net Profit} + \text{Depreciation}}{\text{Long-Term Liabilities} + \text{Short-Term Liabilities}}$$

Investopedia explains *Solvency Ratio*

Solvency ratios can vary from one industry to the next, but as a rule of thumb, a solvency ratio greater than 20% is considered financially healthy. Conversely, the lower a company's solvency ratio is, the greater is the likelihood that the company will default on its debt obligations.

RELATED TERMS:
- Asset Turnover
- Bankruptcy
- Liquidity Ratios
- Balance Sheet
- Fundamental Analysis

SPIDERS (SPDR)

What Does *Spiders (SPDR)* Mean?

The product name for the Standard & Poor's Depositary Receipt, which is an exchange-traded fund (ETF) managed by State Street Global Advisors that tracks the Standard & Poor's 500 Index (S&P 500). Each SPDR share represents one-tenth of the S&P 500 index and trades at roughly one-tenth of the index's dollar value. The term also can refer to the general group of ETFs to which the Standard & Poor's Depositary Receipt belongs.

Investopedia explains *Spiders (SPDR)*
Spiders are listed on the American Stock Exchange (AMEX) under the ticker symbol SPY. SPDRs trade like stocks, are liquid, can be sold short and bought on margin, and are a good source for dividend income. As with a stock, investors pay a brokerage commission when trading SPDRs. Investors buy SPDRs to replicate the performance of the overall stock market. SPDRs are not actively managed and are thus passive investments (index investing).

RELATED TERMS:
- *American Stock Exchange—AMEX*
- *Benchmark*
- *Exchange-Traded Fund—ETF*
- *Standard & Poor's 500 Index—S&P 500*
- *Diversification*

SPINOFF

What Does *Spinoff* Mean?
The creation of an independent company through the sale or distribution of new shares of an existing business or a division of a parent company. A spinoff is a type of divestiture.

Investopedia explains *Spinoff*
Businesses that want to "streamline" their operations often sell less productive or unrelated subsidiary businesses as spinoffs. The spun-off companies are expected to be worth more as independent entities than as parts of a larger business.

RELATED TERMS:
- *Balance Sheet*
- *Discount Rate*
- *Value Proposition*
- *Common Stock*
- *Due Diligence*

SPREAD

What Does *Spread* Mean?
(1) The difference between the bid and the ask price of a security or asset. (2) An options position established by purchasing one option and selling another option of the same class but of a different series.

Investopedia explains *Spread*
(1) The spread for an asset is influenced by a number of factors:
(a) supply or "float" (the total number of shares outstanding that
are available to trade), (b) demand or interest in a stock, (c) total
trading activity of the stock. (2) For a stock option, the spread would
be the difference between the strike price and the market value.

RELATED TERMS:
- Ask
- Bid-Ask Spread
- Strike Price
- Bid
- Premium

STAGFLATION

 What Does *Stagflation* Mean?
A condition in the overall economy that is characterized by slow
economic growth and relatively high unemployment—a time of
stagnation—accompanied by a rise in prices (inflation).

 Investopedia explains *Stagflation*
Stagflation occurs when economic growth declines while prices
keep rising. This economic malady occurred during the 1970s, when
world oil prices rose dramatically, fueling extreme inflation that
became a hindrance to economic growth.

RELATED TERMS:
- Business Cycle
- Deflation
- Inflation
- Consumer Price Index—CPI
- Fiscal Policy

STANDARD & POOR'S 500 INDEX (S&P 500)

 What Does *Standard & Poor's 500 Index (S&P 500)* Mean?
An index of 500 stocks that are chosen on the basis of market size,
liquidity, and industry grouping, among other factors. The S&P 500
Index is designed to act as a barometer for the overall U.S. stock
market; it reflects the risk-return characteristics of the large-cap
universe. Companies included in the index are selected by the S&P
Index Committee, a team of analysts and economists at Standard &
Poor's. The S&P 500 is a market value weighted index: Each stock's
weight in the index is proportionate to its market value.

Investopedia explains *Standard & Poor's 500 Index (S&P 500)*
The S&P 500 Index is one of the most commonly used benchmarks for the overall U.S. stock market. The Dow Jones Industrial Average (DJIA) was at one time the most renowned index for U.S. stocks, but because the DJIA contains only 30 companies, most people agree that the S&P 500 is a better proxy for the U.S. stock market. Other popular Standard & Poor's indexes include the S&P 600, an index of small-cap companies with market capitalization between $300 million and $2 billion, and the S&P 400, an index of mid-cap companies with market capitalization of $2 billion to $10 billion. A number of mutual funds and exchange-traded funds that are sold to investors are based on the S&P 500. This is helpful because it would be difficult and cost-prohibitive for average investors to buy all the companies in the index for their own portfolios.

RELATED TERMS:
• *Benchmark*
• *Dow Jones Industrial Average—DJIA*
• *Index Fund*   • *Large Cap—Big Cap*
• *Weighted Average*

STANDARD DEVIATION

 What Does *Standard Deviation* Mean?
(1) A measure of the dispersion of a set of data from its mean. The more spread apart the data, the higher the deviation. The standard deviation is calculated as the square root of the variance. (2) In finance, standard deviation is applied to the annual rate of return of an investment to measure the investment's volatility. Standard deviation also is known as historical volatility and is used by investors as a gauge for the amount of expected volatility.

 Investopedia explains *Standard Deviation*
Standard deviation is a statistical measure that helps shed light on an investment's historical volatility. For example, a volatile stock will have a high standard deviation, whereas the deviation of a stable blue-chip stock will be lower. A large dispersion indicates how much the return on an investment deviates from the expected normal returns.

RELATED TERMS:

- Beta
- Coefficient of Variation—CV
- Volatility
- Bollinger Bands
- Covariance

STOCHASTIC OSCILLATOR

What Does *Stochastic Oscillator* Mean?

A technical momentum indicator that compares a security's closing price to its price range over a particular period. The oscillator's sensitivity to market movements can be reduced by adjusting the time period or taking a moving average of the result. This indicator is calculated by using the following formula:

$$\%K = 100[(C - L14)/(H14 - L14)]$$

Where C = the most recent closing price, L14 = the low of the 14 previous trading sessions, H14 = the highest price traded during the same 14-day period, %D = 3-period moving average of %K.

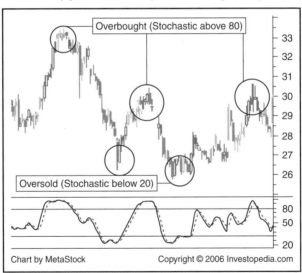

Chart by MetaStock   Copyright © 2006 Investopedia.com

Investopedia explains *Stochastic Oscillator*

The theory behind this indicator is that in an upward-trending market, prices tend to close near their highs; conversely, in a downward-trending market, prices tend to close near their lows. Transaction signals occur when the %K crosses a three-period moving average called the %D.

RELATED TERMS:
- *Downtrend*
- *Moving Average—MA*
- *Moving Average Convergence Divergence—MACD*
- *Technical Analysis*
- *Uptrend*

STOCK

What Does *Stock* Mean?

A security that represents ownership in a corporation and has claims on part of the corporation's assets and earnings per share. There are two main types of stock: (1) common and (2) preferred. (1) Common stock usually entitles the owner to vote at shareholders' meetings and receive dividends when applicable. (2) Preferred stock generally does not include voting rights but has a priority claim on assets and earnings ahead of common shares. For example, owners of preferred stock receive dividends before common shareholders do and are in the front of the line if a company goes bankrupt and is liquidated. Also known as shares or equity.

Investopedia explains *Stock*

A stockholder (a shareholder) has a claim to part of the corporation's assets and earnings. In other words, a shareholder is an owner of the company. Ownership is determined by the number of shares a person owns relative to the number of outstanding shares. For example, if a company has 1,000 shares of stock outstanding and an investor owns 100 shares, that investor owns and has a claim to 10% of the company's assets. Stocks are a major component of investor portfolios because historically they outperform most other investments over the long run.

RELATED TERMS:
- *Assets*
- *Equity*
- *Shareholders' Equity*
- *Common Stock*
- *Penny Stock*
- *Stock Option*

STOCK MARKET

What Does *Stock Market* Mean?

The term for the overall market in which shares are issued and traded on exchanges or in over-the-counter markets. Also known as the equity market, it is one of the most vital areas of a market economy because it provides companies with access to capital and allows investors to own companies and participate in economic growth.

 Investopedia explains *Stock Market*
The stock market is made up of the primary and secondary markets. The primary market is where new issues (IPOs) first are offered, with any subsequent trading going on in the secondary market.

RELATED TERMS:
- *Capital*
- *Dow Jones Industrial Average—DJIA*
- *Nasdaq*
- *New York Stock Exchange—NYSE*
- *Over the Counter—OTC*

STOCK OPTION

 What Does *Stock Option* Mean?
An instrument sold by one party to another party, giving the buyer the right, but not the obligation, to buy (call) or sell (put) a stock at an agreed-on price within a certain period or on a specific date. In the United Kingdom, it is known as a share option.

 Investopedia explains *Stock Option*
American stock options can be exercised any time between the date of purchase and the expiration date. European options may be redeemed only at the expiration date. Most exchange-traded stock options are American.

RELATED TERMS:
- *Call Option*
- *Premium*
- *Strike Price*
- *Index Option*
- *Put Option*

STOCK SPLIT

 What Does *Stock Split* Mean?
A corporate action in which a company's existing shares are divided (split) into multiple shares. Although the number of shares outstanding increases by a specific multiple, the total dollar value of the shares remains the same compared to the presplit amounts. Normally, no real value is added when a stock splits. In the United

Kingdom, a stock split is referred to as a scrip issue, bonus issue, capitalization issue, or free issue.

 Investopedia explains *Stock Split*
As an example, in a 2-for-1 stock split, each stockholder receives one additional share for each existing share owned. Companies often engage in stock splits because a company's share price has grown too high. For example, if XYZ Corp.'s shares were worth $1,000 each, investors would need to spend $100,000 to own 100 shares. If each share was worth $10, investors would need to pay only $1,000 to own 100 shares.

RELATED TERMS:
- *Common Stock*
- *Record Date*
- *Spinoff*
- *Ex-Date*
- *Reverse Stock Split*

STOP ORDER

 What Does *Stop Order* Mean?
An order to buy or sell a security when its price surpasses a particular point (the stop price), thus ensuring a greater probability of achieving a predetermined entry or exit price, limiting an investor's loss or locking in his or her profit. Once the price surpasses the predefined entry/exit point, the stop order becomes a market order. Also referred to as a stop and/or stop-loss order.

 Investopedia explains *Stop Order*
Investors often enter a sell stop order when they know that they will not be able to monitor their portfolios (e.g., while traveling or on vacation). Stop orders do not guarantee an execution price. For instance, if a stock price drops rapidly, a stop order could be triggered (or filled) at a price significantly lower than expected. Traders who use technical analysis place stop orders below major moving averages, trend lines, swing highs, swing lows, and other support or resistance levels.

RELATED TERMS:
- *Limit Order*
- *Stop-Limit Order*
- *Support*
- *Resistance*
- *Stop-Loss Order*

STOP-LIMIT ORDER

What Does *Stop-Limit Order* Mean?

A type of trade order that combines the features of a stop order with those of a limit order. A stop-limit order stipulates that a buy or sell order can be executed only at the limit price or better once the stop price has been reached.

Investopedia explains *Stop-Limit Order*

A benefit of a stop-limit order is that the trader controls when the order can be filled. The downside, as with all limit orders, is that there is no guarantee that the stock price will reach the limit price. If this happens, the order will not execute. A stop order is an order that becomes executable only when a set price has been reached; after that it becomes a market order. A limit order, in contrast, is executed only at a certain price or better. By combining the two orders, the investor has more control over the final trade price. A stop order is filled at the market price after the stop price is reached; therefore, it is possible to get a price very different from what the investor hoped, especially in fast-moving markets. For example, assume that ABC Inc. is trading at $40 and an investor wants to buy the stock once it begins to show some serious upward momentum. The investor places a stop-limit order to buy at a stop price of $45 with a limit price at $46. If the price of ABC Inc. moves above the $45 stop price, the order becomes a limit order to buy at $46 or better (less). As long as the order can be filled at $46 (the limit price) or less, the trade will be filled. If the stock jumps above $46, the order will not be filled.

RELATED TERMS:
- *Bear Market*
- *Limit Order*
- *Stop-Loss Order*
- *Bid*
- *Stop Order*

STOP-LOSS ORDER

What Does *Stop-Loss Order* Mean?

An order placed with a broker to sell a security when it reaches a certain price. It is designed to limit an investor's loss on a security position. A stop order becomes a market order once the stop price has been reached. Also known as a stop order or stop-market order.

Investopedia explains *Stop-Loss Order*
In other words, setting a stop-loss order for 10% below the price an
investor paid for the stock would limit the investor's loss to 10%. It
is a good idea to use a stop-loss order before an investor leaves for
holidays or enters a situation in which the investor will be unable to
watch his or her stocks for an extended period. The downside of a
stop order is that since the order becomes a market order when the
stop price is hit, instead of a limit order, the investor never knows
the price at which the order will be executed.

RELATED TERMS:
- *Buy to Cover*
- *Market Order*
- *Stop-Limit Order*
- *Downtrend*
- *Stop Order*

STRADDLE

 What Does *Straddle* Mean?
An options strategy in which an investor holds a position in both a
call option and a put option with the same strike prices and expiration dates.

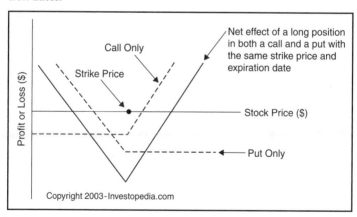

Copyright 2003-Investopedia.com

 Investopedia explains *Straddle*
Straddles are a good strategy for investors who think a stock's price
will move significantly but are unsure about the direction. The stock
price must move significantly one way or the other for the investor
to make money. As shown in the accompanying diagram, if the stock
price does not fluctuate, the investor will experience a loss. As a result,

a straddle is extremely risky. In addition, when stocks are expected to jump, the market tends to price options at a higher premium, which reduces the expected payoff if the stock moves significantly.

RELATED TERMS:
- Hedge
- Risk
- Volatility

- Option
- Stock Option

STRANGLE

What Does *Strangle* Mean?
An options strategy in which the investor holds positions in both a call and a put option with the same maturity and underlying asset but with different strike prices. This option strategy is profitable only when there are large movements in the price of the underlying asset. This strategy is used when an investor thinks that there will be large price movements in the near future but is unsure whether the price movements will be up or down.

Investopedia explains *Strangle*
This strategy involves buying an out-of-the-money call and an out-of-the-money put option. A strangle is generally less expensive than a straddle because the contract premiums are due less to the fact that the options are out of the money. For example, a stock is trading at $50 a share. With the strangle option strategy, an investor enters into two option positions: one call and one put. Say the call option is for $55 and costs $300 ($3 per option × 100 shares) and the put option is for $45 and costs $285 ($2.85 per option × 100 shares). If the price of the stock stays between $45 and $55 over the life of the option, the investor's loss will be $585 (total cost of the two option contracts). The investor will make money when the price of the stock starts to move outside that range, for example, when the stock price goes to $35. In this case, the call option will expire worthless and the loss will be $300, but the put option will be worth $715 ($1,000 minus the initial option value of $285). Thus, the investor's total gain is $415.

RELATED TERMS:
- Hedge
- Maturity
- Straddle

- In the Money
- Stock Option

STRIKE PRICE

What Does *Strike Price* Mean?

The set price at which an option contract can be exercised. Strike prices are associated mostly with stock and index options. For call options, the strike price is the price at which the underlying stock can be bought (up to the expiration date), whereas for put options, the strike price is the price at which the underlying stock can be sold. The difference between the underlying security's current market price and the option's strike price represents the amount of profit per share gained upon the exercise or the sale of the option. This profit results from the options being in the money. In buying an option, the maximum amount that can be lost is the premium paid. Also known as the exercise price.

Investopedia explains *Strike Price*

Strike prices are a key determinant of the premium, which represents the market value (price) of an options contract. Other determinants include the time until expiration, the volatility of the underlying security, and prevailing interest rates. Strike prices are established when a contract is first written. Most strike prices are in increments of $2.50 and $5.00.

RELATED TERMS:
- Call Option
- Exercise
- Put Option
- Common Stock
- In the Money

STYLE

What Does *Style* Mean?

The investment approach or objective that a fund manager uses to make choices in the selection of securities for the fund's portfolio. Although there are a variety of styles, there are nine basic investing styles for both equity and fixed-income funds. For stock funds, company size and value/growth characteristics determine the style. For bonds, style is defined by maturities and credit quality.

Investopedia explains *Style*

The specific size classifications for stocks are large, medium-size, and small companies, as determined by market capitalization. Value, growth, and a value-growth blend are the three basic categories for stocks. Bond maturities are categorized as short-term, intermediate-term, and long-term. Credit quality is determined by a bond's status as a government or agency issue (high) and by credit ratings for corporates and municipals of AAA to AA (high), A to BBB (medium), and BB to C (low). Variations and combinations of these basic categories, as well as consideration of special industries, industry sectors, and geographic location, create investment styles for both stock and bond funds beyond the basic nine categories for each type of fund.

RELATED TERMS:
- *Growth Stock*
- *Mutual Fund*
- *Index Fund*
- *Value Stock*

STYLE DRIFT

 What Does *Style Drift* **Mean?**

The divergence of a mutual fund from its stated investment style or objective. Style drift occurs as a result of intentional portfolio investing decisions made by management, a change in the fund's management, or, in the case of stocks, a company's growth.

 Investopedia explains *Style Drift*

Generally, a portfolio manager's ability to manage and commitment to managing a fund's assets in accordance with its stated investment style over the course of several years is a positive investment quality. For obvious reasons, consistency in this area is preferable to style drift. Managers chasing performance have been known to resort to using different strategies that are often counterproductive and can change the risk-return profile of the fund. Nevertheless, fund investors need to exercise some flexibility in making judgments about a fund's investment style stability. Some funds allow for a "go-anywhere" style, which means that the manager will do just that. Also, it is not unusual for small-cap and mid-cap companies to grow in size, which means that a fund may shift capitalization categories accordingly. Circumstances can justify giving the fund manager some leeway. A history of consistent, above-average total returns may override any concerns about style drift.

RELATED TERMS:
- Asset Allocation
- Growth Stock
- Value Investing
- Diversification
- Style

SUBORDINATED DEBT

What Does *Subordinated Debt* Mean?
A loan (or security) that ranks below other loans (or securities) with regard to claims on assets or earnings; sometimes called a junior security or subordinated loan.

Investopedia explains *Subordinated Debt*
In the case of default, creditors with subordinated debt would not get paid until after the senior debtholders were paid in full. Therefore, subordinated debt is more risky than unsubordinated debt.

RELATED TERMS:
- Bankruptcy
- Debt
- Preferred Stock
- Bond
- Debt Financing

SUBPRIME LOAN

What Does *Subprime Loan* Mean?
A type of loan that is offered at an interest rate far above the prime interest rate; usually extended to individuals who have poor credit and do not qualify for prime rate loans. Quite often, subprime borrowers already have been turned away by traditional lenders because of their low credit ratings or other factors that suggest that they have a reasonable chance of defaulting on the debt repayment.

Investopedia explains *Subprime Loan*
Subprime loans tend to have a higher interest rate than the prime rate offered on traditional loans. This additional interest charge can translate into tens of thousands of dollars in additional interest payments over the life of the loan. However, a subprime loan can be helpful if it is used to pay down other debts with higher interest charges. The specific amount of interest charged on a subprime loan is not set, and lenders will value a borrower's risks differently. Therefore, not all subprime loans are alike.

RELATED TERMS:
- Credit Rating
- Liar Loan
- Subprime Meltdown

- Interest Rate
- Securitization

SUBPRIME MELTDOWN

What Does *Subprime Meltdown* Mean?

A term that refers to the 2008 financial crisis that arose out of the subprime mortgage market collapse brought on by borrowers who defaulted on their loans in record numbers. This led to the collapse of many mortgage lenders, banks, and hedge funds. The meltdown spilled over into the global credit market as risk premiums increased rapidly and capital liquidity was reduced. The sharp increase in foreclosures and the problems in the subprime mortgage market were blamed largely on loose lending practices, low interest rates, a housing bubble, and excessive risk taking by lenders and investors. It is also known as the subprime collapse or the subprime crisis.

Investopedia explains *Subprime Meltdown*

After the tech bubble and the events of September 11, 2001, the Federal Reserve stimulated a struggling economy by cutting interest rates to historically low levels. As a result, a housing bull market arose. Everyone was buying a home, even people with poor credit, and mortgage lenders created nontraditional mortgages: interest-only loans, payment-option ARMs, and mortgages with extended amortization periods. Eventually, interest rates rose, resetting adjustable rate mortgages at higher levels, which led to a record number of homeowners defaulting on their loans. That left mortgage lenders holding properties that were declining in value; more loan defaults occurred until eventually lenders started going out of business and the credit markets froze. Investors and hedge funds also suffered because lenders sold securitized mortgages in the secondary market in the form of collateralized debt obligations (CDOs) and other mortgage-backed securities (MBSs). When the underlying mortgages began to default, those MBSs became nearly worthless.

RELATED TERMS:
- Collateralized Mortgage Obligation—CMO
- Credit Crunch
- Securitization

- Liar Loan
- Subprime Loan

SUPPORT

What Does *Support* Mean?
The historical price level of a security that is used as a point of reference as the security's lowest trading price within a specific time frame. Many investors see this level as a buying opportunity. However, if the security trades below support, some believe that this is a sign that the stock price will drop further. Often referred to as the support level.

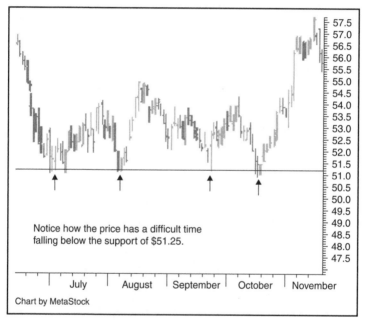

Notice how the price has a difficult time falling below the support of $51.25.

Chart by MetaStock

Investopedia explains *Support*
If the price of a stock falls toward a support level, it is a test for the stock: The support will be either reconfirmed or wiped out. It will be reconfirmed if a lot of buyers move into the stock, causing it to rise and move back up and away from the support level. It will be wiped out if buyers do not enter to buy the stock and the stock falls below the support.

RELATED TERMS:
- *Ask*
- *Resistance*
- *Volume*
- *Bid*
- *Technical Analysis*

SWAP

What Does *Swap* mean?
Traditionally, the exchange of one security for another for the purpose of changing the maturity (bonds), the quality of issues (stocks or bonds), or one's investment objectives. Swaps include currency swaps and interest rate swaps.

Investopedia explains *Swap*
If companies in different countries have regional advantages on interest rates, a swap will benefit both firms. For example, one firm may have a lower fixed interest rate while another has access to a lower floating interest rate. To take advantage of this situation, the companies would do an interest rate swap.

RELATED TERMS:
- Arbitrage
- Credit Default Swap
- Interest Rate Swap
- Commodity
- Currency Swap

SWING TRADING

What Does *Swing Trading* Mean?
A style of trading that is used to capture quick gains in a stock over a one- to four-day trading period. It is done to capitalize on the short-term swings in the market.

Investopedia explains *Swing Trading*
Traders must make quick trading decisions to exploit these short-term price swings in the stock market. This strategy often is used by retail day traders. Large institutions have trouble using this strategy because the size of their trades makes it prohibitive. Swing traders use technical analysis to look for stocks with short-term price momentum. Those traders are not interested in the fundamental or intrinsic value of stocks but in their price trends and patterns. As the saying goes, "Traders trade. Investors invest."

RELATED TERMS:
- Arbitrage
- Stock Market
- Volatility
- Capital Gain
- Technical Analysis

SYNDICATE

What Does *Syndicate* Mean?
A group of bankers, insurers, and others who work together on a large project. A group of brokers (investment banks) involved in selling an initial public offering (IPO) to the public are known as the selling syndicate.

Investopedia explains *Syndicate*
The members of a syndicate work together only temporarily. Syndicates are used commonly for large loans or underwritings to reduce the risk that each individual firm must take on.

RELATED TERMS:
- *Capital Structure*
- *Initial Public Offering—IPO*
- *Underwriting*
- *Equity*
- *Investment Bank*

SYSTEMATIC RISK

What Does *Systematic Risk* Mean?
The risk inherent in the entire market or an entire market segment. Also known as undiversifiable risk or market risk.

Investopedia explains *Systematic Risk*
Interest rates, recessions, and wars are types of systematic risk because they affect the entire market and cannot be avoided even with diversification. Systematic risk affects a broad range of securities, whereas unsystematic risk affects a very specific group of securities or an individual security. Systematic risk can be mitigated only by being hedged. But even a portfolio of well-diversified assets cannot protect against all risk.

RELATED TERMS:
- *Capital Asset Pricing Model—CAPM*
- *Diversification*
- *Standard Deviation*
- *Market Economy*
- *Unsystematic Risk*

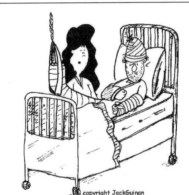

"Great news honey, while you were in a coma, I invested all of our money in the stock market with the help of the psychic hotline!"

copyright JackGuinan

"Dad, if we live in a *free* market economy, why does everything cost so much?"

TAKEOVER

What Does *Takeover* Mean?

A corporate action in which an acquiring company makes a bid for another company. If the target company is publicly traded, the acquiring company will make an offer for the outstanding shares. When the targeted company refuses to be purchased, the takeover is considered a hostile takeover.

Investopedia explains *Takeover*

A welcome takeover usually is a favorable and friendly takeover. Friendly takeovers generally go smoothly because both companies consider this a positive situation. In contrast, an unwelcome or hostile takeover can get downright nasty!

RELATED TERMS:
- Enterprise Value
- Leveraged Buyout
- Poison Pill
- Hostile Takeover
- Merger

TANGIBLE ASSET

What Does *Tangible Asset* Mean?

A physical asset such as inventories, machinery, buildings, and land.

Investopedia explains *Tangible Asset*
This is the opposite of an intangible asset, such as a patent, a trademark, or goodwill. Whether an asset is tangible or intangible is not inherently good or bad. For example, a well-known brand name can be very valuable to a company. In contrast, if a product is produced solely for a trademark, at some point the company will need to have "real" physical assets to produce it.

RELATED TERMS:
- Asset
- Intangible Asset
- Price to Tangible Book Value—PTBV
- Book Value
- Net Tangible Assets

TANGIBLE NET WORTH

 What Does *Tangible Net Worth* **Mean?**
A measure of the physical worth of a company minus any value derived from intangible assets such as copyrights, patents, and intellectual property. Tangible net worth is calculated by taking a firm's total tangible assets and subtracting the value of all liabilities and intangible assets. Tangible net worth is calculated as shown here:

$$\text{Tangible Net Worth} = \text{Total Assets} - \text{Liabilities} - \text{Intangible Assets}$$

 Investopedia explains *Tangible Net Worth*
In personal finance, tangible net worth is the sum of all of a person's tangible assets (cash, home, cars, etc.) minus any liabilities that person may have. In the financial markets, tangible net worth represents the amount of physical assets a company has net of its liabilities. Thus, it represents the liquidation proceeds a company would fetch if it shut down and sold off all its assets.

RELATED TERMS:
- Intangible Assets
- Net Tangible Assets
- Tangible Asset
- Liquidity
- Net Worth

TAX DEFERRED

 What Does *Tax Deferred* **Mean?**
Refers to investment earnings such as interest, dividends, and capital gains that accumulate free from taxation until the investor withdraws

and takes possession of them. The most common types of tax-deferred investments are those in individual retirement accounts (IRAs) and deferred annuities.

 Investopedia explains _Tax Deferred_
By deferring taxes on the returns from an investment, the investor benefits in two ways. The first benefit is tax-free growth: Instead of paying tax on the returns from an investment, taxes are paid at a later date, allowing the investment to grow tax-free. The second benefit of tax deferral is that investments usually are made when a person is earning higher income and is taxed at a higher tax rate. By deferring withdrawals until later in life when his or her tax bracket may be lower, the investor is able to pay lower taxes on the income at that later time.

RELATED TERMS:
- _Capital Gain_
- _Roth IRA_
- _Unrealized Gain_
- _Qualified Retirement Account_
- _Traditional IRA_

TECHNICAL ANALYSIS

What Does _Technical Analysis_ Mean?
A method of evaluating securities by analyzing statistics and data such as historical prices and trading volumes. Technical analysts do not attempt to measure a security's intrinsic value but instead use charts, graphs, and other analytic tools to identify patterns that they believe will help predict future activity.

 Investopedia explains _Technical Analysis_
Technical analysts believe that the historical performance of stocks and markets provides indications of future performance. In a shopping mall, a fundamental analyst would go to each store, study the product that was being sold, and then decide whether to buy the store. By contrast, a technical analyst would sit on a bench in the mall and watch people go into the stores. Disregarding the intrinsic value of the products in the store, he or she would base the decision on the patterns or activity of people going into each store.

RELATED TERMS:
- _Behavioral Finance_
- _Head and Shoulders Pattern_
- _Quantitative Analysis_
- _Fundamental Analysis_
- _Moving Average_

TED SPREAD

What Does *Ted Spread* Mean?
The difference in price between three-month futures contracts for U.S. Treasuries and three-month contracts for Eurodollars with identical expiration dates.

Investopedia explains *Ted Spread*
The Ted spread is used as an indicator of credit risk because U.S. T-Bills are considered risk-free whereas the rate associated with Eurodollar futures is thought to reflect the credit ratings of corporate borrowers. As the Ted spread increases, default risk is considered to be increasing and investors will have a preference for safe investments. As the spread decreases, the default risk is considered to be decreasing.

RELATED TERMS:
- Credit Spread
- Futures
- U.S. Treasuries
- Currency Swap
- Interest Rate Swap

TERMINAL VALUE (TV)

What Does *Terminal Value (TV)* Mean?
The value of an investment at the end of a period, taking into account a specified rate of interest.

Investopedia explains *Terminal Value (TV)*
The formula for calculating terminal value is the same as that for compound interest:

$$TV = P \times (1+r)^t$$

Where TV = total amount, P = principal amount, r = interest rate, t = period of time.

RELATED TERMS:
- Amortization
- Depreciation
- Present Value
- Asset
- Par Value

TICK

What Does *Tick* Mean?
The minimum price movement—up or down—of a security.

Investopedia explains *Tick*
Historically, stocks traded in minimum increments of 1/16. Now they trade in decimals. A stock would move in amounts of 1/8, 1/16, or 1/32 of a dollar (the tick). This changed when the decimal system was brought in. Now they trade in fractions of pennies.

RELATED TERMS:
- Basis Point
- Short Sale
- Uptrend
- Downtrend
- Uptick

TIER 1 CAPITAL

 What Does *Tier 1 Capital* Mean?
A term used to describe the capital adequacy of a bank. Tier I capital is core capital, which includes equity capital and disclosed reserves.

 Investopedia explains *Tier 1 Capital*
Equity capital includes instruments that cannot be redeemed at the discretion of the holder.

RELATED TERMS:
- Capital
- Mezzanine Financing
- Venture Capital
- Capital Structure
- Private Equity

TIME VALUE OF MONEY

 What Does *Time Value of Money* Mean?
The idea that money available today is worth more than the same amount of money in the future, based on its earnings potential. This principle asserts that money can earn interest and grow, and so any amount of money is worth more the sooner a person has it so that that person can put it to use now rather than later. Also referred to as present discounted value.

 Investopedia explains *Time Value of Money*
Everyone knows that money deposited in a savings account will earn interest. Because of this, the sooner it starts earning interest, the better. For example, assuming a 5% interest rate, a $100 investment today will be worth $105 in one year ($100 multiplied by 1.05). Conversely, $100 received one year from now is worth only $95.24 today ($100 divided by 1.05), assuming a 5% interest rate.

Related Terms:
- Discount Rate
- Net Present Value—NPV
- Present Value Interest Factor—PVIF
- Future Value
- Present Value

TIMES INTEREST EARNED (TIE)

What Does *Times Interest Earned (TIE)* Mean?

A metric used to measure a company's ability to meet its debt obligations. It is calculated by taking a company's earnings before interest and taxes (EBIT) and dividing it by the total interest payable on bonds and other contractual debt. It usually is quoted as a ratio and indicates how many times a company can cover its interest charges on a pretax basis. Failing to meet these obligations could force a company into bankruptcy. Also referred to as interest coverage ratio and fixed-charged coverage.

Investopedia explains *Times Interest Earned (TIE)*

Ensuring interest payments to debtholders and preventing bankruptcy depend mainly on a company's ability to sustain earnings. However, a high TIE ratio can indicate that a company has an undesirable lack of debt or is paying down too much debt with earnings that could be used for other projects. The rationale behind TIE is to determine whether there are other projects that yield greater returns than existing ones or whether current borrowing costs (interest rates) should be reduced in exchange for lower borrowing costs.

Related Terms:
- Cash Conversion Cycle—CCC
- Credit Rating
- Earnings before Interest, Taxes, Depreciation, and Amortization—EBITDA
- Interest Rate
- Cost of Capital

TOTAL ENTERPRISE VALUE (TEV)

What Does *Total Enterprise Value (TEV)* Mean?

A valuation measurement used to compare companies with varying levels of debt. It is calculated as follows: TEV = Market Capitalization + Interest-Bearing Debt + Preferred Stock − Excess Cash.

Investopedia explains *Total Enterprise Value (TEV)*
Some investors look only at market capitalization when valuing a company, but some companies issue more equity than others; this is why debt is included.

RELATED TERMS:
- *Book Value*
- *Enterprise Value—EV*
- *Preferred Stock*
- *Debt*
- *Market Capitalization*

TOTAL RETURN

 What Does *Total Return* **Mean?**
The actual rate of return of an investment or a pool of investments over a particular evaluation period. Total return includes interest, capital gains, dividends, and distributions realized and reinvested over a particular period.

 Investopedia explains *Total Return*
Total return consists of both income and capital appreciation. Income includes interest paid by fixed-income investments, distributions, and dividends. Capital appreciation represents a positive change in the market price of an asset.

RELATED TERMS:
- *Absolute Return*
- *Dividend*
- *Interest*
- *Capital Gain*
- *Expected Return*

TRACKING ERROR

 What Does *Tracking Error* **Mean?**
A divergence between the price behavior of a position or portfolio and the price behavior of a benchmark. It often is used in the context of a hedge or mutual fund that did not perform as effectively as intended, creating an unexpected profit or unexpected loss.

 Investopedia explains *Tracking Error*
Tracking errors are reported as a "standard deviation percentage" difference. This measure reports the difference between the return an investor received and the return on the benchmark the investor was trying to match or beat.

RELATED TERMS:
- Benchmark
- Index
- Total Return
- Expense Ratio
- Mutual Fund

TRADITIONAL IRA

What Does *Traditional IRA* Mean?

A qualified retirement account that allows individuals to direct pretax income, up to specific annual limits, toward investments that can grow tax-deferred (no capital gains or dividend income is taxed). Individual taxpayers are allowed to contribute 100% of compensation up to a specified maximum dollar amount to a Traditional IRA. Contributions to a Traditional IRA may be tax-deductible, depending on the taxpayer's income and tax-filing status and other factors. Other variants of the IRA include the Roth IRA, SIMPLE IRA, and SEP IRA.

Investopedia explains *Traditional IRA*

Traditional IRAs are held by custodians, such as commercial banks, mutual fund companies, and retail brokers; investors can use IRA funds to invest in stocks, bonds, funds, and other financial assets. Assets such as real estate come with heavy restrictions from the IRS and may be taxed differently. Distributions from a Traditional IRA are treated as ordinary income and may be subjected to income tax. This is different from a Roth IRA, which can offer tax-free distributions. For people over age 50, higher annual contribution limits may apply for a relatively new IRA or one that was underfunded in previous tax years. IRA withdrawals must begin when the IRA owner reaches age 70.5 years.

RELATED TERMS:
- Annuity
- Individual Retirement Account—IRA
- Required Minimum Distribution—RMD
- Roth IRA
- Tax Deferred

TRANCHES

What Does *Tranches* Mean?

Refers to a piece, portion, or slice of a deal. The portion is one of several related securities that are offered simultaneously, but with each having different risks, rewards, and/or maturities. "Tranche" is the French word for "slice."

Investopedia explains *Tranches*
This is a term often used to describe a specific class of bonds within an offering in which each tranche offers varying degrees of risk to the investor. For example, a collateralized mortgage obligation (CMO) that offers a partitioned mortgage-backed security (MBS) portfolio might have mortgages (tranches) that have 1-year, 2-year, 5-year, and 20-year maturities. Tranches can also refer to segments that are offered domestically and internationally.

RELATED TERMS:
• *Asset-Backed Security*
• *Collateralized Debt Obligation—CDO*
• *Collateralized Mortgage Obligation—CMO*
• *Mortgage-Backed Securities—MBSs*
• *Underwriting*

TREASURY BILL (T-BILL)

What Does *Treasury Bill (T-Bill)* Mean?
A very short-term debt obligation issued and backed by the U.S. government with a maturity of less than one year. T-bills are sold in $1,000 denominations up to a maximum purchase of $5 million; common maturities are one month (4 weeks), three months (13 weeks), and six months (26 weeks). T-bills are issued through a competitive bidding process at a discount from par, which means that rather than paying fixed interest payments as conventional bonds do, the purchaser buys at a discount and then gets the full face amount at maturity.

Investopedia explains *Treasury Bill (T-Bill)*
If an investor buys a 13-week T-bill priced at $9,800, essentially, the U.S. government (and its nearly bulletproof credit rating) writes the investor an IOU for $10,000, which will be paid to the investor in full at maturity (13 weeks). T-bills do not pay interest the way other bonds do. Instead, the difference between the discounted value paid and the maturity value received is the income component. In this case, the T-bill pays a 2.04% interest rate ($200/$9,800 = 2.04%) over a three-month period.

RELATED TERMS:
- Discount Rate
- Risk-Free Rate of Return
- U.S. Treasury
- Equity Risk Premium
- Treasury Bond—T-Bond

TREASURY BOND (T-BOND)

What Does *Treasury Bond (T-Bond)* Mean?

A marketable, fixed-interest U.S. government bond that has a maturity of more than 10 years. Treasury bonds make interest payments semiannually, and the income that holders receive is taxed only at the federal level.

Investopedia explains *Treasury Bond (T-Bond)*

Treasury bonds are issued in a minimum denomination of $1,000. The bonds initially are sold in a treasury auction with maximum purchases set at $5 million if the bid is noncompetitive or 35% of the offering if the bid is competitive. A competitive bid states the rate that the bidder is willing to accept; it will be accepted depending on how it compares with the set rate of the bond. A noncompetitive bid ensures that the bidder will get the bond but must accept the set rate. After the auction, the bonds can be sold in the secondary market.

RELATED TERMS:
- Bond Ladder
- Interest Rate
- U.S. Treasury
- Debenture
- Treasury Note

TREASURY INFLATION PROTECTED SECURITIES (TIPS)

What Does *Treasury Inflation Protected Securities (TIPS)* Mean?

Refers to a Treasury note or bond that is adjusted for inflation. Like other Treasuries, an inflation-indexed security pays interest every six months and pays the principal when the security matures. The difference with TIPS is that the coupon payments and underlying principal are increased automatically to compensate for inflation as measured by the consumer price index (CPI). Also referred to as Treasury inflation-indexed securities.

Investopedia explains *Treasury*
Inflation Protected Securities (TIPS)
If U.S. Treasuries are the world's safest investments, one might say that TIPS are the safest of the safe. This is the case because the real rate of return, which represents the growth of the investor's purchasing power, is guaranteed. The downside is that because of that safety, TIPS offer very low interest rates. Other countries have similar securities. For example, TIPS in Canada are called real return bonds (RRB).

RELATED TERMS:
- *Consumer Price Index—CPI*
- *Inflation*
- *Real Rate of Return*
- *Government Security*
- *Interest Rate*

TREASURY NOTE

 What Does *Treasury Note* **Mean?**
A marketable U.S. government bond with a fixed interest rate and a maturity generally between 1 and 10 years. Treasury notes are sold directly from the U.S. government or through a bank. When buying Treasury notes from the government, an investor can put in a competitive or a noncompetitive bid. With a competitive bid, the investor specifies the yield he or she wants; however, this does not mean that the bid will be approved. With a noncompetitive bid, the investor accepts whatever yield is determined at the auction.

 Investopedia explains *Treasury Note*
Treasury notes are extremely popular not only because they are backed by the full faith and credit of the U.S. government but also because there is a large secondary market for the notes; this makes them highly liquid. Interest payments on the notes are made every six months until maturity. The income from the interest payments is not taxable on a municipal or state level but is federally taxed.

RELATED TERMS:
- *Debt*
- *Treasury Bill*
- *U.S. Treasury*
- *Interest Rate*
- *Treasury Bond*

TREND ANALYSIS

What Does *Trend Analysis* Mean?

A type of technical analysis that is used in an attempt to predict the future movement of a stock on the basis of past data. Trend analysis is rooted in the idea that historical trading trends can give traders an idea of what may happen in the future. There are three main types of trends: short-term, intermediate-term, and long-term.

Investopedia explains *Trend Analysis*

Trend analysis is used to predict a trend such as a bull market so that investors can ride that trend until data suggests a trend reversal (e.g., bull market to bear market). Trend analysis is helpful because moving with trends, as opposed to against them, can lead to profits for an investor.

RELATED TERMS:
- *Bear Market*
- *Downtrend*
- *Uptrend*
- *Bull Market*
- *Technical Analysis*

TRIPLE WITCHING

What Does *Triple Witching* Mean?

An event that occurs when the contracts for stock index futures, stock index options, and stock options all expire on the same day. Triple witching days happen four times a year on the third Friday of March, June, September, and December. This phenomenon sometimes is referred to as Freaky Friday.

Investopedia explains *Triple Witching*

The final trading hour for that Friday is the hour known as triple witching. The markets are quite volatile in this final hour, as traders quickly offset their options and futures orders before the closing bell. Triple witching has a minimal impact on a long-term investor.

RELATED TERMS:
- *Expiration*
- *Index Option*
- *Strike Price*
- *In the Money*
- *Stock Option*

TURNOVER

What Does *Turnover* Mean?

(1) In accounting, the number of times an asset is replaced during a financial period. (2) The number of shares traded in a specific period expressed as a percentage of the total shares in a portfolio or traded on an exchange.

Investopedia explains *Turnover*

(1) In accounting, turnover often refers to inventory or accounts receivable. A quick turnover is desired because it means that inventory is not sitting on the shelves for too long. (2) In a portfolio, a low turnover is desired because it means that the investor is paying less in trading commissions. Excessive trading by a broker for the sole purpose of generating commissions is called churning. This practice is both unethical and illegal.

RELATED TERMS:
- Accounts Receivable—AR
- Asset Turnover
- Inventory Turnover
- Asset
- Cash Conversion Cycle—CCC

TURNOVER RATIO

What Does *Turnover Ratio* Mean?

The percentage of a mutual fund or another investment vehicle's holdings that is replaced ("turned over") by other investments during the course of a specific period. A mutual fund's investment objective, along with the portfolio manager's active management, plays an important role in the amount of turnover that occurs in a portfolio.

Investopedia explains *Turnover Ratio*

As an example, a stock index fund that is not actively managed has a very low turnover rate, but a nonindex fund or a bond fund typically has more turnover because active trading is an inherent part of active portfolio management, particularly as bonds mature and are replaced with new bonds. An aggressive small-cap growth stock fund generally experiences higher turnover than does a large-cap value stock fund. Investors should avoid mutual funds with high turnover

because they incur higher trading costs and can produce additional tax liabilities, which in the end translate into lower returns. Turnover ratios for a mutual fund vary from year to year, but a fair approximation can be ascertained by looking at turnover over a few consecutive years.

RELATED TERMS:
- *Expense Ratio*
- *Index Fund*
- *Mutual Fund*
- *Index*
- *Liquidity Ratios*

"My husband invests in the futures market. Unfortunately, his losses occur in real-time."

copyright JackGuinan

UNDERWRITING

What Does *Underwriting* Mean?

(1) The process employed by investment bankers to raise investment capital on behalf of a corporation. This is done mainly through stock offerings but also may be accomplished through selling bonds. (2) The process of issuing insurance policies.

Investopedia explains *Underwriting*

The word "underwriter" is said to derive from the practice of having each risk taker write his or her name under the total amount of risk he or she was willing to accept at a specified premium (price). In a way, this is still true, as new issues usually are sold to the market by an underwriting syndicate in which each firm takes the responsibility (and risk) of selling its specific allotment.

RELATED TERMS:
- *Capital*
- *Initial Public Offering—IPO*
- *Syndicate*
- *Capital Structure*
- *Rights Offering (Issue)*

U.S. TREASURY

What Does *U.S. Treasury* Mean?
Created in 1798, the United States Department of the Treasury is
the government (Cabinet) department responsible for issuing all
Treasury bonds, notes, and bills. Some of the government branches
operating under the U.S. Treasury umbrella include the IRS, the U.S.
Mint, the Bureau of the Public Debt, and the Alcohol and Tobacco
Tax Bureau.

(I) **Investopedia explains *U.S. Treasury***
Generally, the U.S. Treasury is responsible for the revenue of the
U.S. government, but it also has other key functions: (a) printing
of bills, postage, and Federal Reserve notes and minting of coins,
(b) collection of taxes and enforcement of tax laws (through the
IRS), (c) management of all government accounts and debt issues,
and (d) overseeing U.S. banks.

RELATED TERMS:
- *Monetary Policy*
- *Treasury Bond—T-Bond*
- *Treasury Inflation Protected Securities—TIPS*
- *Treasury Note*
- *Treasury Bill—T-Bill*

UNEMPLOYMENT RATE

What Does *Unemployment Rate* Mean?
The percentage of the total labor force in a certain period that is
unemployed but actively seeking employment and willing to work.

(I) **Investopedia explains *Unemployment Rate***
The unemployment rate is considered a lagging indicator, confirm-
ing what happened in the past but not predicting what may happen
in the future. Unemployment numbers often are revised up or down
months after they have been reported. Therefore, it may not be wise
to base investment decisions on initial unemployment figures.

RELATED TERMS:
- *Business Cycle*
- *Gross Domestic Product*
- *Quantitative Analysis*
- *Fundamental Analysis*
- *Market Economy*

UNLEVERED BETA

What Does *Unlevered Beta* Mean?

A type of metric that compares the risk of an unlevered company with the risk of the market in general; the unlevered beta is equal to the beta of a company without any debt. Unlevering a beta removes the financial effects from leverage. The formula to calculate a company's unlevered beta is shown here:

$$B_U = \frac{B_L}{[1+(1-T_C)\times(D/E)]}$$

Where B = the firm's beta with leverage, T= the corporate tax rate, D/E = the company's debt/equity ratio.

Investopedia explains *Unlevered Beta*

This measure shows the amount of systematic risk inherent in a firm's equity compared with the overall market. Unlevering the beta removes any beneficial effects gained by adding debt to the firm's capital structure. Comparing companies' unlevered betas gives investors a better idea of the amount of risk associated with a firm's stock.

RELATED TERMS:

- *Beta*
- *Debt/Equity Ratio*
- *Systematic Risk*
- *Capital Structure*
- *Leverage*

UNREALIZED GAIN

What Does *Unrealized Gain* Mean?

A profit that exists only on paper as a result of holding on to an asset rather than actually selling it.

Investopedia explains *Unrealized Gain*

Let's say an investor owns a stock that has doubled in price but he or she hasn't sold it yet. This is said to be an unrealized gain. The opposite of an unrealized gain is an unrealized loss. Either way, no tax consequences are incurred until the investor actually sells the security.

RELATED TERMS:

- *Capital Gain*
- *Return on Investment*
- *Tax Deferred*
- *Market Order*
- *Stop Order*

UNSYSTEMATIC RISK

What Does *Unsystematic Risk* Mean?

Company- or industry-specific risk as opposed to overall market risk; unsystematic risk can be reduced through diversification. As the saying goes, "Don't put all of your eggs in one basket." Also known as specific risk, diversifiable risk, and residual risk.

Investopedia explains *Unsystematic Risk*

As an example, news that affects a small number of stocks, such as a sudden labor strike, is a type of unsystematic risk.

RELATED TERMS:
- *Macroeconomic*
- *Microeconomics*
- *Risk*
- *Risk-Return Trade-Off*
- *Systematic risk*

UPTICK

What Does *Uptick* Mean?

A securities transaction that occurs at a price above the previous transaction. For an uptick to occur, a transaction price must be followed by another transaction at a higher price. This term is used commonly in reference to stocks but also can refer to commodities and other securities.

Investopedia explains *Uptick*

As an example, suppose stock ABC previously traded at $10. If its next trade occurs at a price above $10, say, $10.05, ABC is on an uptick.

RELATED TERMS:
- *Commodity*
- *Stock*
- *Stock Market*
- *Uptrend*
- *Volume*

UPTREND

What Does *Uptrend* Mean?

Describes the price movement of a financial asset when the overall direction is upward. A formal uptrend occurs when each successive peak and trough is higher than the ones earlier in the trend.

Notice in the accompanying chart how each successive peak and trough is above the previous ones. For example, the peak at Point 4 is higher than the peak at Point 2. The uptrend will be considered broken if the next low on the chart falls below Point 5. Uptrend is the opposite of downtrend.

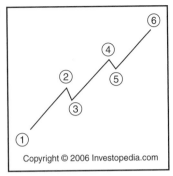

Copyright © 2006 Investopedia.com

 Investopedia explains *Uptrend*
The goal of most technical traders is to identify a strong uptrend and profit from it until it reverses. Selling an asset once it has failed to create a new peak or trough is one of the best ways to avoid the large losses that can result from a reversed trend. Many technical traders also draw trend lines to identify an uptrend and use this tool as a guide for when to sell as it can be an early indication of a trend reversal.

RELATED TERMS:
- *Average Directional Index—ADX*
- *Trend Analysis*
- *Uptick*
- *Downtrend*
- *Volume*

VALUE INVESTING

 What Does *Value Investing* **Mean?**
The strategy of selecting stocks that trade for less than their intrinsic value. Value investors try to identify companies that through no fault of their own are out of favor with the market. Value investors believe that the market tends to overreact to short-term news, good or bad, resulting in stock prices that do not reflect a company's long-term fundamentals. The result is an opportunity for value investors to profit by buying when the price is deflated. Typically, value investors select stocks with lower than average price-to-book or price-to-earnings ratios and/or high dividend yields.

 Investopedia explains *Value Investing*
A challenge with value investing is estimating a company's intrinsic value. There really is no "correct" intrinsic value. Two investors with identical information could arrive at two different intrinsic values for a company. Therefore, value investors consider a "margin of safety," which simply means that they buy at a big enough discount to allow

for errors in calculations of intrinsic value. One should keep in mind that the entire concept of value investing is subjective as some value investors look only at present assets/earnings and do not place any value on future growth, whereas other value investors base their evaluations on future growth and cash flow estimations. Whichever method is employed, value investors' decisions come down to buying a stock for less than what they believe it is actually worth.

RELATED TERMS:
- Earnings
- Intrinsic Value
- Style
- Growth Stock
- Value Stock

VALUE PROPOSITION

What Does *Value Proposition* Mean?
A business or marketing statement that summarizes why a consumer should buy a product or use a service. The statement should convince a potential consumer that a particular product or service will add more value or solve a problem better than will other similar offerings.

Investopedia explains *Value Proposition*
Companies use this statement to target customers who will benefit most from their products. The ideal value proposition is concise and addresses a customer's strongest decision-making drivers. Companies risk losing customers if their products' value proposition is not communicated properly to their customers.

RELATED TERMS:
- Asset
- Intangible Asset
- Tangible Asset
- Goodwill
- Spinoff

VALUE STOCK

What Does *Value Stock* Mean?
A stock that trades at a lower price relative to its fundamentals (dividends, earnings, sales, etc.); value stocks are considered undervalued by a value investor. Common characteristics of such stocks include a high dividend yield, a low price-to-book ratio, and/or a low price-to-earnings ratio.

Investopedia explains *Value Stock*

A value investor believes that the stock market is often inefficient and that it is possible to find companies trading for less than what they actually may be worth. One popular way to identify value stocks is to check the "Dogs of the Dow" investing strategy: buying one of the 10 highest dividend-yielding stocks on the Dow Jones at the beginning of each year and adjusting it every year thereafter.

RELATED TERMS:

- *Earnings*
- *Price-to-Book Ratio—P/B Ratio*
- *Value Investing*

- *Growth Stock*
- *Style*

VARIABLE COST

 What Does *Variable Cost* Mean?

A cost that changes in proportion to a change in a company's activity or business.

 Investopedia explains *Variable Cost*

A good example of a variable cost is fuel for an airline. This cost changes with the number of flights and how long the trips are.

RELATED TERMS:

- *Accrual Accounting*
- *Law of Diminishing Marginal Utility*
- *Operating Leverage*

- *Contribution Margin*

- *Operating Margin*

VENTURE CAPITAL

 What Does *Venture Capital* Mean?

Private financing used to fund a new business; in other words, money provided by investors to start-up firms and small businesses with perceived long-term growth potential. This is a very important source of funding for start-ups that do not have access to capital markets. It typically entails high risk for the investor, but it has the potential for above-average returns.

 Investopedia explains *Venture Capital*

Venture capital also can include managerial and technical expertise. Most venture capital comes from a group of wealthy investors, investment banks, and other financial institutions that pool such investments or partnerships. This form of raising capital is popular among new companies, or ventures, that have a limited operating history and cannot raise funds through a debt offering. The downside for entrepreneurs is that venture capitalists usually get a say in company decisions in addition to a portion of the equity.

RELATED TERMS:
- Capital
- Initial Public Offering—IPO
- Private Equity
- Capital Structure
- Mezzanine Financing

VIX (CBOE VOLATILITY INDEX)

What Does *VIX (CBOE Volatility Index)* Mean?
VIX is the ticker symbol for the Chicago Board Options Exchange (CBOE) Volatility Index, which numerically expresses the market's expectation of 30-day volatility; it is constructed by using the implied volatilities of a wide range of S&P 500 Index options. The results are meant to be forward-looking and are calculated by using both call and put options The VIX is a widely used measure of market risk and often is referred to as the investor fear gauge. There are three variations of the volatility indexes: (1) the VIX, which tracks the S&P 500, (2) the VXN, which tracks the Nasdaq 100, and (3) the VXD, which tracks the Dow Jones Industrial Average.

Investopedia explains *VIX (CBOE Volatility Index)*
The first VIX Index was introduced by the CBOE in 1993 and was a weighted measure of the implied volatility of eight S&P 100 at-the-money put and call options. In 2003, it was expanded to use options that were based on a broader index, the S&P 500 Index, which provides a more accurate picture of investors' expectations of future market volatility. VIX values that are greater than 30 generally are associated with a large amount of volatility as well as greater investor fear and uncertainty. VIX values below 20 generally signal less volatile times for the market.

RELATED TERMS:
- Beta
- Moving Average
- Volatility
- In the Money
- Standard Deviation

VOLATILITY

What Does *Volatility* Mean?

(1) A statistical measure of the dispersion of returns for a particular security or market index. Volatility can be measured by using the standard deviation or the variance between returns from the same security or market index; normally, the higher the volatility, the riskier the security. (2) A variable in option pricing formulas showing the extent to which the return on the underlying asset will fluctuate between now and the option's expiration date. Volatility, as expressed as a percentage coefficient within option-pricing formulas, arises out of daily trading activities. The way volatility is measured affects the value of the coefficient used.

Investopedia explains *Volatility*

In other words, volatility refers to the amount of uncertainty or risk regarding the degree and size of changes in the value of a security. A higher volatility means that a security's value potentially can be spread out over a larger range of values. This means that the price of the security can change dramatically over a short period in either direction. A lower volatility means that a security's value does not fluctuate dramatically but changes in value at a steady pace over a period of time. One measure of the relative volatility of a particular stock to the market is its beta. A beta approximates the overall volatility of a security's returns versus the returns of a relevant benchmark (usually the S&P 500 Index). For example, a stock with a beta of 1.1 historically has moved 110% for every 100% movement in the benchmark (based on price). Conversely, a stock with a beta of .9 has historically moved 90% for every 100% movement in the underlying index.

RELATED TERMS:

- Beta
- Hedge
- VIX—CBOE Volatility Index
- Futures
- Standard Deviation

VOLUME

What Does *Volume* Mean?

The number of shares or contracts traded in a security or in an entire market during a specific period. It is simply the total amount of shares that change hands between buyers and sellers. If a buyer of a stock purchases 100 shares from a seller, total trading volume increases by that transaction, or 100 shares.

 Investopedia explains *Volume*
Volume is an important indicator in technical analysis as it is used to measure the worth of a market move. If the markets move significantly up or down, the perceived strength of that move depends on the volume of trading in that period. The higher the volume during that price move, the more significant the move.

RELATED TERMS:
- Ask
- Bid
- Downtrend
- New York Stock Exchange—NYSE
- Uptrend

VOLUME WEIGHTED AVERAGE PRICE (VWAP)

 What Does *Volume Weighted Average Price (VWAP)* Mean?
A trading benchmark that is used most often in pension plans. VWAP is calculated by adding up the total dollar value traded for all transactions (share price multiplied by number of shares traded) and then dividing by the total quantity of shares traded for the day (see the accompanying formula).

$$VWAP = \frac{\Sigma \text{Number of Shares Bought} \times \text{Share Price}}{\text{Total Shares Bought}}$$

 Investopedia explains *Volume Weighted Average Price (VWAP)*
The theory is that if the price of a buy trade is lower than the VWAP, it is a good trade. The opposite is true if the price is higher than the VWAP.

RELATED TERMS:
- Ask
- Bid
- Weighted Average
- Benchmark
- Volume

"I think my stock portfolio is the only thing not on growth hormones."

WARRANT

What Does *Warrant* Mean?
A type of security known as a derivative that gives the holder the right to purchase securities (usually equity) from the issuer at a specific price within a certain time frame; warrants often are included in a new debt issue as a "sweetener" to entice investors.

Investopedia explains *Warrant*
The main difference between warrants and call options is that warrants are issued and guaranteed by the company, whereas options are exchange-traded instruments that are not issued by the company. In addition, a warrant's lifetime is often measured in years, whereas the lifetime of a typical option contract is measured in months.

RELATED TERMS:
- Call Option
- Put Option
- Rights Offering (Issue)
- Derivative
- Premium

WEIGHTED AVERAGE

What Does *Weighted Average* Mean?
An average in which each quantity that is being averaged is assigned a weight. The weightings determine the relative contribution of each

quantity to the average. Weightings are the equivalent of having that many like items with the same value involved in the average.

Investopedia explains *Weighted Average*
To demonstrate this concept, take the value of letter tiles in the game Scrabble.

Value: 10 8 5 4 3 2 1 0

Occurrences: 2 2 1 10 8 7 68 2

To average these values, do a weighted average by using the number of occurrences of each value as the weight. To calculate a weighted average, do the following: Step 1: Multiply each value by its weight. (Answer: 20, 16, 5, 40, 24, 14, 68, and 0.) Step 2: Total all the values from Step 1. (Answer: sum = 187.) Step 3: Total the occurrences (weights). (Answer: sum = 100.) Step 4: Divide the total of the values by the total occurrences (weights). (Answer: 187/100.) Step 5: The average value of a Scrabble tile is 187/100 = 1.87.

RELATED TERMS:
- *American Stock Exchange—AMEX*
- *Dow Jones Industrial Average—DJIA*
- *New York Stock Exchange—NYSE*
- *Price-Weighted Index*
- *Weighted Average Market Capitalization*

WEIGHTED AVERAGE MARKET CAPITALIZATION

What Does *Weighted Average Market Capitalization* Mean?
A stock market index weighted by the market capitalization of each stock in the index; in such a weighting scheme, larger market cap companies carry greater weight than do smaller market cap companies that are in the index. Most indexes are constructed in this manner, with the best example being the S&P 500.

Investopedia explains *Weighted Average Market Capitalization*
As an example, if a company's market capitalization is $1 million and the market capitalization of all the stocks in the index is $100 million, the company is worth 1% of the index. The alternative to weighting by market cap is a price-weighted index such as the Dow Jones Industrial Average.

RELATED TERMS:
- Benchmark
- Market Capitalization
- Standard & Poor's 500 Index—S&P 500
- Index
- Price-Weighted Index

WINDFALL PROFIT TAX

What Does *Windfall Profit Tax* Mean?
A tax levied by governments on certain industries when economic conditions allow those industries to have above-average profits. Windfall taxes are levied primarily on the companies in a targeted industry that have benefited the most from an economic windfall, most often commodity-based businesses such as big oil companies.

Investopedia explains *Windfall Profit Tax*
As with all government taxes, there are those who support them and those who are against them. The benefits of collecting a windfall tax include increased revenues to the government that can be used for social programs. However, windfall taxes can be a disincentive to a company to pursue projects or promote innovation that potentially could result in less profit as a result of a windfall tax. Windfall taxes will always be a contentious issue among shareholders, corporate executives, the government, and the citizens.

RELATED TERMS:
- Capital Gain
- Gross Profit Margin
- Unrealized Gain
- Income
- Profit and Loss Statement—P&L

WORKING CAPITAL

What Does *Working Capital* Mean?
A measure of a company's efficiency and short-term financial health; a company's working capital is calculated as shown here:

$$\text{Working Capital} = \text{Current Assets} - \text{Current Liabilities}$$

Positive working capital means that the company is able to pay off its short-term liabilities, whereas negative working capital means that a company is unable to meet its short-term liabilities out of its current assets (cash, accounts receivable, and inventory). Working capital also is referred to as net working capital.

Investopedia explains *Working Capital*

If a company's current liabilities exceed its current assets, it may have trouble paying back its creditors in the short term. The worst-case scenario is bankruptcy. A declining working capital over a longer period should be a red flag to investors. For example, it could signal a decrease in a company's sales, and as a result, its accounts receivable (future cash flow) will shrink, meaning that future cash flows will be reduced. Working capital also reveals a company's operational efficiency. Money that is tied up in inventory or money that customers still owe (accounts receivable) cannot be used to pay off any of the company's current obligations. Therefore, if a company is not operating in the most efficient manner (slow collection), that will show up as an increase in working capital. This efficiency can be deduced by comparing working capital from one period to another; slow collection may signal an underlying problem in the company's operations.

RELATED TERMS:
- *Acid-Test Ratio*
- *Current Assets*
- *Inventory*
- *Capital Structure*
- *Current Liabilities*

copyright JackGuinan

"Congratulations grandma, you're no longer a long-term investor!"

YIELD

What Does *Yield* Mean?

The income return on an investment; the interest or dividends an investor receives from a security. Yield usually is expressed annually as a percentage of an investment's cost, its current market value, or its face value. Bond yield is calculated as shown here.

$$\text{Bond Yield} = \frac{\text{Coupon Rate}}{\text{Current Market Price of Bond}}$$

Investopedia explains *Yield*

This seemingly simple term often perplexes investors. For example, if an investor bought a stock at $30 (cost basis) and its current price rose to $33 with an annual dividend of $1, the "cost yield" would be 3.3% ($1/$30); however the "current yield" would be 3% ($1/$33). Bonds have four types of yields: (1) coupon yield (the bond interest rate fixed at issuance), (2) current yield (the bond interest rate as a percentage of the current price of the bond), (3) yield to maturity (an estimate of what an investor will receive if the bond is held to its maturity date), and (4) for tax-free municipal bonds, a tax-equivalent (TE) yield (determined by the investor's tax bracket). Mutual fund yields are an annual percentage measure of income (dividends and interest) earned by the fund's portfolio, net of the fund's expenses. An SEC yield is the percentage yield on a mutual fund based on a 30-day period.

RELATED TERMS:
- *Annual Percentage Yield—APY*
- *Dividend Yield*
- *Yield to Maturity—YTM*
- *Current Yield*
- *Yield Curve*

YIELD CURVE

What Does *Yield Curve* Mean?
The line on a chart that plots the interest rates, at a set point in time, of bonds that have equal credit quality but different maturity dates. The most frequently reported yield curve compares 3-month, 2-year, 5-year, and 30-year U.S. Treasury debt. This yield curve is used as a benchmark for other debt in the market, such as mortgage rates and bank lending rates. The curve also can be used to predict changes in economic output and growth.

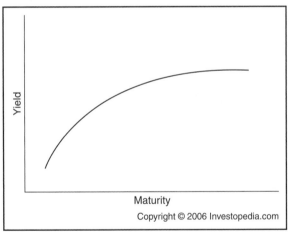

Copyright © 2006 Investopedia.com

Investopedia explains *Yield Curve*
The shape of the yield curve is scrutinized closely because it can indicate future changes in interest rates and economic activity. There are three main types of yield curve shapes: (1) normal, (2) inverted, and (3) flat (or humped). (1) A normal yield curve (pictured here) is one in which longer-maturity bonds have a higher yield than do shorter-term bonds because of the risks associated with time. (2) An inverted yield curve is one in which the shorter-term yields

are higher than the longer-term yields; this can be a sign of an upcoming recession. (3) A flat (or humped) yield curve is one in which the shorter-term and longer-term yields are very close to each other; this is also a predictor of an economic transition. The slope of the yield curve also is considered important: the greater the slope, the greater the gap between short-term and long-term rates.

RELATED TERMS:
- Corporate Bond
- Inverted Yield Curve
- U.S. Treasury
- Interest Rate
- Risk-Free Rate of Return

YIELD TO MATURITY (YTM)

What Does *Yield to Maturity* Mean?
The expected rate of return on a bond if it is held until the maturity date; YTM is a long-term bond yield expressed as an annual rate. The calculation of YTM takes into account the current market price, par value, coupon interest rate, and time to maturity. It also assumes that all coupons are reinvested at the same rate. Sometimes YTM is referred to simply as yield.

Investopedia explains *Yield to Maturity*
An investor can approximate YTM by using a bond yield table. However, because calculating a bond's YTM is complex and involves trial and error, it usually is done with a programmable business calculator.

RELATED TERMS:
- Bond
- Interest Rate
- Yield
- Coupon
- Par Value

"Don't mind us, we're here from the SEC to audit your year-end performance."

ZERO-COUPON BOND

What Does *Zero-Coupon Bond* Mean?

A debt security that does not pay interest (a coupon) but is traded at a deep discount and paid in full at face value upon maturity; also called an accrual bond.

Investopedia explains *Zero-Coupon Bond*

Some zero-coupon bonds are issued as such, whereas others are bonds that have been stripped of their coupons by a financial institution and then repackaged as zero-coupon bonds. Because they offer the entire payment at maturity, zero-coupon bonds tend to fluctuate in price more than coupon bonds do.

RELATED TERMS:
- Bond
- Discount Rate
- Maturity
- Coupon
- Face Value

Index

About the Editor and Cartoonist

Photograph by Nancy Spencer

Jack Guinan is a veteran Wall Street insider who has worked for some of the world's leading financial services firms including Citi Smith Barney, Fidelity Investments, and Chase/BrownCo. Guinan also is the author of *The Online Trading Survival Guide: Insights from an Insider*. His cartoons, *The Closing Bell by JackGuinan*, are enjoyed by millions of people worldwide in newspapers, magazines, investment calendars and on the Internet.